MY
BOYHOOD
WAR

'Told with the wisdom of one who survived the deafening noise of war, as well as the deafening silence of the peace that followed, this riveting story of heroism and betrayal is indispensable for understanding political events today. Narrated with elegance, gravity and a writer's eye for the harrowing details that shaped life on the front, Hryniewicz's book reminds us all of the urgency of the past ...'

Krystyna von Henneberg
Historian

'An intensely personal yet politically significant account of a major World War II battle ... It also enhances a better understanding of Russia's current goals in East–Central Europe.'

Zbigniew Brzezinski
Former US National Security Advisor

'Hryniewicz' engrossing and detailed memoir of the Warsaw Uprising adds the unvarnished insights of an adolescent "runner" for the underground to a story that never fails to move the reader with its tragic consequences for Poland and for the Poles.'

Norman M. Naimark
Professor of East European Studies, Stanford University

'A fascinating personal memoir ...'

Halik Kochanski
Historian and Author

'This first-hand memoir is a welcome addition to our knowledge of what [the Warsaw Uprising of 1944] meant for ordinary people.'

Count Adam Zamoyski
Historian and Author

MY
BOYHOOD
WAR

WARSAW 1944

BOHDAN HRYNIEWICZ

To Andrzej,
and all the boys and girls who so bravely
gave their lives in Warsaw, 1944.

Cover illustrations.
Front, top: Bohdan Hryniewicz, Szczecin, February 1946 (author's archive); *bottom*: German gun next to the opera house, end of August 1944. (Wałkowski Z.) *Back*: German police car captured during the first days of the Uprising on Swietokrzyska Street. (Author's archive)

First published 2015
By Spellmount, an imprint of
The History Press
The Mill, Brimscombe Port
Stroud, Gloucestershire, GL5 2QG
www.thehistorypress.co.uk

British Library Cataloguing in Publication Data.
A catalogue record for this book is available from the British Library.

ISBN 978 0 7509 6210 0

Typesetting and origination by The History Press
Printed and bound in Great Britain by TJ International Ltd

Contents

Author's Note

When I wrote my dedication to my older brother Andrzej – and all the young boys and girls who died in the sixty-three days of the Warsaw Uprising – I automatically wrote … gave their lives 'for Poland'. There is no question in my mind that they believed they did. So did I. But did they really? What did they achieve by giving their young and very promising lives? We will never know. It has been, and will be, debated for years.

On one hand, there was the complete destruction of Warsaw, the deaths of over 200,000 human beings, the loss of the Polish nation's most valuable human asset. The impact on Polish society and potential, from the loss of its best and brightest, can never be assessed. We all know now that the Uprising was doomed from day one. Stalin deliberately stopped the Russian Army from liberating, or even helping Warsaw, giving the Germans free rein. The Allies, turning a blind eye, did not help either.

After the Second World War ended, nobody talked about it. The story of the Battle for Warsaw, the largest and longest urban battle of the Second World War, between lightly armed, irregular forces and the most experienced, well-equipped army of the day, was virtually unheard of until the fall of communism. It was simply an 'inconvenient truth'.

The Germans obviously did not want to have their war crimes exposed: the indiscriminate murder of combatants and a defenceless civilian population – men, women and children – the bestial murder of wounded soldiers and nurses; rapes; the unnecessary destruction of an evacuated city where, after 80 per cent of the buildings were looted and burned, the remaining structures of any historically significant buildings were systematically dynamited.

The Russians could have taken Warsaw, and at little cost, in the first few weeks of the Uprising. They opted instead to give the Germans total freedom to liquidate that element of the Polish population they knew would always resist communism. They also prevented the Allies from airdropping badly needed supplies to the insurgents.

The Allies – particularly the US under President Roosevelt – did not want to disclose that they had sold out Poland, and the rest of Central Europe, to Stalin at the 1945 Yalta Conference.

On the other hand, many believe that the rise of *Solidarność* (Solidarity), which later precipitated the fall of communism, would not have happened without the Uprising. I believe (or do I desperately *want* to believe?) that those lost lives, given so willingly, were not lost in vain. That the generation that produced Solidarity was inspired by those sacrifices, as they were by the sacrifices of their forebears in the Polish-Bolshevik War of 1920, the failed Uprisings of 1863 and 1831, and the Polish participation in the Napoleonic Wars.

* * *

In November 2009, at the celebration of Independence Day at the Polish Embassy in Washington, the Polish Ambassador presented me with the Commander's Cross with the Star of the Order of Merit, awarded by the President of Poland. In my acceptance speech I said (or rather I *tried* to say as I became overwhelmed with emotion) that the Chinese curse 'May you live in interesting times' applied to me. I wanted to share the three most significant days of my life during those 'interesting times': the saddest day was 19 September 1939, when I woke to the sound of Russian tanks arriving in Wilno; the happiest day was 1 August 1944, when the Polish national colours, red and white, once again flew from the highest building in Warsaw; and the most disappointing day was 3 October 1944, when my commanding officer would not allow me to go to a prisoner of war camp with the other soldiers of our battalion.

* * *

For many years my children, and others, have been after me to write my memoirs. I did live in interesting times, times of significant change in Poland. I am old enough to remember life before the Second World War in the Second Republic of Poland, newly reborn in 1918. I also remember conversations and stories of life before the First World War, of times and a way of life that will never return. I lived through the Second World War, the Russians crossing the Polish border seventeen days after the Germans in 1939; the brief annexation of Wilno by the Lithuanians; the return of the Russians; the arrival of the Germans in June 1941; the German occupation and Warsaw Uprising in 1944; the re-entry of the Russians and the end of the

Second World War in May of 1945; the communist takeover and the creation of the Polish People's Republic; and finally the fall of communism and the rebirth of the Third Republic of Poland. I lived to see, once again, a free, independent and democratic Poland.

I would like to stress that my experiences in the Second World War and particularly in the Warsaw Uprising were not at all unusual or unique. Many boys and girls my age, both younger and older, took an active part in the fighting and the Polish Underground. The figures speak for themselves. After the capitulation of the Uprising, about 15,000 men, 2,500 women and 1,100 adolescent boys were transferred to German POW camps. One of those camps, Stalag 334 at Lamsdorf, held 5,800 men and boys, and 1,000 women including 14–17-year-old girls. On 18 October 1944, the Germans held a special roll call for underage POWs. From about 550 young POWs present, there were eight between the ages of 11 and 13, fifty-seven between 13 and 14, 115 aged 15, and 175 aged 16. Among them were two recipients of the Order Virtuti Militari, the highest Polish military decoration for valour, eighteen recipients of the Cross of Valour and 206 who received promotions.

* * *

I thank my daughter Elisabeth and my cousin Andrew Korab, who edited parts of this memoir. I am grateful for the support and encouragement of all my children, Andrew, Sarah, Elisabeth and Gregory. My special thanks to Elisabeth, who on her own decided to be my literary agent and was successful in having this book published.

I would like to thank my wife Anne, whose love and friendship I cherish. Her strength and support were invaluable through the difficult process of reliving some of the experiences while writing.

I dedicate this book to the memory of two of the most important women in my life. My mother Janina (1906–2001), who awed and inspired me with her strength, fortitude and *sang-froid* in the face of life's adversities, her ability to go on and never give up under the weight of personal loss, the love that she always gave Andrzej and me. To Linda Kelly Hryniewicz (1937–2001), always loved and never forgotten, life companion of forty-two years, mother of our children. And to the new generation: my grandchildren Janina (Nina), Sophia-Linda, Alexander, Bryce and Neve in the hope that they never have to live in 'interesting times'.

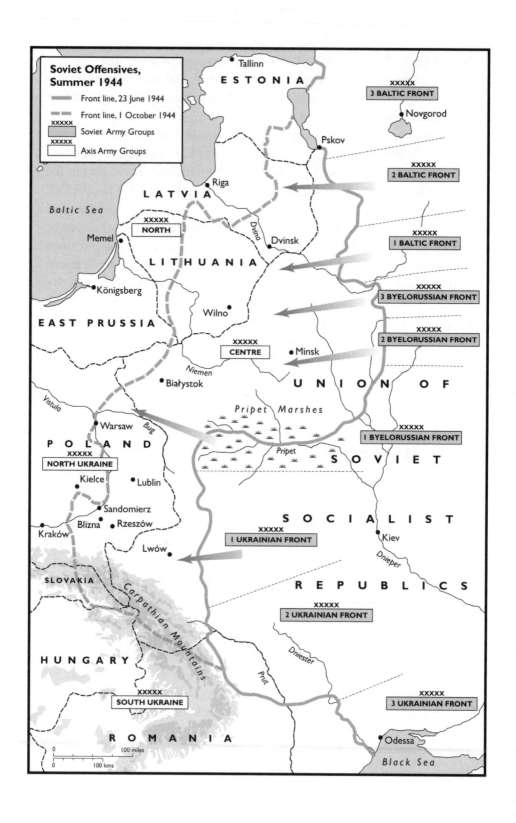

Soviet Offensives, Summer 1944

Front line, 23 June 1944
Front line, 1 October 1944
XXXXX Soviet Army Groups
XXXXX Axis Army Groups

Tallinn

ESTONIA

XXXXX
3 BALTIC FRONT

Novgorod

Pskov

XXXXX
2 BALTIC FRONT

Riga

LATVIA

XXXXX
1 BALTIC FRONT

Baltic Sea

XXXXX
NORTH

Dvina

Dvinsk

Memel

LITHUANIA

XXXXX
3 BYELORUSSIAN FRONT

Königsberg

Wilno

XXXXX
2 BYELORUSSIAN FRONT

EAST PRUSSIA

XXXXX
CENTRE

Minsk

Niemen

Białystok

UNION OF

Vistula

Pripet Marshes

Warsaw

Bug

POLAND

Pripet

XXXXX
1 BYELORUSSIAN FRONT

XXXXX
NORTH UKRAINE

Kielce

Lublin

SOVIET

Sandomierz

Blizna

Rzeszów

Kraków

Lwów

XXXXX
1 UKRAINIAN FRONT

Kiev

Dnieper

SOCIALIST

SLOVAKIA

Carpathian Mountains

REPUBLICS

HUNGARY

XXXXX
2 UKRAINIAN FRONT

Dniester

XXXXX
SOUTH UKRAINE

Prut

XXXXX
3 UKRAINIAN FRONT

ROMANIA

Odessa

0   100 miles
0   100 kms

Black Sea

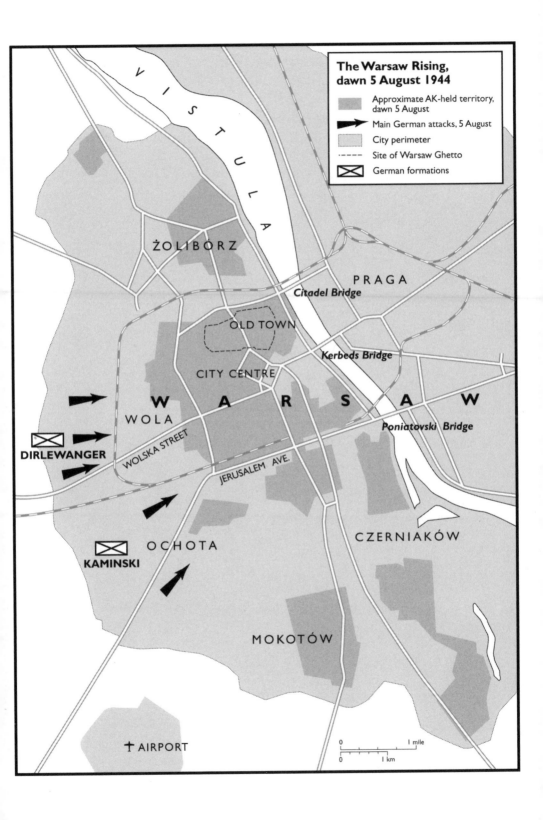

The Warsaw Rising, dawn 5 August 1944

- Approximate AK-held territory, dawn 5 August
- ➤ Main German attacks, 5 August
- City perimeter
- ----- Site of Warsaw Ghetto
- ⊠ German formations

V I S T U L A

ŻOLIBÓRZ

PRAGA

Citadel Bridge

OLD TOWN

CITY CENTRE

W A R S A W

WOLA

Kerbeds Bridge

⊠ DIRLEWANGER

WOLSKA STREET

JERUSALEM AVE.

Poniatovski Bridge

CZERNIAKÓW

⊠ KAMINSKI

OCHOTA

MOKOTÓW

✝ AIRPORT

0   1 mile
0   1 km

PART I

OUTBREAK OF THE SECOND WORLD WAR

1

The Summer of 1939,
June–19 September 1939

I awoke to the sound of metallic clatter on cobblestones. It was early morning and grey light filtered into the bedroom I shared with Andrzej, my older brother. I got out of bed and sat on the windowsill clutching my knees, still in my nightshirt, and was quickly joined by my brother. The noise was getting louder and louder, punctuated by the sound of shots. Looking through the second-floor window towards Arsenal Street, about 200ft away, I could see a column of tanks against the outline of the trees in Cielętnik Park, advancing towards Cathedral Square. The tanks were much larger than the Polish ones I was familiar with. From time to time I saw a puff of blue-grey smoke accompanied by the sound of a shot – but they weren't shots; their engines were backfiring. Red stars stood out on the turrets, growing larger and more menacing as they approached. The Russians were here, just as my father warned us late last night.

I was in Wilno (Vilnius), Poland. It was 19 September 1939, nineteen days after Germany attacked Poland and started the Second World War, and two days after the Russian Army also invaded us from the east. I was eight and a half years old and could feel excitement building inside me.

The summer of 1939 began like any other. My older brother and I had just completed our fourth and third years of primary school in Wilno, Andrzej with all As, while I barely passed. Older by a year and two months, Andrzej was a very serious and studious boy. I, on the other hand, was a hellraiser who did not like to study.

Every summer we would move to the country house with our governess, Miss Krysia. Our property was in Kolonia Wileńska, a summer community 3 miles from Wilno. In the morning we would commute to school by train with our father, who worked in the Military Bureau of the Polish State Railway, returning in the afternoon by ourselves. Kolonia was halfway between Wilno and Nowa Wilejka, a small town with a very large military garrison comprising the 85th Wilno Rifles (father's old regiment), the 13th Wilno Ułans and the horse artillery regiment. Because of its proximity to the Russian border, Wilno had a significant military presence. It was the headquarters of the entire military district, with an infantry division and cavalry brigade. Several regiments were stationed there, including an armoured battalion where my favourite uncle, Lt. Karol Smolak, commanded a squadron of armoured cars. Our immediate neighbours in Kolonia were all families of army officers serving in the nearby regiments.

School ended on the last Friday of June. Miss Krysia left for her usual one-month holiday and was replaced by our maid and cook, Pola. Our mother stayed in Wilno to run her beauty salon, and joined us on the weekends. Every summer we would reconnect with our old buddies: next door were Ryszard and Zdziś (sons of Major Kulczyński, company commander of the Wilno Rifles, with whom father served during the Polish-Bolshevik War), next were the three sons of Capitan Misiewicz and last, to complete the pack, was our slightly younger sidekick Staś Slusarski, son of a local farmer and cavalry sergeant from the Polish-Bolshevik War.

As summer progressed, we fell into our usual routine of playing our own version of cowboys and Indians (Polish Army and the Bolsheviks), and generally raising hell. When the area near us was used for manoeuvres by troops from the nearby regiments, that was real fun! We would follow either 'reds' or 'blues', betraying one side or the other in exchange for a ride on a horse, a meal from the field kitchen or some other special treat.

The day we most eagerly awaited was 24 June, St John the Baptist's day, important for two reasons. Firstly, it was mother's name day (in Poland we did not celebrate birthdays only *imieniny*, the day of the patron saint after whom you are named); secondly, and more importantly, it was the day we could start swimming. It didn't make any difference what the temperature was, you could not swim until 24 June.

Mother was born on 23 June and the closest acceptable patron's day was St John's, so she was named Janina, a female version of John. The whole custom of *Noc Swiętojańska*, or St John's Night, originated from pagan times. Originally, it was celebrated a few days earlier, during the vernal equinox, the longest day of the year. The pagan Slavs celebrated this festival of fire, water, sun, moon, fertility, happiness and love by frolicking in the woods, lustfully chasing one another. The Roman Catholic Church very cleverly embraced this custom, minus the lustful frolicking, as the church holiday of St John the Baptist. Mother's name day was always celebrated in the country house and was a reliably merry affair with lots of people. This summer, I eagerly awaited the arrival of my Aunt Marysia and her husband Lt. Karol Smolak, who had a soft spot for me. However, to my great disappointment, she showed up without him, explaining that duty had kept him away.

The much-awaited first swim took place in the River Wilejka, a tributary that joined the Wilja in the centre of Wilno. A fifteen-minute walk from our country house took us to a place where the Wilejka was dammed, forming a reservoir which fed a water mill. The dam was wooden, about 12ft high, with water overflowing onto a wooden spillway below. The long spillway was covered with moss, creating a wonderfully slippery surface. The water cascaded over the top of the dam making a tunnel over the spillway, which we entered from the sides, and made our way towards the middle, inching along on our behinds until the water hit our backs. The force of the water would send us flying down the spillway landing in the water below with an enormous splash. This was great fun, which we repeated *ad infinitum*, rubbing large holes in our bathing suits in the process.

Our greatest collective achievement that summer was making gunpowder. Uncle Karol jokingly gave me the recipe: take three parts sulphur, three parts charcoal and four parts saltpetre; pulverise each separately; gently mix together; wet and mix more thoroughly; spread thinly and dry out in the sun and finally, when dry, break up by hand and pulverise very gently. Getting charcoal was no problem, but the other two ingredients presented a greater challenge. We used Staś, our *factotum*, to purchase the missing ingredients. We gave him money and sent him to the general store with the following stories: first, 'we have bedbugs and my mother wants to fumigate, so we need 9oz of sulphur'; then 'we slaughtered a pig and my daddy needs 9oz of saltpetre'. With all the ingredients in hand, we proceeded to manufacture our first small batch. We 'borrowed' a brass pestle and mortar from Misiewicz's kitchen and proceeded according to the recipe. When our concoction had dried out in the sun, we gently pulverised it into real gunpowder. The time to test it finally arrived, and we decided to make a small petard first. We used a little metal pillbox, made a small hole in the side, into which we placed a miniature firecracker to be used as a primer. We filled it with our newly made gunpowder and wired the box securely. We decided to test the powder by exploding it around the corner of Mr Slusarski's barn. I placed our masterpiece on a brick in such a way that only the fuse protruded around the corner. Since it was my recipe and my idea, I had the honour of lighting the fuse. With great anticipation, and using a very long match, I lit the fuse. The resulting explosion, producing a large amount of bluish black smoke, was very satisfying. As the ringing in our ears cleared and we congratulated ourselves, a very angry Mr Slusarski, who we had assumed was absent at the time, appeared. After ascertaining that none of us were hurt, he confiscated the rest of the gunpowder. He promised not to tell our parents if we gave him our word of honour that we would never repeat the experiment.

On 1 July Miss Krysia returned from her holiday and Pola left. Pola went to her sister and brother-in-law's small farm near Troki every August, returning more tired than when she left, since she spent the whole time helping to bring in the crops. Pola had been with our family since before I was born and was very devoted to my mother and family. Her previous employers had thrown her out when they discovered she was pregnant, a detail mother was not aware of when she hired her. Pola gave birth to a boy, the day before I was born, who unfortunately died in childbirth. As a result, she transferred her love to me and we had a very close bond.

As August unfolded we noticed changes from the year before. Father, who normally spent as much time as possible in the country, hardly showed himself. Mother, who always closed her business in August to holiday at some spa, cancelled her trip. Uncle Karol did not visit us at all. We also saw much less of our friends' fathers and other neighbours, most of whom were officers in the nearby regiments.

Around the third week of August we returned to our apartment in Wilno. This too was unusual as we normally stayed in the country until mid-September, commuting to school with our father. All the adults seemed very preoccupied; we overheard talk about war with Germany. Personally, I was looking forward to it since I was sure that our Polish Army would quickly win any war. Did we not have the best army in the world? Did we not win against the Bolsheviks in 1920? Did we not regain lost territories from Germany after the world war? Wasn't our cavalry the best fighting force in the world? I had seen our soldiers marching smartly in national holiday parades right under our balcony. I had been to the barracks, ridden in tanks and armoured cars, watched the cavalry horse shows and military manoeuvres, visited army shooting ranges, stood in the chow line with soldiers to get food from the field kitchens. I knew officers like Uncle Karol and Major Kulczyński … I *knew* they were the best!

A few days later, we bid a tearful goodbye to Miss Krysia, who had to return to her family. Mother hired a woman to cook and clean temporarily, but my brother and I didn't want another governess. Father started spending more and more time in his office, sometimes overnight, coming home only to grab a quick meal and change clothes. He seemed completely preoccupied and more unapproachable than ever.

Mother decided we should all have gas masks. She obtained patterns from the Government League for Air Defence (Liga Obrony Powietrznej i Przeciwgazowej, LOPP) and proceeded to make them from sheets of latex taped together with surgical tape. The eyepieces where cut out from stiff cellophane and the inhalers were purchased already loaded with activated charcoal. We had a bit of fun trying them on but they certainly were not comfortable. After a few minutes you would start sweating, the latex would stick to your skin and the eyepieces would fog over, but you could breathe without a problem. Mother's next project, which we helped with, was to glue paper strips onto the windows in the form of an 'X' to stop glass fragments from flying if they were blown out by bombing.

During the last days of August the radio blared martial music, which was broadcast on the streets through loudspeakers. The military choir would sing, 'Marshal Rydz-Smigły is a gallant commander; nobody will take anything from us as long as he is with us.' The streets were plastered with posters showing pictures of the Marshal, resplendent in his uniform, superimposed on planes, guns, tanks and marching columns of infantry. An inscription in bold letters stated, 'Violation by Force Must be Repelled by Force,' and further down, 'In case of war, every man regardless of age and every woman will be a soldier.' I was sure that the latter applied to me: I was a 'man,' age did not matter. After all, I knew that young boys and even girls, called 'Young Eagles of Lwów', fought to defend their city from Ukrainians and Bolsheviks in 1918–19. One of them, only 13 years old, was the youngest recipient of the Order Virtuti Militari, the highest Polish decoration for bravery under fire. And the youngest Eagle was only 9 years old. 'Well', I thought, 'in a few months I'll be 9.'

On 30 August, around noon, the streets were plastered with large yellow posters. The President of the Republic, Ignacy Mościcki ordered the general mobilisation of the military. Large groups of men were gathering to read the orders; there was a new feeling of excitement in the air. We noticed long columns of troops marching out of their barracks towards the railway station, cheered along by the gathering crowds. That night uncle Karol came to say his goodbyes while his staff car waited downstairs. He looked splendid in his officer's black riding boots and black leather coat of the tank troops over his elegantly tailored uniform. He had a brown leather Sam Browne belt; his large, heavy 9mm VIS pistol hung in a triangular tan leather holster on the right side of his belt with a pleated leather lanyard around his neck. A leather map case hung on his left side while field glasses and a gas mask in a metal canister completed his equipment. Brown leather gauntlets where wedged under his belt and a black beret of the tank troops, with the Polish eagle and two silver stars signifying his rank of first lieutenant, capped his head. His orderly stood behind him carrying his helmet and holding Rex on a leash. Rex used to be our dog, a big male cross between an Alsatian shepherd and a Great Dane. Our old white female Spitz didn't want him in our city apartment and constantly attacked him so uncle Karol took him in. Now, I thought, with uncle Karol *and* Rex going to war we were certain to win. On the last day of August, more troops marched towards the railway station. Father briefly stopped by our apartment to discreetly speak with my mother; after he left we did not see him again for a while.

The next morning was 1 September 1939. I was awakened by the sound of the radio in the living room, where mother was sitting on the couch and listening. She looked at us and very quietly said, 'the war has started, the Germans attacked us this morning,' and then she hugged us.

The next couple of days were uneventful but the radio was on all the time, alternating between solemn and martial music periodically interrupted by a grave voice saying, 'attention, attention, arriving …' followed by co-ordinates that meant nothing to us. The Air Defence was giving coded positions of German planes on bombing raids over Poland. Then on 3 September, there was great jubilation: France and England had declared war on Germany! Now we were sure that the war would end soon with a quick German defeat. There was no way they could stand up to the combined might of the Polish, French and English armies. After all, weren't the French supposed to attack Germany immediately? And wouldn't the British bomb them and send us new planes through Romania?

One day, when the air sirens sounded we ran to the balcony and looked up. I spotted a few small planes in the distance and heard explosions from the direction of Porubanek Airport. Then I noticed one small plane rising up to meet them, two planes came from above to attack it. They were circling each other, sparks appearing on the wings of the attacking planes and on the fuselage of the small plane. They looked just like the sparks from my toy tank. I had a wind-up toy tank with a gun that had a lighter flint. In the evening I would turn off the lights in my room, making my tank march forward over obstacles, its guns blazing sparks, just like the planes were doing. The air battle did not last very long. We watched in stunned silence as heavy black smoke started to trail behind the small plane, which was now falling. There was an explosion. Andrzej and I looked at each other in disbelief, how could this happen? Weren't our pilots and our planes the best?

The next few days were again uneventful. Being in the far north-eastern corner of Poland, Wilno was not attacked by the Germans or their planes in the early days of the war. In the drive to capture Warsaw, their army concentrated on overcoming the resistance of the Polish Army in the west of the country. Radio and newspapers gave accounts of heavy fighting, lost battles, withdrawals to new lines of defence and the heavy bombing of Warsaw. The streets of Wilno were deserted since all cars, trucks and buses were requisitioned by the army, the only vehicles still moving were horse-drawn. Lines started to form in front of shops and food became harder and harder to find. A few days after the war started we hoarded one sack each of flour, groats, sugar and salt in the maid's room. Later on, we added a few sides of smoked bacon and a few smoked hams. Our parents had been through the First World War and knew that food would be in short supply. At night the streets were dark and streetlights were turned off but the blackout was not strictly observed. During that period father hardly left his office, spending most nights there, coming home only occasionally to bathe, change clothes and grab a bite to eat.

On the morning of 16 September, air sirens blared again. We heard the drone of planes and then heavy explosions from the direction of the railway station. It didn't last very long and soon the all-clear sounded, but as soon as people started to emerge from wherever they had taken shelter a second wave of planes descended. Realising that we had no anti-aircraft artillery, the German pilots started bombing from a very low altitude, strafing the people below. The air raids lasted for several hours, leaving many fires burning into the night. On the next day, the 17th, Andrzej and I snuck out to see the bombing damage near the railway station. We saw collapsed buildings and big craters in the street with broken pipes leaking water and sewage. We saw people trying to salvage their belongings from the ruins. We stared in fascination at a three-storey apartment building whose front was completely gone, as if it had been cleanly cut off. Pictures were still hanging on the exposed back walls and furniture still stood on what remained of the floors. When we returned home we expected to be punished or at least chastised by our mother since we had left without her permission and had been gone for quite a while. I was surprised that her only reaction to our unauthorised absence was admonishment that in the future we must always tell her in advance where we were going. She seemed so preoccupied and sad. Again she hugged us, making me uneasy: I sensed that something was not right but I didn't know what. Later that day father again came home to speak to mother briefly and in private, returning again to his office.

On the 18th, mother told us that we had to stay at home. We lived on Mickiewicz Street, the main street in the centre of town. From our balcony we could see Cathedral Square, some of the streets feeding onto the square, and up and down our own street as well. We noticed a lot of unusual activity in the city, people moving in and out of government offices, large lines forming in front of shops and banks. There was tension in the air. Then, in the early afternoon, great news was announced on the radio through public loudspeakers and in a special edition of the newspaper: the Polish Army had broken through the German defences! Revolution was taking place in Germany! The Allies had started an offensive on the Western front! People were cheering in the streets. In the fading afternoon light long columns of troops marched under our balcony, towards the west. The loudspeakers continued churning out information on the breakthrough in the German front in Eastern Prussia, where the remaining troops of the Wilno Garrison would now take part in the offensive. Mother, Andrzej and I were standing on our balcony, watching people cheer the marching troops in the fading light. As the dark of night descended, father came and stood behind us in silence. When the last marching columns of soldiers disappeared in the distance I heard him say to mother, 'this is all a lie, the Russian troops are already at the outskirts of Wilno; our troops are escaping to Lithuania.' After a moment of silence he added in a soft, sad voice, 'the Russians will be here tomorrow morning.'

2

Soviet Occupation,
19 September–28 October 1939

While we watched the last Russian tank rumble through the streets from our window, early on the morning of 19 September 1939, an eerie silence descended on the town. We left our room and joined our parents in the kitchen. As mother hugged us they tried to reassure us that this was only temporary, that in the spring the French and British armies would attack, defeat Germany and liberate Poland. Once again I asked about uncle Karol, and once again I was told that no one had heard from him. Father said the fighting with the Germans was still going on and that many Polish troops were withdrawing to Hungary and Romania and would go to France to re-form the Polish Army, just as they had in the First World War. We all knew that the German Army had overrun large parts of Poland but Warsaw, the capital, was still defending itself. A few days before the arrival of the Russians, my uncle Richard and aunt Fela arrived from Warsaw (Fela was originally from Wilno and had family there). It took them more than a week to reach Wilno. They told us of indiscriminate bombing in Warsaw, strafing of civilian trains by German pilots and congestion on the roads as people fled the advancing Germans. Thousands of refugees had already flocked to Wilno. As the day progressed we saw more and more Russian troops pouring into town. There were cavalry units mounted on small shaggy horses; they looked so different from the Polish cavalry on their much better, larger horses. There were infantry units marching and singing. Each unit had a soloist who would start the first verse, in a very loud voice, and then the unit would boom out the refrain. They all had strong voices and the streets would echo with 'Moskva moya, moguczaya, ty samaya lybimaja' (my Moscow, powerful, only you are my love). Trucks and artillery roared by. Supply columns of wagons drawn by small, long-haired Siberian horses bivouacked in the centre of the city. Soldiers lit open fires to cook their meals and warm themselves. The troops looked tired, dirty, covered with dust, dressed in coarse grey overcoats – a stark contrast to our soldiers.

The streets were deserted and we all stayed at home. Slowly the Russian troops moved out of the centre of town and into the barracks vacated by the Polish Army. Starting the next day, bit by bit, the population of Wilno re-emerged onto the streets. There was no traffic except for Soviet troops and vehicles. The Polish population remained almost completely silent. This contrasted starkly with the segment of the Jewish population with communist leanings, mostly young men, even teenagers, who came out wearing red armbands, carrying rifles and pistols, welcoming the Russians. That day we watched from our windows and balcony; the next day, we were finally allowed out. Russian tanks with soldiers sitting on top of them were still parked in Cathedral Square. They didn't object when people approached.

When I first saw the tanks in the grey light of the morning two days before, I immediately spotted their Christie suspension. After visiting my uncle's squadron a few months before, he showed me different types of tanks and armoured vehicles in his military books. He pointed out the Christie tank, designed by an American engineer, as the best. He couldn't understand why the American Army never embraced Christie's design. Polish officers had recognised its superiority and the government entered into a contract with him to buy one tank and a licence to produce them in Poland. After Christie received payment, he broke the contract and sold the same thing to the Russians for more money, which is why only the Russians had these tanks with their superior suspension.

As I was standing right next to this tank, admiring its four large rubber-covered wheels with treads running on top and bottom, I saw somebody climb onto the tank and start to yell. I noticed he was wearing a Polish uniform and field cap. His army overcoat, lacking a belt, was hanging unbuttoned sloppily. As I watched him, the red band on his arm jumped out at me as he welcomed the Russian Army as 'liberators'. He proceeded to take his army cap off, rip off the Polish eagle insignia, spit on it and throw it to the ground. He continued by ripping off his army buttons – stamped with the Polish eagle – and throwing them to the ground while still praising the Russians. The small crowd that had silently gathered around started to become restless and hostile towards him. Finally the Russian soldiers told him to get off and get lost. He sulked away, acquiescing to the hostility of the crowd and the lack of support from the Russian soldiers. I stood there shocked, unable to comprehend how a Polish soldier could behave that way.

Soon the Russian soldiers disappeared from the streets, confining themselves to their barracks. There were no bad incidents with soldiers as they were not allowed to enter private dwellings and generally did not bother civilians. The families of Russian officers started to arrive in large numbers and bought everything in sight. In a matter of days all the shops were stripped bare and there were shortages of all goods. Pola complained that food was impossible to find, even to get bread she had to wait in line for hours. Our parents' foresight in stocking sacks of staples at the beginning of the war kept us from going hungry. The most valuable commodity turned out to be the sack of salt, which Pola used for bartering. Even matches were hard to come by, I remember father using a razor blade to cut each match into four slivers, with which he very carefully lit his cigarettes.

The Russian authorities ordered all Polish officers to report to their headquarters for registration. The very few who did were detained and sent to Russia, most of them never to be heard from again. Father did not register, nor did he return to work. A few days after the Russian troops arrived, the People's Commissariat for Internal Affairs (Narodnyj Komissariat Wnutriennich Dieł, NKWD) came in and took over the old Polish court building a few blocks down our street. Their officers were very noticeable as their uniforms were different from the army: they wore army tunics with navy blue trousers and their army caps were blue with a red band. With the arrival of the NKWD, the arrest of prominent Poles began, usually carried out in the middle of the night. Father decided to move to our country house, a very remote property near the end of a long country lane that terminated at Mr Slusarski's farm. Because of its secluded location, any car approaching the property would be noticed in time to allow him to escape into the woods.

Life in the city started to return to quasi-normality. The Russians formed a new administration and militia, which replaced the Polish police. Our school reopened with the same Polish teachers and books but more crowded classes. A few weeks after we went back to school, my brother started to complain about a pain in his knee. Mother examined his leg and found nothing more than a small black mark on the upper part of his right knee, so she told him to go to bed. I woke up early next morning while it was still dark, to the sound of Andrzej sobbing quietly. He showed me his knee, which by then was very swollen and red. Mother immediately sent Pola to get a *droshky* (carriage) and took him to the hospital, where he was operated on right away. His knee was opened from both sides and a drain was inserted through it. He had a very serious infection and was on the verge of getting gangrene. As the hospital was overcrowded with war casualties there were shortages of medical supplies and medicines, including sulfa powder, which my mother found on the black market. In the days before penicillin and antibiotics, this was the only medicine against infection. My mother and Pola took turns staying with Andrzej in the hospital. Every few hours a nurse would come and pull back and forth on the drain that went through his knee to keep the wounds from scabbing over. It was very painful. After a few days, when the drains were removed, Andrzej came home sporting scars two inches long and half an inch wide on each side of his knee. Eventually he told us what happened. One morning at school, before the teacher arrived, some boys were playing with peashooters. Andrzej held a pen with a steel nib dipped in ink between his teeth and as he instinctively ducked to avoid being shot, he had jammed the steel nib into his knee.

In October we started to hear rumours that the Russians would give Wilno to Lithuania. At the same time they started very openly to remove and cart away all manner of equipment, machinery, furniture and art from office buildings, universities and private residences. One day, coming from school I watched as all the merchandise was removed from a very large, five-storey department store of the Jabłkowski Brothers. I saw trucks full of upright pianos, radios, furniture, carpets, all being carted away and taken to the railway station. In the last week of October, as the Russian Army started to move out, the NKWD intensified its arrest of prominent Poles, who were then all shipped to Russia. I watched convoys of military trucks loaded with equipment and soldiers, confiscated city buses with officers' families, guns and tanks all moving out. The same tanks that I first saw six weeks before were now rumbling through the streets of Wilno on their way out of town.

Lithuanian Annexation, 28 October 1939–17 June 1940

The day the Lithuanian Army entered Wilno, 28 October 1939, was overcast and gloomy under a light drizzle. Later, a parade was held. Just as they had before the war, troops marched down our street and under our balcony to Cathedral Square. We all watched, including our father, who had come back from the country house. The previous few weeks, when the Russians were here, he visited us a few times during the day, always using the kitchen entrance and wearing simple workman's clothes. Parading Lithuanian troops, infantry, cavalry and horse artillery looked almost like the Polish Army, which had very similar uniforms in the same khaki colour. The only differences were their German helmets and double-breasted officers' overcoats. The departure of the Russians and arrival of the Lithuanians brought immediate relief to the city. The fear of the Russian secret police (NKVD), arrests and deportations abated. There was also an immediate improvement in the food supply; there were no more shortages. Lithuania had a very advanced agriculture geared towards export. The two principal co-operatives, *Miastas* for meat products and *Pienocentras* for milk products, immediately opened several very well-stocked shops. However, the problem was that those stores accepted only Lithuanian currency – *litai*. Before banks started to exchange a very small amount of old Polish currency (equivalent to £4 per family), only the newly arrived Lithuanians were able to shop there. Father found enough *litai* in his box of foreign coins to buy some wonderful fresh ham.

After the arrival of the Lithuanians, uncle Karol appeared dressed as a labourer. He had avoided capture by the Germans and the Russians and made his way to our country place when the Russians were still there. When I finally got him to myself I bombarded him with questions: how many Germans had he killed, how many tanks he had destroyed, what had happened to Rex, and on and on. Well, to my great disappointment Rex was not a hero. At the beginning of the second week of war, when they were under heavy artillery shelling, Rex ran away. He ran from the edge of the woods where my uncle and his troops were in position, through the open fields, towards a village where the Germans were. Through his binoculars my uncle later saw Rex on a leash led by a German officer. I was hurt that Rex was not only a coward but a traitor too. My uncle said that German superiority in the number of troops, tanks and planes made fighting very difficult. Nevertheless, the Polish Army fought well and bravely, inflicting heavy casualties on the Germans. In the engagement where Rex ran away, the dismounted cavalrymen destroyed several German tanks with their 37mm *Bofors* anti-tank guns. In the same engagement, uncle ambushed and destroyed three German trucks loaded with troops in his armoured car. The accompanying armoured car with its machine gun inflicted heavy losses on German soldiers. Eventually, all eight of his armoured cars were lost. The Poles were making a fighting withdrawal towards Hungary when the Russians entered from the east. My uncle and some of his soldiers managed to escape and avoid capture, making their way to Wilno. He holed up in our country house with my father and one other officer.

Life started to return to normal except that now, instead of the white and red Polish flag, a very large yellow, red and green Lithuanian flag flew from the tower on Castle Hill visible from our bedroom windows. Mother reopened her beauty salon. Pola no longer had a problem buying food as the shops were full once again. More and more Lithuanians moved into Wilno, taking over the administration of the city. A very aggressive policy of de-Polonisation began in the city. Lithuanian was made the official language and all the streets where renamed in Lithuanian. Wilno University, the second oldest in Poland, was closed. Many Polish university teachers were laid off and Lithuanians took their place. This influx of Lithuanians, combined with the thousands of Polish refugees who arrived in September, created overcrowding and shortages of accommodation. The Lithuanian administration started to requisition rooms in private dwellings. One of our rooms, the one with the balcony, was taken over for a Lithuanian teacher. She turned out to be quite pleasant, spoke Polish and created no problems.

The capital of Lithuania was transferred from Kaunas to Wilno (Vilnius), bringing with it embassies of neutral nations, opening a window of escape to the West. Under pressure from Germany, men of military age (between 18 and 50) were not allowed the necessary permits to leave Lithuania. Mother used her professional skills to make some Polish officers look either younger or older. Her success rate with the 'older' group was 100 per cent but not so good with the younger. Most of them made their way through Sweden and joined the Polish Armed Forces in France.

Two months after the Lithuanians arrived, their government made sweeping changes in all schools and we were assigned to a different one. Half of the Polish teachers were laid off and substituted with Lithuanians. There were more classes every day, including intensive Lithuanian lessons, as well as Lithuanian history and geography, taught in Lithuanian. Teaching of the Polish language was greatly reduced. Lithuanian is a Baltic language with no similarity to Polish. What especially irked everybody was the forcible change in our names to correspond with Lithuanian. I, Bohdan Hryniewicz became Bohdanas Hryniewičius. We all tried to rebel against this change. We had one young male teacher who was very chauvinistic. Any infraction of the rules, such as speaking in Polish during his class, or giving our names in the Polish version, had been immediately and harshly punished. His favourite punishment was to have a boy stand in front of him with both hands covering his eyes while he snapped a heavy rubber band into his nose. I can attest that the pain was quite excruciating.

The first Christmas of the war arrived. There was no joy and all festivities were very subdued. During Christmas time a letter came from mother's older brother, Stefan, postmarked from Portugal. Before the war he was in the Polish Air Force Reserve and was mobilised. Poland managed to evacuate a large portion of Air Force personnel through Hungary to France, where the Polish Armed Forces where re-formed. He wrote this letter from France. It was mailed through the Red Cross and postmarked in Portugal because France was a belligerent nation.

As soon as snow began to fall we started skiing again. Now we skied on Three Crosses Hill. It took us about fifteen minutes of cross-country skiing through parks to get there. There were no lifts. We walked up the hill for ten to twenty minutes in order to ski down in three to five. We built small jumps and started learning to jump. It was a lot of exercise and a lot of fun.

We dreaded the return to school because of the tension between us Polish students and the Lithuanian teachers. We particularly hated the teacher who used rubber bands on our noses and we all wanted our revenge. One fine spring day we got it. This teacher was always elegantly dressed and on this day he was sporting a new white linen summer suit. We had previously noticed that upon entering the classroom he usually sat down on his chair without looking at it. His chair had a dark brown concave plywood seat. During the break between classes we poured ink on the chair seat. He entered staring at us sternly and sat down without looking. As we watched him he started to wiggle, and got up touching his backside. The look of rage and horror on his face, when he brought his hand to his eyes, more than compensated for our previous suffering. Unfortunately, this prank had severe repercussions. All parents were given heavy penalties for our bad behaviour.

The first half of 1940, the second year of the war, destroyed our hopes that the war would end soon. Instead of an imagined French offensive that would defeat Germany, the opposite happened. The complete collapse of France made us realise that the war would go on much longer. Nevertheless, everybody still believed that Germany would be defeated and Poland would be independent again. The only consolation was that our national honour was preserved since France, with a much larger army and helped by the British, did not last much longer in May–June 1940 than Poland had in September 1939.

While the world's attention was occupied with France, Stalin took over all the Baltic states. On 17 June 1940, Russian troops entered Wilno for the second time. A few days later, on 22 June, France capitulated.

4

Return of the Soviet Occupation, 17 June 1940–22 June 1941

The entry of Soviet troops to Wilno did not go according to plan. The troops entered the city from several directions and were supposed to meet at the Green Bridge over the Wilja and continue towards the interior of Lithuania. A tremendous bottleneck formed at the bridge. Several units arrived at the same time, each trying to force its way first. The tanks were forcing their way through horse-drawn artillery, the cavalry through the infantry. Nobody wanted to give way to the others. It took some time for the officers to establish order and the units to start moving on again. The appearance of the soldiers was worse than when they came the first time in September 1939. Soldiers in the same unit were dressed in different uniforms and hats. The equipment looked uncared for. The Russian troops disappeared into the barracks. From then on, a solitary Russian soldier was never seen on the streets of Wilno. From time to time a unit would march through the streets singing. Once I saw a Russian platoon marching with the officer leading and the sergeant behind him. Hanging by a string from the sergeant's neck was a large alarm clock.

On the surface there were no noticeable changes; Lithuanian police were still on the streets and in charge while Lithuanian soldiers wore their same uniforms and insignias. The NKVD arrived but kept a low profile. There were no mass arrests, apart from some prominent Poles. The arrival of the Soviets terminated our school year. And again I barely managed to complete Year 4.

After the Russians gave Wilno to the Lithuanians, father returned from our country house to the apartment. This arrangement did not last long and he moved back to the country. His return visits to the city were becoming less and less frequent. There was also a visible change in the interaction between our parents, much colder and more restrained. That did not seem to bother me; I did not feel much closeness to my father, only to mother. Andrzej, on the other hand, was definitely affected. When the summer of 1940 started we did not go to our country house. Instead we played with our school friends in town. We reconnected with the Kulczyński brothers, who were now living in town with their mother. They had not heard from their father since he left for the September 1939 campaign. At the end of July, mother told us that we would stay with father in the country for the rest of the summer. We packed our knapsacks and when father came we left immediately with him. He told us that we would not take a train but would walk instead. It was not far, slightly more than four miles. This visit to the country was no longer fun. Neither Kulczyński nor the Misiewicz boys were there. Staś Slusarski had to work on the farm as his father had not returned from the September 1939 campaign. Father was working on his garden, orchard, beehives and a new venture of raising rabbits. He was occupied all the time. We were asked to help and were assigned different tasks, removing weeds, picking fruit and vegetables, collecting grass for the rabbits. The fun and gaiety of pre-war summers was not there anymore. After three weeks, and well before the summer was over, I wanted to return home and father walked us back to the city.

The autumn of 1940 brought many changes to Wilno. The independent country of Lithuania ceased to exist but, together with Latvia and Estonia, became a Soviet socialist republic: the Lithuanian SSR. The Lithuanian police were transformed into a Russian-style militia. In place of the previous operetta-style uniforms, which had earned them the sobriquet *kalakutas* (turkeys), they were now wearing Russian navy blue uniforms. Their ranks were swelled with Russians and Belarusians. Lithuanian soldiers wore their same uniforms but now sported red stars on their caps. Shortly thereafter, they disappeared from the streets of Wilno altogether. There was a large influx of Russians and their families. There were officers, government officials and NKVD. Many Lithuanians started to return, including the teacher who used to live in our requisitioned room. Instead of her, we got two young Russian officers with their wives. Our large dining room was divided into a passageway and two small rooms, by a 7ft high partition that left a 3ft space beneath the ceiling. I imagined the Russians were used to the lack of privacy. They turned out to be very pleasant and well-behaved people. Since mother was fluent in Russian there was no problem with communication. The young wives asked mother's advice on how to dress and behave. They lived with us for almost a year without any problems. Individually and in private, Russian people can be very warm and hospitable. Russian women, the wives of officers and officials, started coming to mother's beauty salon. One of them was the wife of an Air Force colonel. She and her husband were cultured and educated people from the upper classes of old Imperial Russia. They were saved from the purges by his degree in aeronautical engineering. Once they became friendly with mother, in the privacy of our apartment, they told her what life was like in Stalinist Russia.

At the end of the summer, when we returned from the country, we had found a new housekeeper. I missed Pola and never warmed to the new housekeeper. She was not a typical maid from the countryside, but an educated woman whose husband had been arrested and deported to Russia in 1939. The other big change was school. Once again we were assigned to a new school, even further away. The Russian model was now imposed. The Lithuanianisation of Polish students was replaced by Soviet indoctrination and Lithuanian was no longer the sole language of instruction. Instead, classes were taught in Polish, Lithuanian, Russian or Yiddish, depending on the location and student body of the school. We were pleased with this change; however, we still had to take both Lithuanian and Russian as a second language. We even had to learn the 'Internationale' in Lithuanian, which we were required to sing practically every day. To this day I still remember, in Lithuanian, the opening verse of this Anthem of International Socialism:

Stand up, damned of the earth,
Stand up, prisoners of starvation …

Our new school was farther away in a different part of the city, with predominantly working-class children. It was part of the social engineering programme in the new Socialistic Republic to disperse the children of the bourgeoisie. All of us kids got along quite well, being united as Poles. The authorities tried to introduce Pioneers, an entry organisation to Komsomol, the youth organisation of the Communist Party, without success. The few boys who joined were tormented whenever they appeared in their white shirts and red kerchiefs. The arrival of the Russians brought several diseases: typhus, cholera and dysentery. There was even talk about cases of the plague. We all got vaccinated against cholera at school. I had a severe reaction, my arm swelled up, became very tender and I ran a very high fever. Shortly after, I became quite ill with bloody dysentery; it was not fun. I was prescribed opiates, burned toast, boiled flaxseeds and apple sauce made on a glass grater. I made a quick recovery.

We started skiing again when winter came. The winter of 1940 was not as severe as 1939, one of the coldest on record. All the Polish coal mines were in Silesia, annexed by Germany, which caused a tremendous shortage. The lack of fuel created great hardships. We were lucky because father had arranged for a larger shipment of coal to be delivered to our cellar in the summer of 1939. It was enough to last for two winters.

Father came by, on the morning of 24 December, bringing Christmas presents for Andrzej and me. After we opened our gifts, he left and we did not see him for the rest of the Christmas holidays. Our parents divorced in March of 1941.

There was a noticeable increase in the number of NKVD troops towards the end of spring 1941. Their officers' superior uniforms, short black leather coats and black riding boots, and the blue bands on their caps, made them easily recognisable. Around Easter, we began to hear of sporadic arrests. Mass arrests and deportations started in the middle of June. Very early one June morning, I was woken by the sound of truck engines. Trucks loaded with people, men, women, children and NKVD guards, came from two directions, passing under our windows. The trucks on Arsenal Street followed the same route as the Russian tanks in 1939. Others came down Mickiewicz Street. They merged on Cathedral Square and continued in the direction of the railway station. As the trucks went by, life in the city continued, just more subdued and quieter. Later that day we snuck out and followed the trucks to the railway station. The train yards were full with cattle cars loaded with people from the trucks. This mass deportation continued throughout the next couple of weeks. After a few days it became clear who was on the arrest list: prominent public figures; members of government, military and police; members of the judiciary; estate owners; professionals; factory and business owners; bankers; doctors; engineers; university professors and teachers; and refugees from German-occupied territories. They were mostly Poles, but Lithuanians, Belarusians and Jews were taken as well.

The trucks rumbled by in the daytime; arrests were made at night. Those arrested were given very little time to get ready. Mother laid out heavy winter clothing and backpacks for all of us, just in case. Twice over the following week, we heard cars stop in front of our building in the middle of the night, followed by shouts and heavy banging on the entry door. The first time the heavy boots continued up past our floor. People from the third floor were taken. A few nights later, the footsteps stopped on our floor. There was banging on the door opposite ours. Elderly Mrs Szymanska lived there with her son, his wife, and their son Tadek (two years older than Andrzej), refugees from Warsaw. That night Tadek's parents were taken. In the winter of 1947 I bumped into Tadek at a Polish military hospital in England. His mother had survived and left Russia with the Polish Army, but his father had perished in Siberia.

One day a Polish railway worker brought mother a folded piece of paper that had been thrown from a train departing to Russia. It was a note from uncle Richard: he and his wife had been arrested and separated. We learned later that his train, loaded with men only, crossed into Russia and stopped at Novosibirsk in Siberia. They were transferred to a riverboat and taken north on the River Ob, past the Arctic Circle. After a journey of three weeks he arrived at a gulag. The men in the gulag were mostly Latvians and a few Poles, labouring cutting trees. Aunt Fela was taken to Kazakhstan, with other women and children, where she worked in a *kolkhoz* (farming co-operative). Luckily, they both survived. They left Russia separately with the Polish Army. In the spring of 1942 they were reunited in Iran. The army went to Iraq and Palestine and from there to Italy. They both went through the entire Italian campaign, aunt Fela as a nurse in a field hospital and uncle Richard in the anti-aircraft regiment. They immigrated to the United States from England.

At daybreak on Sunday 22 June 1941, Germany launched Operation Barbarossa, the invasion of the Soviet Union, attacking in full force along the border of occupied Poland. Later that day, one of the two Russian officers living in our apartment arrived in a very agitated state. He said the war had started. We already knew that. Their wives packed up very quickly and after a hurried goodbye they all left in an army truck.

PART 2

GERMAN OCCUPATION

5

German Arrival,
23 June 1941–June 1942

T he next day, Monday 23rd, German bombers reached Wilno around midday. They concentrated their bombing around the railway station, just as they had in 1939. There was visible panic in the city as Russian families tried to escape. Throughout it all the trucks with deportees kept rumbling through the streets. Eventually the German air attack prevented the Russians from continuing their arrests. The lists, found after their departure, bore many more names, including ours. Polish railway workers sabotaging engines saved some of the last people arrested.

In the evening, shooting was heard from the direction of the military barracks, Lithuanians were attacking the remaining Russian soldiers. The next morning I woke up to the sight of the Lithuanian flag flying, once again, from the tower on Castle Hill. Smoke and the sound of explosions were coming from the direction of the barracks. German military vehicles were parked, by 10 o'clock, on Cathedral Square, the same place as the Russian tanks two years before. People slowly re-emerged onto the streets. The Lithuanians alone waved and greeted the German troops as saviours. Swastika flags appeared in the windows of a few Lithuanian households. The Poles were reserved but not hostile; after all, the Germans were supposed to be *civilised people*, not like the Bolsheviks. The border that divided the German and Russian occupation zones in Poland was very tight and news about German atrocities trickled only very slowly into Wilno.

The look of the German soldiers contrasted greatly with the Soviet troops. There was a notable difference in the quality of their armaments, uniforms, bearing and their general appearance. My brother and I went out to explore the city. A few blocks away on Wileńska Street, German tanks rolled towards Green Bridge on their way north. They were the biggest tanks I had ever seen. We crossed the street and continued past Łukiszki Square, packed with Soviet soldiers sitting on the ground under German guard. We continued towards the next bridge, where there were signs of the previous day's bombing, destroyed buildings and craters in the street. In one of the craters we saw two bodies. They looked rather peaceful, as if asleep, with only a trickle of congealed blood on the ground beside them. These were the first war dead I saw.

For days thereafter, large columns of defeated Russian soldiers were marched through the streets of Wilno escorted by very small numbers of German soldiers. Their appearance was pitiful; many were walking wounded, with bloody bandages. They all begged for food and water. Whenever a local tried to give them some bread or water, the German guards prevented it, mercilessly kicking and rifle-butting any Russian trying to pick up the offered bread or water. They tried to prevent civilians taking pity on the prisoners.

A few days later, a school friend of mine told us that there were Russian rifles to be salvaged in the burned-out barracks. We picked up some old sacks from our cellar and joined him on this expedition. When we arrived at the barracks we found them unguarded and several people already scavenging. We found the armoury and in the smouldering rubble there was a large number of rifles with the wood stocks burned off. We each picked one up, wrapped it in our sacks and headed home. I also found a box of flares for a signalling pistol and added that and a bayonet to my hoard. When we got home, we secreted our 'arsenal' in the cellar.

Shortly after the Germans arrived, mother came to our room, sat down and told us she had very bad news that we would have to take bravely: uncle Karol was dead, murdered in his sleep by a Soviet deserter. I just stood there, biting my lip in silence. I did not cry. In bed later that night, I cried silently. Tears ran down my cheeks, tears of sadness at never being able to see him again and tears of frustration and disappointment: why was he just shot in his sleep, why didn't he die fighting?

Later we learned what had transpired. Uncle Karol had been living in our summer home together with father. Under an assumed identity he worked as a labourer on a construction site a few miles away. When the mass arrests started a few weeks prior, they decided not to sleep in the house but in the nearby woods. On the evening of the 19th, as night was falling, father said it was time to leave the house. Uncle Karol replied that he was too tired to go and would sleep there. He did not respond to my father's insistence that they go together into the woods. In the early morning, before sunrise, there was a single shot. When father returned he found uncle Karol dead in bed, shot in the head. A Russian Army rifle was lying on the floor and the house was ransacked. Through the serial number on the rifle it was determined that an NKVD deserter from the nearby post shot him in order to take his civilian clothes. His uniform was found abandoned in the house. The day before Germany invaded Russia, uncle Karol was buried under his assumed name.

In the middle of July, mother introduced us to Wiktor Rymszewicz. They had met recently through mutual friends and he had been coming to visit her. From the moment I met him I liked him. He had a military bearing. He was mobilised as a reserve cadet officer in the Polish Army Signal Corps. In the September 1939 campaign he was severely wounded and narrowly avoided being sent to a POW camp. While recuperating he was sheltered by a cobbler's family and learned the trade. Later, he worked for a watchmaker and was living with his younger cousin, Zygmunt, who arrived from Warsaw at the beginning of the war.

Towards the end of July, mother told us to go and spend the rest of the summer with father in the country house. I did not look forward to it. I very much looked forward to Wiktor's visits; he always took an interest in what I was doing. At that time I was involved in making airplane models. He was a great help, he had a knack for anything mechanical. He gave me a lot of pointers and help. The first week of August, father arrived and we again walked back to our summer house. It was no longer any fun; none of our old friends where there. The only pleasure was playing with father's new dog, a mutt called Max. Two weeks later, we walked back to town.

Upon our return Wiktor took us aside, in mother's absence, and said that he loved our mother and would like to marry her but she kept turning him down. He wanted to know how we felt about it. I was immediately enthusiastic; Andrzej was more reserved but did not object. Wiktor asked for our help to persuade her. Over the next month or so we wore down her objection about his being younger than her. They were quietly married in the middle of September 1941.

After our return I noticed that the office supply store on the ground floor had closed. Mother told us that the Germans had created a ghetto in the Jewish part of the city. Most of the Jewish population was locked up there, including the old lady who owned the store. I was saddened to learn this, she had always been very nice to us and we bought our school supplies from her. She had a large supply of 2 x 3ft sheets of light cardboard printed with cut-outs that one could make into castles, buildings, etc. What interested me most were the sheets with soldiers from different armies and periods. They were printed facing right on the left half of the sheet and facing left on the right half. Thus they could be cut out and glued together to make a cheaper version of lead soldiers. I would spend a long time going through all the sheets before spending my pocket money on one. She was always indulgent, rewarding my small purchase with a candy.

The Jews had been in Wilno for over 600 years and they represented a third of the population. Most of them lived in a Jewish area set within three streets, Dominican, German and Grand. There the Germans established the first ghetto. Through the centre of this area ran Jewish Street, where the Great Synagogue, dating from 1572 with a capacity of over 5,000, was located. In the oldest part of this area the cobbled streets were narrow and winding with deep gutters. The interconnecting alleyways and passages were even narrower. There were shops and workshops everywhere. I had been to that part of town several times as most of our clothes were made there. Practically everything, from underwear to overcoats, was custom-made. Only the owners of the stores and workshops who served mother spoke Polish. It felt like being in a foreign country, teeming with people speaking only Yiddish and wearing different clothing.

At the beginning of September, a huge column of men, women and children moved slowly beneath our windows escorted by Lithuanian paramilitary and a sprinkling of German SS. They carried suitcases and bundles, pushing and pulling baby carriages and carts loaded with personal belongings. The second ghetto was created on the other side of German Street. Both ghettos were surrounded by a brick wall. German Street, running between them, was open to traffic. The rest of Wilno's Jews, mostly professional and assimilated, were being moved there. My mother was very upset; she knew several of them and some were good friends. We learned that the Lithuanians and Germans had been executing large numbers of Jews and some Poles in Ponary Forest.

The school reopened and I started Year 5. As soon as the Germans arrived, the Lithuanians aggressively restarted the Lithuanianisation of the city: street names were changed, and Lithuanian and German were made the only official languages. They tried, unsuccessfully, to reintroduce Lithuanian as the language of instruction in all schools. The Lithuanians' hopes for the rebirth of an independent Lithuanian state were quashed by the Germans. The whole area, including the pre-war Lithuanian state, was made part of Reichskommissariat Ostland, one of the two German administrative districts created by Hitler for the administration of conquered parts of Russia (the other was Ukraine). The Germans were in charge, with Lithuanian advisors. Nevertheless, it was Lithuanians who administrated and controlled the police. The German Gestapo took over the old NKVD building. The same Lithuanian security police, previously helping Russians, were now working for the Germans.

My school friends showed me a gadget that made a sound just like a pistol shot. It was very easy to make from an old-fashioned key that had a hole at the inserting end and a large nail that fit tightly into the hole. The nail's end was cut square and a string, about 3 or 4ft long, was tied from the key handle to the nail's head. The hole in the key was filled with scrapings from match heads, lightly thumbed towards the end, and the nail inserted. The key-nail combo was swung so that the head of the nail hit a wall. The explosion sounded just like a pistol shot and, if made in the entrance to a building or hallway, it sounded much louder. It was fun to annoy the Lithuanian police and gun-shy German soldiers ... I spent a lot of money on matches.

The German administration imposed the same draconian rules, regulations and penalties against the Polish population as it had occupied in 1939. All Polish secondary schools and universities were closed and only Lithuanian ones were allowed. Ownership of cars and motorcycles was forbidden. All radios were confiscated and a severe penalty imposed for owning or listening to one. Food rationing was introduced. A new currency, the *Ostmark*, was introduced. It was the third change of currency since the beginning of the war, each one limiting the exchange amount and all at confiscatory rates of exchange, resulting in the pauperisation of the population. Another item requisitioned by the Germans was men's bicycles, but not ladies'. All the 'male' bicycles disappeared from the streets and a new type of 'ladies' bicycle appeared. It was made by cutting the top bar of the frame next to the seat and welding it much lower. Wiktor's cousin's bicycle was one of those that changed sex.

Wiktor found a great hiding place for our radio in the cellar. It was brought up almost every night and we all listened to the BBC's Polish programme from London. Bedsprings were used for an antenna and the reception was very clear. Wiktor started to teach us Morse code. First we memorised all the letters and then we would practise on the set he produced. One of us would be in one room tapping on a key. The wires led to another room, where the other one would listen to the battery-powered buzzer and transcribe the message. It was great fun and we both became quite proficient.

I decided to show Wiktor our 'armoury' hidden in the cellar, containing the two Russian rifles salvaged from the fire, a couple of bayonets and several leather holsters for Polish Army pistols. We had salvaged those holsters after the Lithuanians took over Wilno. My school friend's father was a janitor in an office building of the pre-war government, where they also lived. We would go and play with him there and my friend showed us an underground air shelter where Polish Army military equipment had been stored. We smuggled out about ten holsters in our school bags. Wiktor said that the rifles were useless and he would get rid of them. However, the holsters were made from good leather. He traded them with his shoemaker friend for skiing boots for us, which he helped to make. This was the same shoemaker who had sheltered him while he was recuperating from the wounds he received in the September 1939 campaign.

In the middle of the November, shortly after he proudly gave us our new boots, Wiktor was arrested by the Gestapo. There was a wave of arrests of Polish reserve officers and young men from academic circles. Apparently the Gestapo, with help from the Lithuanian secret police, had managed to penetrate some underground organisations. Fortunately, some members of the Gestapo were bribable, unlike the NKVD, which was incorruptible. Mother found the necessary channel and, in exchange for a large emerald ring and a pair of matching earrings set in diamonds, Wiktor was released after a couple of weeks. This jewellery was a wedding gift from her mother, the only items left from her pre-First World War jewels. Wiktor returned, late in the evening, emaciated, unshaven and dirty, with signs of severe beatings. The first order of business was delousing. As he soaked in the bathtub, his linens were boiled and all the seams of his suit were pressed with a hot iron. Next morning, clean and shaven, in fresh clothing, he looked much better, even if the bruises were still visible on his face and he smelled faintly of creosote from the anti-lice soap.

As the snow fell we started skiing again. We both outgrew our skis. I took over Andrzej's skis and he, mother's. The Germans requisitioned all skis above a certain length for their army. My mother's skis, like many others, had been shortened to avoid confiscation. As the winter progressed and the temperature fell, we noticed how woefully unprepared for winter the German Army was. Their soldiers were shivering in their thin overcoats. One day, as I was walking from school, a German officer riding in a motorcycle sidecar suddenly stopped and got out. He grabbed a passing Polish woman wearing a Persian lamb fur coat. He made her take the coat off and cut off the sleeves with his penknife. He took off his thin army overcoat, put on the sleeveless fur coat, replaced his overcoat and drove off leaving the unfortunate woman shivering in -20°C.

At the beginning of December 1941, we heard great news on the radio: America had declared war on Germany. Now everybody believed that the war would soon end, maybe even by the following summer. We also heard of German reverses near Moscow. It sounded like what had happened to

Napoleon 130 years before would now happen to Hitler. The bitter Russian winter and the lack of proper winter clothing created a large number of frost-bite casualties in the German Army. We started to see convalescing German soldiers without fingers, ears, noses and even eyelids.

Christmas of 1941 was very subdued and we celebrated with only one guest, Wiktor's younger cousin Zygmunt, whom I liked. He was a stamp collector and advised and helped me with my collecting. I do not remember any contact with my father. When 1942 started, we did not return to public school. Mother hired a tutor, a young man who had been a student at Warsaw Polytechnic before the war. Tadek Szymanski from across the hall joined us. The three of us had lectures from noon, which allowed us to go skiing in the morning. In addition, we had French lessons twice a week from an older lady in her home. According to my mother, she had a proper 'Parisian' accent. Once a week, late on Friday afternoons, a group of boys met clandestinely at the Church of St Casimir. Jesuit priest lectured us on religion and Polish history, subjects that were forbidden in the schools.

That winter, again, there was no heating coal. Our stock of coal was completely finished. In most cellars, however, there was a deposit of coal dust that had accumulated on the floor over the years. In our case, it was almost 2ft deep. An ingenious somebody was making cast-iron stoves specifically designed to burn coal dust. They were spherical in shape, about 18in in diameter with a hinged cover on top through which the coal dust, previously wetted, was loaded. There was a grate and removable ash box at the bottom. They were installed in front of the opening to the firebox of the tile stoves. They were difficult to light, but once lit they were kept burning around the clock. One had to be careful moving around as these protruding stoves could get red hot.

Our tutor emphasised mathematics and science. In one of his lectures he talked about the forces created when water changes state from liquid to steam or ice. I decided to conduct experiments to prove his teachings. The first was the expansion of water when it freezes. That one was easy. I took a beer bottle, filled it completely with water, closed the ceramic cork with a rubber washer and placed it outside the window. Next morning, as expected, I found that the bottle was cracked. In the second experiment I planned to prove the force exerted by steam. This was more challenging. I found an empty bottle of mother's eau de cologne. It was made of very thick glass and had a metal screw top. I half filled it with water and closed the metal top tightly. Accompanied by Andrzej and Tadek, I opened the lid of the potbelly stove in the dining room, where we had lectures, placed the bottle on top of the red-hot coals and closed the lid. We all retired behind the door and waited. Nothing happened for a while. After what I thought was sufficient time I decided to check. I entered the room by myself and lifted the lid of stove with a poker. I saw that the water in the bottle was boiling. I closed the lid and as I turned away the bottle exploded. The noise of the explosion was rather subdued but created a shockwave, alerting mother in her salon. As we were frantically trying to put out the glowing pieces of coal that had fallen on our furniture and carpets, mother's young assistant arrived to see what had happened. The young lady immediately brought wetted towels that finally stopped the fires. The damage was quite spectacular: the carpet had a multitude of small holes burned through, the furniture likewise had charred black spots and the white gypsum plaster ceiling above the stove was grey with embedded pieces of black coal. There was grey dust everywhere. By the time mother arrived, about half an hour later, the room looked a little bit better. Between our maid, my mother's assistant and the three of us, the dust was cleared away but the little black holes and spots remained on our furniture and carpet, to say nothing of the ceiling.

Mother called all three of us and asked for an explanation, zeroing in on me. I told her that it was my idea and why and how I did it. She explained in a stern but quiet tone that I had not exercised good judgment; not only did I cause considerable damage but, more important, I endangered everyone and could have been blinded by the explosion. She let us go saying that we would discuss the matter further. Later that day she told me that she had decided not to punish me, but I had to promise never to conduct any more experiments without first checking with her or Wiktor. I abandoned all future scientific experimentation and directed my efforts to making a slide projector. This project was approved by Wiktor, who also helped. I built a plywood box with an electric bulb inside; it was ventilated so it would not catch fire. I used a magnifying lens from a torch to concentrate the light into a cardboard tube where a second movable lens from a watchmaker's loupe allowed focusing. I made slides from strips of drafting paper on which I traced figures of Napoleonic soldiers in ink. The projector worked fine but I soon lost interest.

Some time during the spring, while walking the streets of Wilno, Wiktor found himself approaching a German officer. They recognised each other as they had been close friends when studying at the Vienna Technical University before the war. He was an Austrian drafted into the German Army. He was in charge of the Wilno office of the *Große Heeresbaudinstellen*, a German Army heavy construction office that constructed facilities for the German Army using local labour. Anybody working for it was issued special ID documents that protected them from casual arrest and gave them more freedom to move around. As a result of this chance meeting, not only Wiktor, but also his cousin Zygmunt, was immediately employed and received the coveted IDs. Later on, several other friends, all members of the Polish Underground, were also employed there.

6

The Best Holiday,
June–August 1942

Some time in June of 1942 mother arranged for us to spend the summer at the Powidaki Estate, 12.5 miles north-west of Wilno. This large estate belonged to some descendant of my father's maternal great-grandfather, Zenon Jan Dłuski, who had eight daughters and forty granddaughters. We were told that there would also be three young girls, relatives of the owners. This did not make me happy; I would have much preferred if they had been boys.

The day of our departure finally arrived. In the late morning a simple one-horse farm wagon pulled into the courtyard. Even though I knew that most of the good riding and carriage horses had been confiscated in the war, I was still hoping for a team of horses with a carriage. After saying our goodbyes, we mounted a wooden bench behind the coachman and went off with a rattle of iron rims on the cobblestones. We crossed the River Wilja by the Green Bridge and started the long climb up Cavalry Street. When we left town, we left the street for the old highway heading north from Wilno, right through Lithuania and on to Latvia. The road was straight and lined with old trees on both sides. It led to the countryside, through rolling hills, farmlands and patches of forest. We saw villages and glimpses of lakes and streams along the way. After about a three-hour drive, we turned into a long straight driveway framed by poplar trees on both sides. The drive stopped at a roundabout with an enormous beech tree in the centre, in front of a manor house. Fifty-two years later, when I returned to Powidaki, that tree was the only recognisable thing left standing. The manor house, its stables, service buildings, poplar trees, park and orchards were all destroyed by the Soviets. This was the case with all the manors in the former Polish territories annexed by Russia in 1944. Russians completely eradicated all Polish presence in what became the Lithuanian, Belarusian and Ukrainian socialist republics.

As the cart stopped we jumped off and went up the front steps of the manor. The lady of the house met us, a beautiful woman in her late thirties flanked by three young girls a little older than us. We had previously met her in Wilno. We bowed to her and she offered her hand to be kissed, as was the custom, and then introduced us to the girls. After the appropriate bows, curtsies and handshakes were exchanged, we stared at each other in awkward silence. It was broken by the arrival of the maid, who led us to our room. We first entered a large hallway. To the right, through opened double doors, we caught a glimpse of a large living room, to the left the dining room and, at the end of the hall, the stairway to the next floor. We followed the maid upstairs to our room, a large one at one end of the manor, above the short side of the building and overlooking the park. The girls' room was also upstairs, another large room with a balcony over the front porch.

The maid showed us where we could clean up, then led us to the kitchen to eat; we had missed our dinner at three o'clock and were quite hungry after our long ride. We then met the housekeeper, a small old woman in black, who had laid out the food for us. Everything was fresh and home-made, and tasted delicious. After that we went to explore the lay of the land, starting with the manor house. It was a large rectangular building typical of the Polish borderlands, about 200 years old, built with heavy logs plastered on both sides and painted white with a wood-shingled roof. There was a large living room with a parquet floor, a richly ornate gypsum ceiling and a tiled heating stove in one corner. There were card tables and seating groups throughout, overlooked by portraits of stern old men and beautiful women. Across the main hallway, the dining room had a huge table surrounded by at least a dozen chairs with more chairs, a serving table and a huge credenza against the walls.

As soon as we had completed our cursory examination of the manor we made a beeline for the stables, a large masonry building with stalls for about thirty horses and an adjoining carriage house. The stable master told us they only had about fifteen horses left now, about six in the stables and the rest working in the field. All the best horses had been requisitioned by the Polish Army, then the Russians and finally the Germans. The stable master told us to come back the next morning and he'd teach us to ride. We got up the next day at sunrise to start what turned out to be the best summer holiday I ever had. For the next two months we had complete freedom to do whatever we wanted and go wherever we chose, provided we didn't interfere with or disrupt the farm work. Powidaki was a medium-sized estate, about 500 hectares. Two-thirds was cultivated land and the rest was made up of pastures and forests. The principal crop was grain but potatoes, sugar beets and tobacco were also cultivated.

The stable master was an older man who had served in the imperial Russian cavalry before and throughout the First World War. After that he had been in the Polish Army during the Polish-Bolshevik War. He was a retired master sergeant of the cavalry. We followed him around while he selected a mare called Old Soviet, bridled her and led her to the paddock. Old Soviet was one of two horses that were somehow acquired from the Russian Army; the other was a younger gelding called Young Soviet. Both were Kazaks, very tough, large ponies accustomed to harsh conditions. They were not used for ploughing but were harnessed to coaches or light wagons, or simply used under the saddle. The stable master told us we first had to learn how to ride bareback before he would put us in a saddle – so we started bareback, holding on to the mane as he led us around the paddock. We eventually progressed to riding independently on bridled horses, and after a couple of weeks were deemed good enough to ride with the men to take the horses to pasture at the end of the day.

Every evening, after field work, the horses were groomed and taken to the pasture for the night. Everybody rode bareback. Each groom led two or three horses and I usually rode on the outside horse of the leader. From the stable yard a country lane led to the fields and pastures about a mile away. The lane was flanked by ditches, fences, balks, trees and bushes that kept our horses on track. We would leave the barn at a walk at sunset, moving to an extended walk once we got to the lane. As soon as the horses broke into a trot we'd push them into a canter as no one enjoyed bareback trotting. Quite often, as we approached the pastures we would let the horses go and run at a full gallop. The pastures were in lowlands with a stream running through them. There were swarms of mosquitoes so we had to close our mouths and squint our eyes while passing through them. When we finally arrived, the horses were hobbled with rope fetters in the pastures; we quickly mastered that. A man who guarded the horses at night would appear from a lean-to surrounded by smoke from a fire meant to deter mosquitoes. He was a big man who loomed even larger than he was because of his full-length sheepskin cape, black fur turned to the outside. He was always smoking a smelly cigarette made from weeds rolled in newspaper, also meant to keep the mosquitoes at bay. After some brief banter, the grooms and us boys would walk home as night fell.

As a result of all this bareback riding my inner thighs developed big, painful scabs. After a few evenings the sores became quite uncomfortable so I decided to ease my pain by switching my sitting position, a trick I had seen done in the movies by Cossacks and Indians. I shifted my lower body to the right while leaning to the left in such a way that the crook of my left knee supported my body over the horse. This worked for a while but when the horse broke into a full gallop I started to lose my grip and slipped off. Luckily, I managed to thrust myself into a ditch to avoid being trampled by the horses behind me; the last groom stopped and helped me remount. The next morning the housekeeper took me to her room, made me drop my trousers, and dressed my scabs with some evil smelling poultice that was very effective.

The old sergeant was a very good instructor and over the next two months we really learned to ride. Whenever we could, we would ride bareback. We loved to take the horses to the lake and swim holding their tails. Whenever any riding horse was available, we would saddle him up and go. But I still loved our evening bareback rides to the pasture and the walk back with the grooms the best.

During that summer we spent most of our time following farm hands working on the estate. They were very difficult times since all agricultural products were controlled by the Germans and every estate and farm had to supply them with a crippling amount of crops and livestock. At the same time, shortages made it difficult to obtain the supplies necessary to run the estate efficiently. The owner actively ran the estate and spent most of his time supervising work in the fields, assisted by his younger brother, Marek. Most of our interactions were with Marek. He was a reserve cadet officer in the cavalry and had been about to start university when the war broke out. He managed to avoid POW camp and made his way to his brother's estate. Throughout the summer he would disappear unexpectedly for days at a time, most probably something to do with the underground. The foreman, who lived in a *czworaki* (quadraplex) next to the manor, also took us under his wing. Altogether, there were eight families living there but only six included men as two had not returned from the 1939 campaign. The rest of the workers came from a nearby village of the same name as the estate, Powidaki. The field work followed the seasons. When we arrived, they were still ploughing some fields in preparation for sowing wheat for the autumn. Dogs always followed the ploughs, waiting for nests of field mice to be unearthed so they could gobble up the little babies. Not really any different from what was going on throughout Europe at the time, the strong devouring the helpless. Haying was next. Grass was cut and laid out in the meadows to dry, then raked into large haystacks mostly by women. The hay was then loaded onto wagons stacked very high; a wooden pole was placed on top and tied down. We would climb on top of the hay and ride to the barn. After it was unloaded, the ride back was great fun as the horses were driven fast. The empty wagon would sway and jump up and down on the country lanes and fields as the pair of horses broke from a canter into a gallop.

Throughout the night many of the young farm hands and girls slept on the hay in the barn. One night we decided to join them. We arrived carrying our bedding to the amazement of everybody there. It was probably the first time someone from the manor had ever joined them. There was a lot of bumping, ribbing and teasing amongst the men and women, but as night fell the bustle died down. I fell asleep to rustling, murmuring, giggling and other noises that I couldn't identify then.

Tobacco was grown in a nearby field. By that time we had already experimented a few times with cigarettes. I convinced Andrzej that we should try again. We went to the fields, broke off a few large green tobacco leaves and dried them in the attic. When they turned yellow we chopped them up and rolled them with newspaper into cigar-sized cigarettes. We sat facing each other and lit them. We coughed and gagged while we smoked them until the bitter end as neither of us wanted to appear chicken. We both got sick after that and I never smoked again. In the middle of August the wheat harvest began. On the first day, as tradition dictated, the owner led his men carrying a scythe. He started at the corner of the field, cutting a wide swath into the grain. As soon as he had moved a few feet, he was followed by the men behind him, the entire staggered line of ten to fifteen men moved forward with slow, measured strokes. They would stop from time to time to re-sharpen their scythes or take a drink of water brought to them by the younger boys. The men were followed by women who used sickles to scrape the fallen grain into piles, which were bundled into sheaves and stacked together. We helped with the stacking. Work continued from early morning until evening, day after day, interrupted only for the noon meal brought out by the older women or children. When the grain stacked in the fields was sufficiently dry it was transported to the barn. Again, we would ride on the fully loaded wagons, help unload the goods and return at high speed. Summer passed very quickly. Besides our forays into the fields, riding horses, swimming in the lake, fishing and picking wild berries and mushrooms, we also watched stallions covering mares, and the village blacksmiths shoe horses and replace the iron rings on cart wheels. We had a great time and to our dismay it passed quickly. At the beginning of September we returned home.

7

From Wilno to Warsaw, September 1942–19 March 1943

Upon our return, Andrzej, Tadek and I resumed lectures with our tutor. I started my last year of primary schooling and Andrzej the first year of the *gimnazium* curriculum (first of six years of secondary education). Shortly thereafter, Tadek's grandmother died and he left for Warsaw to live with his aunt. That autumn there was another fuel shortage and our supply of coal dust from the cellar floor was almost completely exhausted. At that time electricity was rationed at minimal levels. There were draconian penalties for exceeding that allowance: immediate suspension of service, fines and even prison. Wiktor, being an electrical engineer, found a solution. He altered the electricity meter so that at the flip of a switch it would reverse direction and the recorded consumption would decrease. From time to time we would flip the switch and run the meter backwards.

Wiktor then made several space heaters using resistant coils mounted on insulated frames. Each frame was about 18in high and 2ft wide with coils running up and down a couple of inches apart. The frames were mounted in flowerpots filled with cement to give them stability. After a couple of them were turned on they blew the fuses. Wiktor then changed the fuses not only in our apartment but also on the principal lines running into the building. The heaters were very effective but you had to be very careful around them as the resistant coils were red hot.

In late autumn, mother told us she would try to go to Warsaw. At that time you needed a special pass from the German authorities to cross the border between what was considered the *Ostland*, territories captured by Germans after their invasion of Russia, and the *Generalgouvernement*, the part of Poland captured in 1939. After obtaining the necessary pass in November, she left for Warsaw. Before leaving, Zygmunt asked her to deliver a letter to Janek Bytnar, an old friend from secondary school. (Jan Bytnar, code name 'Rudy', became a legendary figure in the Polish Underground). She returned about two weeks later with a letter for Zygmunt and news of all the family: uncle Jozef Emir-Hassan's wife was killed in the September 1939 bombing and he was wounded. Their apartment was damaged. My mother's brother Stefan's apartment was destroyed by bombing. His wife and daughter Danuta moved to a house my grandmother had bought in Babice outside of Warsaw. They were still receiving food parcels from Portugal, indicating that uncle Stefan was alive. After the fall of France he made his way across the channel and rejoined the Polish Air Force in England.

The snows began and we started to ski again. One day before Christmas, as we left our courtyard we noticed a newly built structure at the corner of the park, next to the cathedral. It was a wooden beam about 18ft long supported by wooden posts at both ends, 12ft above ground. The next morning when I woke up to a grey, overcast day I saw from my window that bodies were hanging from the beam. I dressed and quietly left the apartment through the kitchen. There were twelve bodies, two of them women. They had their winter clothes on, but all were bare headed. On the ropes, their heads were bent at an unnatural angle. Some had boards hanging from their necks with 'PARTIZANEN' (partisan) painted in crude black letters. As they passed by, men would take off their hats and women would cross themselves.

Christmas came and went, and was, again, very subdued. As the new year, 1943, began, everybody once again started saying that Germany would be defeated this summer. There was more and more news about the battle at Stalingrad. As always, the BBC and German propaganda presented opposing views. Needless to say, we believed the BBC. Towards the end of January German radio stopped broadcasting news about Stalingrad. On the last day of January 1943, German radio started to play very sombre music. Finally, there was the announcement of defeat. After hearing the scope of the German Army's defeat on clandestine radio from London, mother said, 'We have to move to Warsaw, we will never see Wilno Polish again.' Her words turned out to be prophetic. At the Yalta Conference in February 1945, Roosevelt and Churchill agreed to Stalin's demand to keep the eastern part of Poland, taken previously in September 1939 in accordance with the Molotov–Ribbentrop Pact of 23 August 1939. The Polish population was later resettled in communist Poland. Starting at the end of 1944, about 100,000 Poles left Wilno, taking with them the memory of Polish culture, language and the spirit of the Commonwealth of Two Nations. After 400 years it had died forever.

Wilno became Vilnius; my mother never returned, and I returned for the first time in 1994, fifty-one years later.

At the end of February, mother told us that we would be moving to Warsaw and instructed us not to tell anyone. She had clearly been planning this for some time as our furniture, carpets and even clothing were gradually being sold off. She also sold her beauty salon. The proceeds from all the sales were converted into gold coins, mostly Imperial Russian 10 rouble pieces called *chervonets*, as well as British Sovereign and American dollar gold coins. The challenge was hiding the gold coins so they would not be discovered during an inspection at the border. Wiktor found three big thermoses. He opened them up and very carefully cut out the bottom from the glass casing of the vacuum flask. The space between the outer and inner casings was about half an inch wide. Gold coins were packed into that space with cotton wool to prevent them rattling and the cut-out bottom glued back. The rest of the coins were layered between the stiffening boards on the bottom of mother's bag.

Finally, on a Sunday afternoon in the middle of March, we were told to pack our bags as we were leaving the next day. We could take only hand luggage that we could carry. Andrzej, mother and I would go first; Wiktor and Zygmunt would follow later. We each took just a backpack with a 'golden' thermos and a small suitcase. Mother had her 'golden' bag and thermos and one larger suitcase. The only personal article I took with me was my stamp collection.

Early next morning, while it was still dark, a truck belonging to the *Große Heeresbaudinstellen* Company pulled into our courtyard. Wiktor arranged for us to travel in the truck, which was going to Warsaw on official business. We climbed into the back and sat on our suitcases, the back gate was slammed shut and the canvas top closed. The truck started to move, rattling through the streets of Wilno. When we left the city the truck picked up speed and the wind whistled through the loose canvas. It was very cold, well below freezing. We bundled ourselves in blankets and sat close together for warmth. After a while the truck stopped and the driver invited one of us to sit in the cab to warm up. Every hour or so, we traded places. The truck was an old Russian Army ZiS modified to run on gas generated from wood. The iron furnace, about 18in in diameter and 5ft tall, was mounted outside the cab on the other side of the driver. Every few hours we had to stop and load more wood chips into it.

Around noon we drove through Grodno and crossed the River Niemen, where the truck and our papers were checked. In the afternoon we arrived at the administrative border established by the Germans between the *Generalgouvernement* and *Ostland*. The border check was rather perfunctory as the truck belonged to an official German company and made the same trip almost every week. After the guards examined my mother's documents and took a cursory look at our open suitcases, we were allowed to proceed. No one showed any interest in our thermoses. Shortly after the border we stopped for the night as it was getting dark and very cold. After some warm soup, we slept in our clothes on the floor, wrapped in our blankets.

Our truck left early the next morning, arriving in Warsaw just before noon on 19 March 1943.

8

Warsaw, 19 March 1943–December 1943

W e were dropped off in the Grochów suburb on the Praga side of Warsaw, at my great-aunt Walerja's villa, who greeted us warmly. Walerja was the younger sister of my maternal grandmother and mother's favourite aunt. As a child, mother used to spend her Easter holidays with her. Before the Russian Revolution, Walerja and her husband Zdzisław Modzelewski lived on their *Lubomirka* estate near Kiev. They and their baby daughter survived the Revolution and escaped to Poland. Zdzisław became the administrator of all the estates belonging to Count Grocholski and lived on an estate near Zbaraż in south-eastern Poland. My mother, her brothers and all their Emir-Hassan cousins spent their summer holidays there.

Walerja was a slender, elegant and prematurely grey woman. When she and her husband moved to Zbaraż in the early 1920s they endured an attack on the manor by bandits. Zdzisław was shot and lost an eye, but survived. The bandits threatened to kill their two young children, but luckily the shots were heard by a unit of the Polish Army, which came to their rescue. After the Polish-Bolshevik War, the border areas were a no-man's-land. Bands of Ukrainian partisans, White Russians, Soviet deserters and just plain bandits robbed and burned estates. Aunt Walerja perished in the Warsaw Uprising; her body was never found.

Aunt Walerja's home was about a fifteen-minute walk to the tram stop on the main street, from where it took about half an hour to reach the centre of Warsaw. There was a great shortage of tram wagons because all the new ones had been taken to Germany. On top of that, the front third of the first wagon was *Nur für Deutsche*, reserved for Germans only. The wagons were always overcrowded with people literally hanging on the outside.

Early in April 1943, we moved to a boarding house on Sienna Street in the centre of the city. Mother was busy making contacts and looking for an apartment, which was not an easy task as there was a tremendous shortage of housing. In addition, she needed an apartment in the centre of the city large enough to set up her cosmetic salon. We lived there for one month, a very dramatic month. Mother found out that both Janek Bytnar and his father had been arrested by the Gestapo. Janek's father was sent to Auschwitz; Janek was tortured by the Gestapo, and then rescued in a spectacular armed action carried out by his friends. He died four days later from injuries sustained in torture during his interrogation.

In mid-April the Germans published information regarding the massacre of Polish officers in Katyń Forest by the NKVD. The papers showed pictures of exhumed Polish officers in uniform, hands tied behind their backs with wire, and holes in the back of their skulls. A new list of names with military ranks was published daily in the papers and displayed on wall posters. Groups of people would stand silently before them, checking the names.

On Monday 19 April, news spread about fighting in the ghetto. Over the next few days we heard explosions, sporadic shots and the rattle of machine guns from the direction of the ghetto. At night the glow of burning fires was visible from the same direction. While walking nearby I saw a group of prisoners, guarded by Germans, dumping rubble into manholes to block any escape through the sewers.

Early on the Friday morning before Easter there was a document inspection for everyone in our boarding house. A uniformed Gestapo officer and a civilian speaking heavily accented Polish burst into our room, demanding to see our IDs. Mother's papers were in order but she couldn't find our birth certificates right away. They would not believe mother's insistence that we were her children, shouting that she was too young to be our mother. The Gestapo officer started to yell that she was hiding Jewish boys; looking at my brother he shouted, 'He is a Yid, look at his dark wavy hair.' When mother protested again, he hit her across the face, yelling that he would 'take care of all of us'. As he tried to pull his gun from the holster, the other man told us to drop our trousers. A visual examination revealed that we were not circumcised. After confirming the findings, the Gestapo officer casually holstered his gun and left the room.

On the Monday after Easter we took a tram to go and visit Wacek Wieczorek, a friend of ours from Wilno. He lived on Zakroczymska Street on the other side of the old town, close to the ghetto. When we disembarked near Krasiński Square we could hear explosions and see clouds of dust arising from the ghetto. As we walked close to it we saw a surreal scene: on our side of the wall the trams were running, there was light traffic on the street and a few people walked quickly and purposefully, looking straight ahead. On the other side of the wall there were explosions, burning fires, clouds of smoke and dust. A single Stuka plane circled above, diving down and dropping bombs. A group of German SS men were manhandling a field gun through a breach in the ghetto wall. Polish police were stationed outside to keep people away.

By the middle of May it was over. The last of the heroic fighters perished. On 16 May the Great Synagogue was blown up and the Germans started to methodically destroy all the buildings within the ghetto. Fires burned for a long time and buildings were blown up. The entire area was levelled, becoming nothing more than a great field of rubble.

After a month in the boarding house, mother found a perfect apartment located on the main street, 37 Nowy Swiat (now part of Royal Way, the main thoroughfare to the Royal Castle). Before the war, it was considered one of the most fashionable streets in Warsaw. Most of the buildings were four storeys high, built between 18th and 19th centuries in a neoclassical style. The ground floors were used for commercial purposes while the upper floors were residential. Our apartment was on the second floor. We had four rooms plus a maid's room and a kitchen with a separate service entrance. Shortly after we moved in, Wiktor and Zygmunt arrived from Wilno. Wiktor quietly left his job with the tacit permission of the German lieutenant in charge (his Austrian friend from Vienna Polytechnic), hoping he would not report his disappearance to the Gestapo. Zygmunt moved into the maid's room and for the first few weeks Wiktor slept at mother's aunt's apartment nearby. The Gestapo conducted most of their arrests at night so, had Wiktor somehow been informed upon, he would most likely have been taken at night within the first few weeks of their arrival. At that time, mother started to work in a beauty salon to make contacts before opening her own business.

During June and part of July we spent a lot of time in Babice, where my aunt, the wife of my mother's brother Stefan, lived together with Danuta. There was also another girl, a little younger, who was introduced as her cousin. Many years later, Danuta told me that this 'cousin' was not actually a relative but a Jewish girl her mother had been hiding. Danuta learned the truth after the war, when the girl was repatriated to Israel. The rest of the summer was spent in Swider, close to the town of Otwock, about 20 miles from Warsaw. We stayed in a boarding house within walking distance of a swimmable part of the river. We had a great time as both Tadek and Wacek were there and the rest of the summer passed very quickly.

At that time we knew that there was a very strong and well-developed Polish Underground in Warsaw that incorporated the Boy Scouts. We had seen signs of their activity on the streets: the symbol 'PW', an acronym for *Polska Walczy* (Fighting Poland), was painted in the form of an anchor on buildings and monuments all over Warsaw. We were trying to find a contact so we could join. In Swider I approached Wacek, a native of Warsaw, who was two years older than me and had been back from Wilno for over a year. Without making any commitment, he said he would try to arrange a 'meeting' when he was back in Warsaw.

Upon our return from Swider, mother told us that we would resume our studies. Since the start of the occupation, the Germans had closed all the secondary schools and universities in Poland. Primary schools and a few trade schools had been allowed to stay open. As a consequence, an underground education system was created which the Germans tried to suppress with draconian penalties.

In the first week of August mother took us to see Miss Górska, daughter of Dr Wojciech Górski, who in 1877 had founded a secondary school that became one of the best private and progressive schools in Warsaw. Mother's brothers and most of her cousins completed their secondary education there. Mother contacted Miss Górska to arrange for an interview. She looked like an old maid, a very stern, tall woman. After the interview, we were accepted to the *Gimnazium*, me to the first year and Andrzej to the second. Lessons were given in private homes in small groups called *komplety*; my group had eight boys. A teacher would arrive and lecture us for a few hours on various subjects. Each boy would arrive and depart individually, or in pairs at staggered times. We would meet at different homes and at varying times. Miss Górska taught Latin and French. There were two male teachers, one taught maths and science, and the other lectured on Polish language, literature and history. Religious education was given by a priest in one of the churches. As a first-year student I had to learn how to be an altar boy, which required memorisation of the Latin liturgy. I served mass at a hospital chapel once a week, very early in the morning.

Shortly after we started our education, Wacek came to see me and told me that he could arrange the 'meeting' if we were still interested. 'Of course we are!' I shouted on hearing the good news. The meeting was arranged and the next day he introduced us to 'Jerzy' and 'Wojtek'. Jerzy, the younger of the two, looked about 15 or 16; Wojtek was probably 18. They asked us a lot of questions about our background and family. After the interrogation Jerzy looked at Wojtek, who nodded and I knew that we were in. Jerzy gave us the time and place of our next meeting and then told us to choose code names. I decided on *Sokół*, meaning 'Falcon', and Andrzej chose 'Tarzan'. Much later I learned that Jerzy's real name was Wiśniewski; he became our squad leader.

I never learned Wojtek's real name and never knew where either of them lived. Wojtek was second in command of our troop, 'Number 11'. At our first meeting we met the other six boys and were introduced by our code names. We were told only to use our code names and adhere to the principle that 'what you do not know, you cannot betray'. Nonetheless, we soon learned the others' real names and where some of them lived.

From then on, we would meet once or twice a week at different apartments. Our training followed the pre-war Polish Boy Scouts model, but had a greater emphasis on paramilitary skills – communications, map reading and first aid. We sharpened our observation skills with an exercise in which about twenty different items were placed on a table and covered by a blanket. The blanket was removed for one minute, after which we had to write a description of each object, with as much detail as possible. Another field-related exercise was to observe military vehicular traffic and give detailed reports, like '13:02, Opel Admiral car with driver, escort armed with MP40 and two officers, WH licence plates'. We were also required to know Warsaw inside and out, particularly the transportation system: tramlines, suburban trains and train stations. We had to be aware of all possible escape routes through buildings with additional exits that opened onto a different street from the entrance. We were given the address of all these buildings and had to make sure we knew them all. If we discovered a new pass-through building, we were to report it.

We also learned ordinary Boy Scout skills such as knot tying. We received lectures from Wojtek on the structure of our organisation. Ours was an underground continuation of the ZHP (Związek Harcerstwa Polskiego), the pre-war Polish Boy Scouts. The underground Boy Scout organisation was formed in the autumn of 1939, at the very beginning of the German occupation. It assumed a new name, *Szare Szeregi*, meaning 'Grey Ranks'. It was divided into three groups based on age: the youngest, for boys of 12 to 14, where we started, was called *Zawisza*, the name of a legendary medieval Polish knight. Our mission was to prepare ourselves for auxiliary military service in the case of an uprising. In the meantime, we had to continue our education so that we could contribute to the rebuilding of Poland after the war. The second group, for boys of 15 to 17, was 'BS', an acronym for *Bojowe Szkoły*, meaning 'combat school'. This group underwent military training and took part in small acts of sabotage, a form of psychological warfare against the Germans. The oldest boys, 18 and over, were the assault groups or 'GS', *Grupy Szturmowe*. The GS were incorporated into the *Armia Krajowa* (the AK, or Home Army of the Polish Underground) and used on special operations. These were the elite troops of the Underground.

After the summer of 1943 our lives fell back into a routine. Mother opened her beauty salon and steadily expanded her clientele while Wiktor did small electrical jobs. I have no idea what Zygmunt was doing; he periodically disappeared for prolonged periods of time. There is no question in my mind that he was involved with the Underground. Since we had no maid, Wiktor, Andrzej and I helped with the housework and Wiktor did some of the cooking. Finding food was a problem as it was severely rationed. However, there was a thriving black market where almost anything could be obtained, even if at exorbitant prices. We managed to eat better than the average person, but food was scarce and limited in choice. It was carefully portioned and never wasted; everybody always finished everything on his plate. Meat was the scarcest food item, except for horsemeat, which was not rationed. We ate horsemeat quite often. I loved it, I thought it was good.

Our days were fully occupied. Between the underground secondary school, Boy Scout meetings and exercises, schoolwork and housework, we had little free time. I spent what spare time I had making toy tanks, which I sold to toyshops to bolster the limited pocket money I received from my mother. The tanks were about 2 to 3in long, made of wood, cardboard and clothing snaps that served as the tanks' wheels. They sold quite well as there was a shortage of any toys and my little business did indeed provide me with additional pocket money. Later I increased my production line by making toy submarines, photo albums, gypsum lambs for Easter, and whatever else there was a market for.

We got to know Warsaw inside and out by walking the streets and riding the trams. It was a large and crowded city with a pre-war population of 1.3 million, which included more than 400,000 Jews. Initially, these numbers were increased by the influx of Poles forced out of the western part of Poland annexed to the German Reich. After the liquidation of the ghetto in 1943, the remaining Polish population in Warsaw was reduced to less than 1 million. The habitable areas of Warsaw had decreased due to damage wrought during the September 1939 siege, the destruction of the ghetto and the establishment of a German-only district in the best part of the city. Transportation was a big problem: all city buses and private cars, including taxis, were appropriated by the Germans. Poles were not allowed to own motorcars or motorcycles. What remained for the general population were horse-drawn *droshky* and a new invention: the pedal-powered rickshaw. The only motor vehicles moving through the streets of Warsaw were driven by Germans.

On several occasion, while wandering through the streets of Warsaw, we came across *łapanki*, German roundups. All of a sudden a street would be blocked at both ends by Germans and all working-age men and women were segregated and their IDs checked. Most of them were loaded into *budy* (covered trucks) and driven away. If they were lucky, they ended up as forced labourers in Germany; if not, in a concentration camp or as a hostage to be executed later. Once, when I found myself in one such *łapanka*, I remembered that there was a pass-through in one of the buildings. I quickly directed several people towards it and a large number of them escaped the roundup. Our Boy Scout training was paying off.

In October 1943, the Germans began public executions of hostages on the streets of Warsaw. They would publish a list of the names of hostages and a warning that any hostile act on the part of the population would lead to hostage executions. Following each execution, another list of names and birthdays was published on red paper, stating that they had been executed for such and such a crime, usually killings of Germans or some act of sabotage. Hostages were executed at the rate of ten Poles for one German. The lists were plastered on the streets of Warsaw, some with over 100 names.

On 12 November 1943, in the middle of the day, as I approached our apartment I realised that our block was closed off at both ends. This time it was not a roundup. On the contrary, the Germans allowed all the traffic to leave and the block was absolutely empty. I was at the entrance gate to our building and there were a few other people scattered around the entrances to nearby buildings. Germans were patrolling on both sides of the street. After about fifteen minutes, I heard the unmistakable sound of the German police siren. From the direction of the Old Town, a convoy of two large open German police cars arrived escorting a covered truck, stopping in front of No. 49, about six buildings away from us. The Germans dismounted and pulled thirty men out from the truck, shoving them against the wall. The men were in civilian clothes, gagged and with their hands tied behind their back. When they were all lined up against the wall, a few SS men stepped forward and raked them with machine pistol fire. An officer walking among the bodies delivering a *coup de grâce* with his pistol. Somehow those measured single shots were more unnerving than the rattle of the machine pistols.

After a few minutes, as the Germans stood around and lit cigarettes, a few men in striped concentration camp uniforms were brought out from the same truck. I thought they would be the next ones to be shot, but instead they picked up the corpses and loaded them back into the truck. Once all the bleeding bodies were loaded, the Germans mounted up and departed. Before traffic flow was restored a fire engine arrived and hosed the blood from the pavement. I stood watching the red water flow into the gutter. The blood in the water slowly dissipated, the firemen left, the water stopped flowing and the traffic resumed. Within half an hour the cleanly washed pavement in front of a bullet pockmarked wall stained with blood, was covered in flowers and lit candles. The next day I read posted on a nearby wall the names and birthdays of the thirty men whose executions I had witnessed.

Three weeks later, on 2 December, Andrzej and I witnessed another execution on the other side of our street, conducted in a similar manner. It was a bit further from us, about twelve buildings away at No. 64. According to the next day's announcement, thirty-four men had been shot. These public executions continued into February 1944 and during those four months there were thirty-five executions on the streets of Warsaw. Flowers and lit candles always appeared at the execution sites.

Today there are simple, identical stone memorial plaques at each of these sites around Warsaw, all bearing the same inscription:

A Place Consecrated By The Blood Of Poles Fallen For Freedom And Country
Here On 2 XII 1943 Hitlerites Executed 34 Poles

To this day, on the anniversary of the executions, there are always flowers and lit candles on the pavements under the plaques.

9

Warsaw, December 1943– 31 July 1944

Christmas 1943 and New Year 1944 ushered in a new spirit. The Russian offensive was slowly grinding down the German Army and making its way towards Poland. In early January 1944, the Russian Army crossed the 1939 Polish-Soviet border. Everybody was sure that the war would end this year.

The Boy Scouts' motto was 'Today, tomorrow, and the day after tomorrow'. 'Today' was what we were doing during the occupation: preparing ourselves for 'tomorrow', i.e the armed fight against the Germans. In the 'tomorrow' phase, our mission would be to assist the Polish underground Armed Forces with communication, reconnaissance and other military functions. The 'day after tomorrow' would be the rebuilding of Poland, for which we had to prepare by studying hard now. In a meeting that January we were assigned an assembly place to meet when the fighting started. We were to meet at the apartment of one of our members, near the Square of our Saviour.

In between our clandestine classes, Boy Scout meetings and exercises we travelled all over Warsaw, mostly by foot and tram. These activities, plus our homework and housework, made our days quite full. In addition to our old friends from Wilno, we had a group of friends from school and scouts. We became friendly with Ryszard Budzianowski, who lived across the street from us and was the same age as Andrzej. We started to socialise with girls, mostly sisters of our friends, and I must say I liked that very much.

What we lacked were sports. All the sporting facilities, including tennis courts, swimming pools, gymnasiums and stadiums were closed to Poles. When winter came, we missed skiing. One of the few sporting activities we were able to engage in freely was swimming in the Vistula. On the Praga side of the river there were floating swimming pools made from big barges that had changing rooms and lockers. Part of the deck was cut out, forming a pool with the bottom and sides made of slats through which the river flowed. We kayaked and raced rented bicycles in the velodrome, about the only sporting facilities open to Poles. We played football on suburban fields and large courtyards.

We knew that the Polish Armed Forces in exile were fighting with the Allies. The exploits of Polish fighter pilots in the Battle of Britain were well known thanks to the Polish writer Arkady Fiedler. His book *Squadron 303* was published in England, first in Polish as *Dywizjon 303* and then in English. A copy was parachuted into Poland and secretly reprinted by the Underground. In the winter of 1943–44 our unit was given a copy and each of us had just two days to read it. I spent almost the entire night reading that book by torch while under my covers and managed to finish just as the battery died.

The second book published clandestinely in Warsaw was Aleksander Kaminski's *Kamienie na Szaniec* (*Stones for the Rampart*). The book was based on the actions of a group of older Boy Scouts who, in 1939, all graduated from Stefan Batory secondary school in Warsaw. They were active in the Underground from the very beginning of the occupation. According to the author, the story was about 'magnificent ideas of brotherhood and service; about men who knew how to live and die beautifully'. It was the story of Janek Bytnar. All the men were classmates and friends of Zygmunt. Again we had the book for only two days.

The title referred to a line from Juliusz Slowacki's poem 'My Testament' published in 1840, shortly after the failed uprising of 1831, when Poland lost its independence:

> But I beseech you – do not let the living lose hope
> Lead the nation with a torch
> And one by one, as need be, go to death
> As stones hurled on the ramparts by God.

And that is how this generation lived and died during the occupation and Uprising.

Possession of either one of these books, or any underground press, was a sure-fire ticket to a concentration camp.

Towards the end of March 1944, while we were out, mother received a telephone call from Zygmunt:

> Niusiu, I met Janek Bytnar at the railway station. Please take my suitcase from under the bed and bring it to the station. Do you understand?
>   Yes
>   Thank you, goodbye.

Mother took his suitcase straight to the next-door neighbours, who were good friends, and it was immediately removed from the building. When we came back mother told us that Zygmunt had been 'burned' and gone into hiding. We were told to go through everything to make sure there was nothing incriminating that would connect us to the clandestine school or to 'whatever else you are involved in'. Even though everybody knew, neither our membership in the Boy Scouts or Wiktor and Zygmunt's in the Underground was ever talked about.

Next morning we were told to leave early and stay away all day. We left early, went to classes and meetings, and spent the rest of the time at our friend's apartment, returning home in the evening. For the next several days nothing happened and then, late one afternoon just as we arrived, a very excited gatekeeper was waiting for us in the entryway. He told us that the Gestapo had arrived around noon; three men had gone up to our apartment while the other two remained in the *porte cochère* with a machine gun. The Gestapo was there for about an hour but left without arresting anybody. We ran to our apartment. Mother was sitting alone in her salon – following Zygmunt's telephone call, she had cancelled all her clients and told her two employees not to come to work.

She told us what had happened. She had heard shouting and commotion in the *porte cochère* and seen through the window the gatekeeper pointing to our apartment and three Gestapo men marching through the courtyard towards the staircase. The loud steps stopped in front of our door then there was loud banging. As she opened the door the three men barged in, a young Gestapo officer in a black uniform and two in civilian garb. One of the plain-clothes agents spoke Polish and started to interrogate mother. Instead of replying to him she turned to the officer and asked him if he spoke French. He said yes and told the other two to start searching the apartment while he began to interrogate mother in French. He wanted to know where Zygmunt was. Mother replied that she also wanted to know as she was very worried because he had left about two weeks ago and hadn't come back or called. The relatively short interrogation ended and the conversation switched to Paris. Mother was a very attractive woman and kept her cool. They were interrupted by the Polish speaker, who had found a page of Latin exercises that Andrzej had overlooked (Latin had been taught in secondary schools, which were now closed). To his visible annoyance, the Gestapo officer dismissed this and in less than an hour they left. It was a miracle that she was not arrested and interrogated further by the Gestapo.

Wiktor later told us what had happened with Zygmunt. He had been on his way to a meeting of the Underground. It turned out that the meeting, which was to be held in a second-floor apartment in Warsaw, was compromised. As Zygmunt knocked on the door with the pre-arranged signal, the door opened and he was pistol whipped and pulled inside. Two Gestapo agents were pointing their pistols at Zygmunt. He was told to remove his jacket and sit on the chair next to the door with his hands clasped behind his head. One of the agents stood by the door, pistol in hand, waiting for more arrivals. The other agent took Zygmunt's wallet to the adjoining room. Soon there were sounds of shouting and people being hit. Zygmunt noticed that the entrance door was not locked, the door could be opened by simply pulling the handle. After a few minutes, the first Gestapo agent came back and dropped some rope on the floor in front of Zygmunt, presumably to be used for tying hands. When the Gestapo agent returned to the room, the other standing in front looked down at the rope. In that instant, Zygmunt kicked the pistol out of his hand, pulled open the door, hitting the agent, and ran out of the apartment. Somehow he managed to escape even though he had been running through the streets with his face and shirt covered in blood, without a jacket in cold weather and without any documents. He was now at a safe place outside of Warsaw.

Zygmunt's luck ran out half a year later. On 1 August, the first day of the Uprising, he was killed. His body was never found.

On the Monday morning after Easter, a cold, windy overcast day, Andrzej and I were on a tram travelling down Królewska Street. As always, the tram was overcrowded. Andrzej managed to squeeze inside but I was standing on a step with three other men, hugging onto a handlebar. It was raining that day and the streets were wet with dirty water standing in the gutters. As we passed the large and empty Piłsudzki Square, renamed Adolf Hitler Platz, a gust of wind blew my cap off. I jumped off the tram, motioning to Andrzej to continue home. I picked up my soaking wet cap from a puddle of dirty water and found myself in front of a large plate glass window of a *Soldatenheim*, a restaurant-nightclub for German soldiers. It looked empty inside. A quick look left and right confirmed that the street was also empty. I stepped up to the window and with my wet dirty cap painted a gallows with a swastika hanging from the noose.

Stepping back to admire my handiwork I noticed the door to my right open. As I turned to run away I was grabbed by a German soldier who had snuck up behind me. I was taken inside, shoved and kicked by three soldiers as they started to take off their army belts. At that moment a German lieutenant appeared from the back room. He was in his late middle age, short but large in girth. He didn't look very military, more like the proprietor of a restaurant or hotel, which he most likely had been before the war. He asked the soldiers what had happened and they pointed to the window. I must say that from the darkened inside my art work was impressive: the gallows was about 5ft high, with a 3ft long arm and a 2 x 2ft swastika hanging from its noose.

The officer asked me in German what my name was. 'Jan Kowalski, Herr Oberleutnant', I replied, which is like saying John Smith in English. 'Where is your father?' was the next question. 'On the Russian front, working for *Große Heeresbaudinstellen*', I replied. After yelling and berating me for five minutes, he told the soldiers to let me go. I was taken outside and let go with couple of swift kicks to my backside. I was very lucky; I could have ended up in a concentration camp.

In the spring of 1944 mother finally relented to our request for a dog and we got a female Fox Terrier puppy. We named her Zabcia, meaning 'little frog'. She was a very lovely, active dog, but also very mischievous. She was great company, and we tried to take her with us everywhere.

The weather was unusually warm that summer. By the end of May we had already started to swim in the Vistula, about a month earlier than usual. In just a few months Andrzej had shot up and was now taller than mother, standing about 5ft 7in. He had also filled out and now weighed almost 110lb. I was about half a head shorter.

We continued with our clandestine lessons. My group of eight 13-year-olds, a so-called *komplet*, met at the homes of two different parents. Because my mother ran her business from our apartment, it was not considered advisable to meet there. One of the apartments used was on Królewska Street overlooking the Saxon Gardens. The father of our classmates was a doctor. In his bookcase, his son found a copy of *The Ideal Marriage* by Van de Velde, which we all paged through with great interest. The last chapter was a description of sexual positions … in Latin! We spent a considerable amount of time with a Polish-Latin dictionary trying to translate it – it was definitely more fun than translating Cicero.

Our Boy Scout squad started its field exercises. Every other weekend we took a train to a forest in one of the suburbs. We always dispersed into small groups of two or three, never travelling in a pack. We would go to a secluded area and start our exercises: compass training, estimating distances and heights, finding north without a compass and so on. We would go to the edge of the forest and make a topographical sketch, noting any important features of the surrounding area. We trained in signalling with flags. The other boys were also learning Morse code, which Andrzej and I had already learned from Wiktor in Wilno. We practised first aid, improvising and applying tourniquets and splints, immobilising injured limbs and carrying the wounded. We practised reconnoitring, walking point and hand signals.

During one of these exercises in the middle of May, while walking stealthily through a pine forest near Swider, we came across two Hitlerjugend boys a couple of years older than us. They were in their uniforms: black short trousers and brown shirts with black kerchiefs. They had black belts with knives that were small replicas of an army bayonet. We surrounded them so they couldn't escape, ripped off all their insignias, badges and buttons from their trousers and took their belts and knives. They tried to resist but soon gave up. With a few well-placed kicks we sent them on their way holding their trousers up. We separated into smaller groups and dispersed, making our way towards two different railway stations. Shortly thereafter we heard whistles blowing, shouts in German and the noise of a large group running through the forest behind us. As Andrzej, one other boy and I reached the outskirts of Swider, we spotted a large group of about twenty Hitlerjugend boys emerge from the woods behind us with several SA men brandishing pistols. Luckily, a train was starting to move out just as we reached the station and we managed to jump on. The rest of our group also got away safely.

After we moved to Warsaw, the Russians bombed the city only once, in May 1943, causing considerable damage. By the beginning of 1944 the Germans had improved the anti-aircraft defences in Warsaw: AA guns were placed on bridges and other strategic locations, open water reservoirs were built on large squares and a blackout was enforced. Every building had buckets of sand in the stairwells and all bathtubs had to be filled with water at all times. In June 1944, Russian planes started to appear over Warsaw at night. Air raid sirens would wail and we would take the kitchen stairway down to the shelter in the basement. The planes would drop flares, German AA guns would fire and then the all-clear would sound. In the last week of June, we again made our way to the basement. This time the sirens were not a false alarm, the bombardment was real and the city was bombed, once again suffering considerable damage.

As June ended we completed our studies and graduated to the next class, Andrzej with all As and I with Cs. In our Boy Scout squad we all completed and passed the requirements for the Młodzik rank, the first of five. We were now qualified to take the wartime Boy Scouts oath:

I vow to serve in the Grey Ranks, to safeguard the organisation's secrets, to obey service orders and to never retreat before the sacrifice of my life.

The oath ceremony was scheduled for early August.

Towards the end of July 1944 there was a different feeling in Warsaw. German patrols on the streets where less frequent. There was excitement in the air as people gathered under the 'barkers', the megaphones of the German public address system. They smiled and chuckled hearing pronouncements of 'a planned retreat to prepared positions' or 'shortening of the front lines'. There were no more announcements of public executions.

On Sunday 23 July, the Germans started openly evacuating their families as well as their offices, warehouses and factories. The atmosphere bordered on panic. As Andrzej and I walked through the streets in the centre of Warsaw we saw trucks being loaded in front of German offices. There was much activity around the German offices in Piłsudski and Theatre squares, and at the headquarters of German Governor Fischer in the Brühl Palace courtyard. The entire area was jammed with heavily loaded trucks. Passenger cars full of families, departing in haste, streamed out of the German sector of town.

The most amazing sight of all, which everyone enjoyed watching, was the withdrawal from the Praga district on the eastern side of the Vistula, across the Poniatowski Bridge, heading westward along Jerusalem Avenue. There was a never-ending flow of the most incongruous assortment of vehicles: there where horse-drawn carts, large army horse wagons and little farm carts pulled by small, shaggy tired horses, some loaded with army supplies and others with household goods. On the carts sat women and children driven by Cossacks, Ukrainians and other collaborators. Domestic animals, cows and horses were tied to the carts. There were flocks of sheep and herds of cows. They all looked tired and dejected, in sharp contrast to the Warsovian bystanders, who openly smiled and joked about the motley spectacle. In amongst the human flow were German Army vehicles withdrawing in good order.

Columns of German Army units made up of *kalmuks*, collaborating nationalities such as Azeris, Cossacks and others, marched through the streets. The Hungarian division was withdrawing from the front and moving to the south of Warsaw. Hungarians and Poles had always been friendly with each other and there was friendly contact between their troops and the Warsovians.

A Hungarian cavalry unit was riding down our street. I stood in front of our building watching them as an officer dismounted in front of the ice cream parlour. When he emerged from the shop, his orderly held his horse and stirrup while he remounted; however, the horse shied away, causing the officer's foot to slip and he lost his balance. When the officer remounted he hit his orderly across the face with his crop. Onlookers started to boo as he cantered off. I was stunned as I could never imagine such behaviour in the Polish Army.

After a few days the exodus subsided. Heavily armed German units once again started patrolling the streets. Large open police cars, with submachine guns pointing in all directions, roamed the streets. They started to fortify their offices and facilities, military and security stations, and the entrances to their sector. There were concrete bunkers and a lot of movable barbed wire barricades known as 'Spanish Riders'.

Hitler issued an order demanding that Warsaw become a *Festung Warschau*, a fortress to be defended to the last man. On the afternoon of 27 July the 'barkers' demanded that 100,000 men present themselves for the construction of a fortification in front of Warsaw. This order was also plastered on walls around the city but was completely ignored as no one showed up. Over the next few days shops and places of business started to close. Russian planes flew overhead and the faint sound of artillery was audible to the east.

On Saturday 29th, Wiktor came out of the master bedroom wearing his Polish officer's riding boots, breeches and a windbreaker rather than his customary suit. Mother stood behind him with a sombre face as he told us he would be 'going away for a few days'. Wiktor gave us each a hug, put on his raincoat and beret, and gave us a wink as he walked out the door. We knew what was coming.

A few days before, we had what turned out to be the last meeting of our Boy Scout squad. The same assembly point in case of an Uprising was reconfirmed. On Sunday 30th, Polish Underground publications were openly distributed. I watched an aerial fight between Russian and German planes in the skies over Warsaw. A Russian plane was shot down and a parachute floated down in the distance. On Monday 31st, most businesses did not open. Young people dressed like Wiktor moved briskly about the streets. German patrols were less frequent but larger; instead of the customary two soldiers, there were four to eight. I didn't see anyone confronted or stopped.

The grumble of artillery fire from beyond the Vistula was quite audible. It sounded as though the Russians would soon be in Warsaw.

PART 3

BATTLE FOR WARSAW
GLORIA VICTIS
(GLORY TO THE
VANQUISHED)

'… Polish pride and German shame … We bow today before the sacrifice
and the pride of the men and women of the Polish Home Army'

German Chancellor Gerhard Schröder, on the sixtieth anniversary
of the Warsaw Uprising, Warsaw, 1 August 2004

10

Centre of Town,
1–5 August 1944

On 1 August 1944 I woke up to an overcast morning. It had rained all night. At breakfast mother reiterated the same orders that she had issued since Wiktor left: you may go out but stay close to the apartment and come back to check with me every hour or hour and a half.

There were noticeably more young people moving purposefully about the streets of Warsaw on foot, carrying packages, bags and knapsacks. They tried to look military; some of them were wearing *oficerki*, the black riding boots of Polish officers, windbreakers and raincoats with military-type belts. Young girls carried bags that we recognised as first aid kits. There were young people with packages travelling fast on rickshaws. German patrols walked the streets pretending not to see them. Likewise, open German police cars, bristling with the barrels of Bergman submachine guns, sped through the streets without stopping.

At noon the air raid sirens sounded an all-clear that lasted for a very long time. This was unusual as there was no preceding air raid warning siren and I had not seen any Russian planes that day.

We returned to mother's empty beauty salon for lunch around two o'clock. Ever since the Germans had started evacuating Warsaw her business had dropped off drastically and her two employees had stopped coming to work. After lunch we washed the dishes. Again, we were allowed to venture out but no further than a few blocks in either direction, and only on our street. We noticed a large decrease in foot traffic and the passing trams were only half-full. A large German patrol passed by but they didn't attempt to stop anyone. The soldiers were in Air Force uniforms, most likely from the AA batteries protecting the nearby Poniatowski Bridge. A large open-topped police car carrying about ten policeman holding their Bergmans at the ready drove by a few times. An open-topped Mercedes touring car carrying Gestapo officers clutching MP40s also sped by.

Around 4 p.m. we heard the first shots: single shots followed by the staccato of submachine guns punctured by grenade explosions. The street started to empty. We returned to our apartment and told mother that *it had started* and that we must go to our assembly point on Saviour Square. She replied that we couldn't go anywhere until the situation became clearer, but allowed us to watch events on our street from the entrance to our building. We ran downstairs and joined a small group that had already gathered there. The street appeared empty in both directions but the sound of firing and explosions came from all over.

After 5 p.m. everything intensified greatly. The sound of very heavy fighting came from the direction of Napoleon Square. The large post office building there was protected by concrete bunkers. We heard more machine gun fire punctuated by explosions. No fighting was visible on our street; it was completely deserted except for a few small groups like ours standing in doorways.

Two teenage girls ran by carrying medical bags, hugging the wall, and stopped in our entranceway. They wore red and white armbands on their right arm. Polish red and white flags started to appear on buildings. We ran back across our courtyard to our staircase, then up the stairs to the top landing. I opened the window and listened to the fighting from the direction of the post office. From the window we could clearly see the Prudential building on the other side of Napoleon Square. With its sixteen floors it was the tallest building in the city. From its radio-TV tower flew a large red and white Polish flag. We were very excited, and ran down to our apartment to tell mother. She smiled and hugged us but looked very sad.

As night approached, the intensity of the fighting decreased. We could see the distant glow of fires as it started to drizzle. Again we went upstairs to look out over the city. Several big fires were clearly visible in all directions, including a large one in the direction of the central railway station. When we returned to the apartment we were ordered to go to bed. I lay in bed very excited, I was *sure* that in a few days all of Warsaw would be liberated. I hoped that in the morning we would be able to join our squad. As I drifted to sleep I heard the rain becoming heavier.

On 2 August, the second day of the Uprising, I woke to the sound of heavy fighting from Napoleon Square. I quickly ran up the stairs to make sure the Polish flag was still flying from the Prudential building. It was.

Again Andrzej and I hung around the entrance to our building. The street was still empty. From time to time, someone would run down our side of the street staying close to the wall. Any attempt to cross the street was met with machine gun fire from the BGK bank, about two blocks away at the intersection with Jerusalem Avenue. From the other end of the street we heard machine gun fire. It was impossible to move around the street or to start building barricades. We saw sporadic German military traffic on the avenue. We realised it would be impossible for us to cross the avenue in order to reach our assembly point.

We went back to the apartment and established a position at our 'observation point', next to the highest window in our stairwell. Behind our building was the Blikle coffee house garden, a very popular place that had entertainment in the summer. In the afternoons Mieczysław Fogg, a very famous Warsovian singer, would sing his latest hits accompanied by an orchestra. The stage was directly opposite our apartment so we could hear and see the concerts from our balcony. On the other side of the coffee house gardens was the four-storey W. Górski Gimnazium, which organised the clandestine secondary school programme we had been accepted into a year before. The building was under attack by the insurgents. There were shots, grenade explosions, machine gun and submachine pistol fire. There were shouts and then the fighting stopped. The building was captured.

I realised that if we broke through the wall between our backyard and Blikle's gardens we could establish a connection to W. Górski Street and into the centre of town. I raced to find the gatekeeper who was standing by the entrance with a couple of men. I told them of my plan and the gatekeeper took charge, procuring a sledgehammer and pickaxe. It did not take long to make an opening in the brick wall. On the other side of the gardens we made another opening into the small square at the end of Górski Street.

We found ourselves in front of the *gimnazium* that had just been captured. There were many insurgents in a variety of dress, mostly civilian with a sprinkling of different uniforms, all wearing red and white armbands. There were a variety of head coverings: civilian caps, old Polish Army caps and helmets, mostly German with some Polish. All headgear had Polish eagles or red and white markings. Many people were armed, but not everybody, there were rifles, submachine guns, revolvers and Molotov cocktails. There was excitement, so much excitement after five years of occupation.

Heavy fighting continued at the post office building. That afternoon, the sound of shooting and explosions from Napoleon Square subsided and eventually stopped altogether. Word soon got out that the post office had also been captured and was now in Polish hands. People started to emerge from their buildings and we went to have a look. There were signs of heavy fighting everywhere, walls pockmarked by bullets, broken windows and big holes from tank shells. There was a destroyed German tank and a burned-out truck. There were also very frightened looking German prisoners. The insurgents and population were in great spirits. Later we watched as the soldiers of *Kiliński* Battalion, who had captured the post office, marched down Szpitalna Street. They were there to secure the nearby area, including our building.

When Andrzej and I returned home, I was afraid that we would be scolded for being gone such a long time. Mother just listened sadly as we told her, with great excitement, about everything we had seen. As I fell asleep a red glow from the fires reflected on our ceiling. I wondered where Wiktor and Zygmunt were fighting.

The next morning, 3 August, began with a light drizzle. There were no changes on our street; machine gun fire still made it impossible to build barricades. We went to the Górski Gimnazium, where the units of *Kiliński* Battalion had camped. We spoke with a few of the officers, asking them to take us on as runners, but they already had enough. Again we tried to cross the avenue but the heavy fighting continued and there was no way to get across.

We returned to Napoleon Square to take another look at the destroyed tank, a turretless assault gun. It was used as a centre point of the barricade on Szpitalna Street blocking the entrance to Napoleon Square. On the square there was a large open water reservoir built at the beginning of the year as part of the air raid defences. It made a perfect swimming pool. Several soldiers were swimming and washing themselves in it. Again we approached some officers and, again, had no luck as they were only taking fighters with weapons.

We passed through Napoleon Square and then Warecka Street to the intersection with our street. There was an attempt to build a barricade across our street, Nowy Swiat, with large wooden cable spools. On the other side of our street, the continuation of Warecka Street was called Ordynacka. That street sloped down towards the Vistula area held by the Germans. A short distance down Ordynacka was a barricade manned with a machine gun, and we decided to go there and once again try our luck to see if we could join as runners. We ran across our street using the unfinished barricade for cover and encountered machine gun fire from the police headquarters but it was ineffective.

We reached the barricade and still had no luck, but we did spend some time with the insurgents. They had placed several upside-down dinner plates in front of the barricade with a sign saying 'attention mines'. I wasn't sure if they were serious or if it was a joke. Insurgents were expecting a tank attack and were well prepared with Molotov cocktails, but this was a new, improved Polish version that self-exploded and did not require a lit wick like the original Russian version. We returned home following the same route. Late that afternoon we helped build a barricade on Chmielna Street, at the intersection with our street. There was an attempt to build a barricade on our street at that same intersection but the machine gun fire from the BGK bank made it impossible.

Throughout that day the Germans used Stuka dive-bombers. When Stukas began their dive you could hear a screeching noise made by sirens attached to the plane. We would then see the planes pull up and away from the rooftops, leaving behind an explosion and a cloud of debris flying into the air. We looked in vain for Russian fighters; they were no longer seen over Warsaw.

Day four. After breakfast we once again tried to cross Jerusalem Avenue. There was heavy fighting on parts of this major thoroughfare as the Germans were trying to gain control for their military traffic. There was no way for us to get through and reach our assembly point. When we returned we found two Polish soldiers in our courtyard. They wanted to know if there was a place in our building where they could see the intersection of Jerusalem Avenue and our street. I immediately told them that there was a clear view of the intersection from the attic. In addition to our building being four storeys high, one higher than the adjoining buildings, our street also curved, allowing for a clear view of the whole intersection. 'Show me how to get there', said the one with the Mauser rifle, who looked like he was in charge. I took them to the gatekeeper and told him to get the keys to the attic, a masonry chisel and a mallet. We ran ahead up the service stairs; a few minutes later the keeper arrived, opened the attic, gave us the tools and left.

The empty space was sparsely lit by a few skylights. At the end of the attic, on the wall perpendicular to the street, we chiselled out a small hole at eye level, which gave us a clear view of the intersection about 275yd away. The man in charge enlarged the hole to make a perfect embrasure for his rifle, and then each of us made his own observation holes by removing a single brick at eye level. We introduced ourselves as Boy Scouts who had been in the Underground for a year. The leader said that he was known as 'Tadek' (all insurgents assumed a code name) and that they were from the 'Nałęcz' unit. We watched the intersection for at least fifteen uneventful minutes. There was sporadic machine gun fire into our street from the BGK bank on the south-west corner of the intersection. Then a German staff car emerged from the east, the direction of the Poniatowski Bridge. Tadek fired but the car carried on and disappeared from our line of vision. After a while a motorcycle with a sidecar crossed from the same direction. Again Tadek fired and again the vehicle carried on.

There was no movement for the next half hour, until we heard the faint noise of a tank clatter coming from the same direction. The tank, a Mark IV, slowly entered our line of sight. It reached the centre of the intersection, turned right facing us, and came to a ponderous stop just before our street. I was all excited wondering what would happen next. We waited for a good ten minutes. Nothing moved. The turret hatch opened and a German wearing a black beret stuck his head out. After a few minutes he pulled himself up high enough to raise a pair of binoculars. As he brought them up to his eyes I heard a shot a few feet to my right, where Tadek was standing. I saw the German slump on the tank's turret, binoculars still hanging from his neck. For a moment everything froze. The German's body was pulled inside the turret. The tank's gun barrel moved up. There was a flash at the muzzle, noise of a wall crumbling and the sound of a gun firing. A hole, about 3ft in diameter, opened up in the wall right next to me. Tadek yelled, 'run, run!' As we scrambled down the stairs the tank fired again and we heard the attic wall crumble behind us. Luckily, since the wall was only one brick thick, neither of the two projectiles exploded in the attic but went straight through both walls. The Germans were most likely using anti-tank ammunition. Andrzej and I had had our baptism of fire.

As we regrouped in the courtyard I told Tadek that we wanted to join his unit and asked if he would take us there. He agreed and we made our way to Chmielna Street, then across a courtyard to the Coliseum cinema, or rather where the cinema used to be. It had been bombed out in 1939 and was now a large, empty paved yard surrounded by the tall masonry walls of other burned-out buildings, with remnants of a steel roof structure. About forty soldiers were standing around and sitting on the ground. Most were in their early twenties, some in their late teens, and a few middle-aged. There were also young women with first aid bags. They all had red and white armbands and a variety of uniforms and head coverings with Polish eagles or red and white markings. I was surprised at how well armed they were. I immediately spotted two German MG34s, half a dozen submachine guns and about a dozen rifles, pistols and grenades. There was a small man in a very odd German air defence helmet carrying a *Panzerfaust* (an anti-tank rocket).

We followed Tadek to an officer with a bandage on his cheek standing with a young woman holding a first aid bag. They were Lt. 'Jur' and Tadek's sister 'Baśka'. As he told them our story, another officer approached. He was a tall handsome man, about 30 years old, with a dark complexion and a military bearing. He had a German helmet, Polish officer's riding boots and breeches. A 9mm pistol with a lanyard around his neck was stuck in his belt. In his right hand he carried a *Błyskawica*, a submachine gun produced by the Polish Underground. He was Lt. 'Nałęcz', the officer commanding this unit. Tadek reported to him, describing our adventures. He gave us credit and told the lieutenant that we wanted to join. Standing at attention, I repeated our desire to join explaining that for the last year we had been training in the Grey Ranks and that we would make good runners. I answered his questions about my family and told him about Wiktor and Zygmunt's involvement in the Underground. Lt. Nałęcz said that he would take us on as runners provided our mother personally gave her permission. He said that the battalion was going to move to 4 Boduena Street and if we got her permission, we should bring her there.

We sprinted home. 'We found a unit that will take us as runners!' I shouted as we entered the apartment. 'We need your permission, and if you don't give it we'll run away.' I babbled on about what a great unit it was, how well armed they were, what a great officer Lt. Nałęcz was, just like uncle Karol – he even looked like him. We followed mother into the living room. She sat down and as we stood in front of her she looked at us, silently, for a long time. Tears welled up in her eyes and slowly rolled down her cheeks. There was no sound except Zabcia excitedly jumping between us. After a while she quietly said, 'I will take you there.'

We hugged and thanked her, then ran into our room to get ready. We put on our windbreakers. I put on a belt that uncle Karol had made for me. It was a smaller version of a Polish officer's army belt made of brown leather with elaborate stitching and a brass buckle. I got out my shoulder bag, a Polish Army *chlebak*. I grabbed a couple of shirts, some underwear and socks, a torch and a toothbrush. On my head I placed my uncle's overseas cap with a pennant of the 1st Mounted Rifles Regiment. Mother came out of the kitchen with two small parcels of food.

Boduena Street was very close, just before Napoleon Square. Number 4 was a large apartment building taken over as the headquarters of the *Korpus Bezpieczeństwa* of the *Armia Krajowa* (Security Corps of the Home Army). *Nałęcz* Battalion was one of their units. We found and reported to Lt. Nałęcz. He introduced himself to my mother, kissing her hand as was customary. 'Madame, do you give your permission?' Mother replied, 'Yes, I know I will not be able to keep them at home.' We joined Tadek and his sister Baśka, who was talking to our mother. She realised that we were anxious for her to leave so she said goodbye with a quick hug, not wanting to embarrass us. As she left she turned and said to Baśka: 'Will you take good care of my boys?' 'I will', Baśka replied. With one last wave, mother departed.

We could not know that this was the last time my mother would see Andrzej, and that two weeks later Baśka would be with him when he was mortally wounded.

The unit we joined, 1st Assault Battalion KB '*Nałęcz*', was part of an underground organisation formed in late 1939. In 1942, it was subordinated to the AK, maintaining a degree of internal independence. KB was the acronym for the *Korpus Bezpieczeństwa* or Security Corps. Its full name was abbreviated as AK KB. It was tasked by the AK with the preparation of a military unit for protection of the Polish administration that would take charge once the Germans were expelled. The KB had its own officer school commanded by Lt. Nałęcz. During the Uprising, the KB was under tactical command of the Home Army.

The outbreak of the Uprising found Lt. Nałęcz with a group of about twenty officer cadets. On 1 August at 6 p.m. the lightly armed group joined the fight for the Hala Mirowska – a large market hall used by the Germans as a food warehouse. The German defenders were defeated and the unit captured one machine gun and four rifles. Lt. Nałęcz accepted volunteers if they were armed and the unit grew to almost forty men. Lt. Jur was appointed second in command. Over the next two days, the unit moved towards the headquarters of the KB on Boduena Street. On its way it joined in several assaults on German positions and at 4 p.m. on 3 August it arrived on the south side of Marszałkowska Street. These were buildings held by Germans. As they were clearing the buildings a German vehicle arrived. It was destroyed and its crew wiped out. The unit captured a second machine gun, assorted other weapons, a *Panzerfaust*, boxes of grenades and ammunition.

The unit reorganised into assault groups and initiated a fight for a building which housed the Esplanade, a German-only restaurant. A large number of stranded Germans took refuge there. After a three-hour firefight, the building was taken. More weapons were captured as well as a few POWs, but at the price of one killed and several wounded, including Lt. 'Dąbrowa', who died two days later. Finally, at 9 p.m. Lt. Nałęcz reported to headquarters. Next morning, 4 August, Lt. Nałęcz was ordered to the corner of Nowy Swiat and Jerusalem Avenue, opposite the BGK bank building. He was later relieved by another unit and ordered to return to the headquarters. It was as the battalion was assembling in the Coloseum cinema that Tadek led us there.

Soon after mother left, Lt. Nałęcz told us to see Staff Sgt. 'Mama' and give him our personal data so we could be issued IDs. Andrzej decided to stay with his old code name, 'Tarzan', and I changed mine to my name, 'Bohdan'.

I reported back to Lt. Nałęcz, who was standing with a new officer Lt. 'Pobóg', appointed second in command of the battalion and commanding officer of the 1st Company. Lt. Jur was appointed commanding officer of the 2nd Company. Lt. Nałęcz told me that I would be his personal runner and I was to stick with him at all times. He told me to get to know all the officers and cadet officers. Later that afternoon our battalion, now about seventy men, moved across Marszałkowska Street to our new billets. They were in an apartment building on Sienna Street, Lt. Col. 'Paweł''s quarters, and we spent the night there.

On the next morning, 5 August, we woke up to a clear sunny day. After sleeping on the floor without much cover I realised that I needed to change my shorts for long trousers. Luckily, in another apartment I found a boy's secondary school uniform slightly larger than my size. I changed into long navy blue trousers and a pair of shoes that were more practical than my sandals. That morning our battalion formed into a 1st Company of three platoons, commanded by Lt. Pobóg, and a second, much smaller reserve company commanded by Lt. Jur. At this reorganisation, provisions and uniforms were replenished. Lt. Nałęcz ordered me to follow him to the Boduena Street headquarters. Before we left he gave me a pre-war Polish assault grenade, which I hung on my belt.

After crossing Marszałkowska Street we met a war correspondent with his camera crew, who wanted to film us. After filming us walking towards them, they wanted some action shots. Lt. Nałęcz gave me his Blyskawica submachine gun and on a given signal I ran with it, darting from a building entrance to a destroyed German car and then to a barricade. I stopped a few times pretending to shoot. It was great fun. Unfortunately, this film clip did not survive the Uprising though quite a lot of footage shot during the fighting has been preserved.

Our visit to headquarters was brief. While I waited outside Lt. Nałęcz reported to Col. 'Doliwa', KB Chief of Staff, and received his final orders. As they emerged together I stood to attention. Lt. Nałęcz said: 'this is Bohdan, my runner'. I saluted and the colonel returned my salute. I felt very proud and thought: 'Now I am a soldier in the Polish Army.'

When we returned, we found the building adjoining our billets demolished by a bomb. The front of the building had taken a direct hit and crumbled onto the street. Bodies had been removed from the wreckage and were lying on the pavement: two women and a child. They lay peacefully on their backs, with no sign of blood or injury, all covered in grey dust as if somebody had sprayed rye flour over them.

For the previous two days Stukas had been bombing Warsaw at will. We had no anti-aircraft defence. Russian planes had disappeared completely from Warsaw's skies, even though the Russian Army was only on the other side of the Vistula. The Stukas were flying very low, diving with sirens screeching; their bombs clearly visible as they fell. As the planes pulled up they were followed by an explosion that shot up a geyser of debris and clouds of dust and smoke. Fires burned in several directions.

Lt. Nałęcz summoned his officers and platoon leaders to brief them on his orders. We were to move to the Wola district. Our first objective was 13 Leszno Street, one of the KB assembly points. The seventy men of our unit assembled in the courtyard and started to move out in the early afternoon. We walked single file starting with a couple of point men, followed by a forward guard of three or four men with submachine guns, Lt. Nałęcz and I, then the rest of the battalion. At the beginning it was easy as this part of Warsaw was under Polish control. We moved from barricade to barricade gathering local intelligence. There were signs of fighting, broken windows, pockmarked walls, holes from artillery and tank fire, and bombed out buildings. We reached Krochmalna Street, which formed the Polish defence perimeter. The situation in front of us was unclear. To our right we knew the Germans were in the Saxon Gardens and we heard sporadic shooting from that direction. From Wola to the left came the sound of heavy fighting. Germans were trying to break through to connect with their positions in the Saxon Gardens. They wanted to establish a corridor to the Kierbedz Bridge in order to connect with their troops facing the Russians on the other side of the Vistula.

We moved towards two large pavilions at Hale Mirowskie, the city's old food markets. Poles had captured them at the beginning of the Uprising but we didn't know who held them now as they had changed hands a few times. Cautiously we entered one of the buildings, which appeared to be vacant, and moved through, shattered glass from broken skylights crunching under our feet. We emerged on the other side of the building and crossed the street. We continued on the short block of Mirowska Street, turned right on Elektoralna Street and then left on Orla Street, reaching Leszno Street. We turned left and found the KB assembly point.

There were several soldiers from the KB, including Lt. 'Holski'; they all joined our battalion. We learned that Polish units defending Wola were under heavy attack and were withdrawing towards the old town. Ours was the last unit that managed to move into the old town. The next day the Germans managed to break through from Wola and connect with their troops in Saxon Gardens. The old town was now surrounded and cut off from the rest of Warsaw.

Lt. Nałęcz made a decision to leave the 3rd Platoon on Leszno Street and move the rest of the battalion towards the old town to new quarters in the Spiess pharmaceutical company building behind the town hall. Later that evening Lt. Nałęcz led a detachment to the end of King Albert Street to provide security from the direction of Saxon Gardens. Having placed them in a defensive position, he and I returned and I dozed off. After midnight, Lt. Nałęcz woke me up saying, 'Let's go, we're going to take a look at Brühl Palace'. The large two-storey, two-winged rococo palace faced Pilsudski Square. The south wing bordered the Saxon Gardens and the other was on Wierzbowa Street. Before the war, Brühl Palace housed the Ministry of Foreign Affairs but now served as the offices and residence of Ludwig Fischer, Nazi Governor of the Warsaw district.

An assault group of about ten men was made ready and we proceeded along Wierzbowa Street, passing the Opera House on our left. It was dark, there was sporadic firing from different directions and illuminating flares were fired from the Saxon Gardens. We walked single file, hugging the wall on our right. The point man was followed by a second man watching the left side, then Lt. Nałęcz and I were followed by a sapper section, with their explosives, led by Abczyc, and at the rear was an assault group armed with submachine guns, pistols and grenades.

We reached King Albert Street, where our security detachment had previously taken position. There was a short exchange with the post: 'nothing to report, all is quiet sir'. We crossed King Albert Street and proceeded towards the next corner of Fredry Street. The back of the palace was on that street. The point men crossed; one was scanning forward and the other along the back of the palace. We crossed one by one and kept close to the palace walls. We proceeded quietly, examining the windows as we moved forward. They were high, the parapet about 5ft above the pavement; they had heavy grates on the outside with steel-plated shutters behind. Nałęcz conferred with Abczyc. It was a no-go: we did not have enough explosives to blow the necessary openings. At that moment we heard German voices behind the windows and a flare shot upwards from the courtyard of the palace. We remained motionless against the wall. From the direction of the Saxon Gardens we heard an engine start, followed by the clatter of tank treads. Nałęcz signalled the retreat and we went back the way we had come.

It was well past midnight when we reached our quarters. I tried going to sleep but I was very cold. I heard a rustling of paper and saw some men sleeping with their legs in large paper sacks. There was a stack of them in the corner. I grabbed one and crawled in almost to my chest. I had no problem falling asleep immediately.

11

Old Town – Town Hall, 6–11 August 1944

We bow in shame today at the crimes of the Nazi troops
Chancellor Gerhard Schröder, Warsaw, 1 August 2004

On Sunday 6 August, a warm and sunny day, I was awoken in the early morning by the sounds of bombing: Stukas were concentrating on the old town.

The remainder of the battalion that had been on Leszno Street re-joined us with a new officer, Lt. 'Skóra'. We were ordered to move into the town hall building and take over its defence. We were under the overall command of Lt. 'Barry', who had taken the town hall at the outbreak of the Uprising. The town hall was the old Jabłonski Palace, a very large four-storey building on Theatre Square facing the opera house. It occupied practically the whole block with the Convent of the Canoness Sisters (Kanoniczki) and the Church of St Andrew on the south-west corner of the square by Bielańska Street. On the opposite corner was the two-storey Blank's Palace. The whole complex had several interconnecting courtyards accessed from the square through a massive wooden gate. We were assigned the defence of the main building.

Most of the day was spent preparing defences. I accompanied Nałęcz as he walked through the building giving dispositions for the defence points and machine gun positions. He ordered openings to be broken through the walls to allow easy movement of the defenders. We came across large stores of food and Nałęcz ordered them to be secured together with the municipal pawnshop. We moved on to explore Blank's Palace, a small and beautiful baroque building. Before the war it was used by the President of the City of Warsaw for official receptions. During the occupation it was the residence and office of Ludwig Leist, the German mayor of the city. At the back of the palace there was a garden with a pond full of large golden carp. Nałęcz took out his colt pistol, 'let's see if we can get some', and shot into a large group of fish. Nothing happened. One of the soldiers accompanying us said, 'Lieutenant, sir, let me show you how to do this properly,' and tossed a concussion grenade into the pond. There was an explosion, a geyser of water shot up, and the surface of the pond was covered with golden fish floating belly up. That afternoon we all had a very tasty fish soup.

While exploring the palace I found the butler's pantry between a large dining room and a kitchen. There were partially opened drawers with silver utensils and cutlery. Most of them were gone but I managed to find a fork, knife and spoon. They were solid silver with the Warsaw coat of arms, a mermaid holding a shield and a sword. From that moment on I ate in style!

On the way back we heard the sound of a racing car engine. When we entered the main courtyard we were greeted by the sight of a large black limousine, running boards loaded with men, speeding around with squealing tyres. Seeing Nałęcz, the car came to a screeching halt. It was a pre-war Cadillac, the official car of the pre-war City President and later of the German mayor. Nałęcz ordered the car back into the garage to preserve the petrol.

During the day more volunteers joined the battalion. Most were men who hadn't managed to connect with their units. Cpl. 'Grisza', a Russian soldier freed from the municipal jail, joined us. He was wounded a few days later and died of his wounds.

In the evening the detachment that had been sent to King Albert Street returned. They reported that that morning their sharpshooter had successfully picked off Germans digging trenches in the Saxon Gardens from the top floor of the building. The Germans had responded with heavy machine gun and tank fire, and in the fighting that followed they managed to destroy one tank but lost four of their own soldiers and several others were wounded.

That night I slept in the same clothes I had been wearing since I left home, but on a real bed in the guards' barracks of the municipal prison behind the town hall. The next day Col. 'Wachnowski' took over as commanding officer of the old town, which was renamed 'Group North'. He assigned Lt. Nałęcz overall command of the town hall area. Lt. Barry was made head of military police. Our battalion was to defend the town hall and the adjoining Convent of the Canoness Sisters. We were reinforced by Lt. 'Leszek''s twenty-man platoon from Barry's unit. On our right flank, Company P-20 under Lt. 'Tadeusz' was defending the barricade on Bielanska Street and the surrounding buildings at the junction with Theatre Square. P-20 Company was placed under the tactical command of Lt. Nałęcz. The 2nd Company of the *Łukasiński* Battalion, defending Blank's Palace on our left flank, was also placed under his command. Our total strength increased to over 150 men. We were made part of the Kuba Sector, commanded by Lt. Col. 'Kuba', and were the southernmost defences of the old town.

Stukas were again concentrating on bombing and strafing the old town, although it was relatively quiet in our immediate area. We heard the noise of tank movements and fighting to the east, from the direction of Castle Square. There were also sounds of motor vehicles and fighting coming from the direction of the Saxon Gardens. Nałęcz sent well-armed patrols along both sides of the opera house towards the Saxon Gardens. He surmised that a German thrust from Wola had succeeded and that the old town was now fully surrounded. We were the last unit to cross over from the centre of Warsaw. He expected the next German attack to be made against our position.

The work to prepare the defence of the buildings continued. The ground-floor windows were blocked while the basement and other floors were interconnected by holes broken through the walls. The superintendent of the building asked for help transferring important paintings and documents to the city archives in the Arsenal building.

When we made openings in one of the walls of the basement we made an interesting discovery. At one point the pickaxe easily broke through one layer of brick, which was unusual since the other walls were 3 to 4ft thick. The second blow produced the sound of broken glass. The rest of the wall was carefully removed, brick by brick, revealing a cache of about fifty bottles lying on their sides. Covered in dust, they were shaped like brandy bottles, made of dark glass and only half-full. Nałęcz was called in and he sent me to find the superintendent. When I brought him in, he was as surprised as everybody else: nobody knew about this hidden cellar. We examined a bottle; it was sealed with wax and stamped with the date 1792, the reign of the last King of Poland. The seal was removed, there were only remnants of a cork left. The liquid was syrupy and sweet. It was opined that it was *Tokay*, a Hungarian sweet wine or Polish mead. The bottles were removed and secured, but somehow their number greatly diminished.

Throughout the morning Nałęcz and Poróg discussed the possibility of making some sort of catapult that could compensate for the lack of mortars by increasing the range of the Molotov cocktails and grenades. A soldier who overheard the discussion said that he had an idea. When he had been a young teenager he and his friends had made a catapult capable of shooting a brick up to 220yd. Abczyc was called in and after further discussion it was decided to build a catapult capable of shooting bombs and that he would make it. A sketch was made of the proposed contraption. The body was made of a shallow, u-shaped wooden channel about 5ft long. The propelling force was provided by a steel leaf from a car spring mounted on the front end like a giant crossbow. A rubber truck tyre inner tube connected the slide to the ends of the steel bow. There was some sort of mechanism to cock the slide. In a few hours, it was ready. In the meantime, the sapper section was making bombs from empty oilcans found in the garage. They were pre-war American Pennzoil quart cans with a conical top and a small cap. The bottom half was filled with nuts, screws, nails and whatever else could be found in the garage. The top half was filled with crushed TNT from an unexploded bomb. A priming fuse with a length of Bickford cord cut to burn for six seconds was inserted. The screw top, with a small hole made for the priming cord, enclosed the bomb. About twenty such bombs were made.

Nałęcz sent me with a dispatch to Lt. Jur at the Spiess building. After I delivered the dispatch I found Andrzej. We had not seen each other for the last three days. I immediately noticed that he had a pistol in a holster on his belt. He showed me his Belgian FN 5mm, a so-called *damka* (lady's) pistol he had gotten from Jur. I was very glad that he had a weapon but also jealous that I only had a grenade. I noticed that he was wearing German Army jackboots. Jur had got hold of a car and they had gone to Stawki, where a large warehouse with uniforms and food had been captured from the Germans on the first day. Jur was trying to get the necessary authorisation to go back and get uniforms for our battalion. In the meantime, he got Andrzej new jackboots.

When I returned, our catapult was ready for a trial. A mock bomb without TNT was loaded. I got Nałęcz, and on his signal Abczyc tripped the trigger. The bomb flew up at about a 30° angle and landed ... twenty paces away! There was a moment of stunned silence and then everybody burst out laughing. This was the ignominious end of our 'artillery'.

Another sunny day dawned on 8 August. It was the day that, after successfully opening a corridor from the Wola district to the Saxon Gardens surrounding the old town, the Germans began their attack on our sector. The *Great Illustrated Encyclopedia of the Warsaw Uprising* describes the military actions of that day as follows:

> The enemy attacked the sector of Theatre Square, the town hall, Bielańska (Street) herding civilians before tanks. The defenders repulsed those attacks; as a result of all-day fighting in this region, the Germans only managed to breach one barricade. Germans dug in in front of the opera house.
>
> *Wielka Ilustrowana Encyklopedia Powstania Warszawskiego*, vol. 3, p. 129

Historian Antoni Przygoński also describes the day's events:

> The fighting that day on Theatre Square was unusually dramatic, continuing from morning to late afternoon. The German attack started with a few tanks entering Theatre Square from Wierzbowa Street, proceeding directly towards the town hall, defended by Battalion KB of Lt. 'Nałęcz' (Stefan Kaniewski). The attempt to break the insurgents' defences was unsuccessful. After bunched grenades were thrown from the top floors of the building, the tanks quickly withdrew to the other side of the square towards the ruins of the opera house, where they started systematically firing on the insurgents' positions. The insurgents managed to immobilise one of the tanks and liquidate the crew trying to escape. After a short barrage, the enemy infantry attacked from the direction of the opera house, herding before them a large crowd of frightened civilians, mostly women, children and elderly. However, the insurgents allowed the attackers to approach to within a short distance, called to the civilians to escape to the side and repulsed the Germans, inflicting heavy losses. The fighting was momentarily stopped and stretcher-bearers from both sides entered to remove the wounded. Corpses of dead German soldiers and Polish civilians covered the square. In the meantime, the soldiers of (SS) Dirlewanger (Brigade) herded in a new group of civilians, placing them in the middle of the square in front of the tanks as a live shield. Awaiting near-certain death, people knelt on the pavement singing 'Boże coś Polskę' (a religious patriotic hymn). Shortly after, more tanks entered from Wierzbowa Street but the following infantry could not deploy to attack under the concentric fire from insurgent machine guns located in barricades on Bielańska and Daniłowiczowska streets, the town hall and positions in Senatorska Street. Twice more the Germans tried to attack without success and withdrew around 5 p.m., losing over thirty killed and many wounded, taking the surviving civilians with them.
>
> Przygoński, *Powstanie warszawskie w sierpniu 1944 r.* [*The Warsaw Uprising in August 1944*] (Warsaw, 1980), vol. 1, p. 426

The previous day's defence preparations proved their worth on this day. To plan for the defence, Lt. Nałęcz placed his two machine guns on both flanks to provide crossfire over Theatre Square; soldiers with rifles were placed on the highest floors to give them a better field of fire from a greater height; and assault groups with submachine guns and grenades were on the ground floor to deal with any breach of the walls. The right flank machine gun was manned by the Mirowski brothers, who were all cadet officers: the oldest, Zbigniew or 'Gryf', was the gunner while Jerzy, 'Wilk', and Henryk 'Dąb' were crewmen. Their friend and future brother-in-law 'Runiek' and their uncle, 2nd Lt. 'Zew', completed the section. On the left flank, the gunner was C. Off. 'Delfin', a Pole from Silesia who had been forcibly drafted into the German Army. An experienced soldier, he fought on the eastern front and then managed to desert in Warsaw. The sapper section commanded by Abczyc prepared anti-tank grenades by taping TNT blocks to German 'potato masher' grenades.

I became very familiar with the location of our defence forces, all the strongpoints and officer command posts. I knew the quickest way to get from point to point. Over the previous two days I had not only accompanied Nałęcz everywhere, but also done a lot of exploration on my own. This morning I was with Nałęcz as he was making his rounds. We were on the top floor of the town hall when we heard the noise of tanks. We looked towards the direction of the clatter and saw three thanks emerging from Wierzbowa Street, proceeding slowly towards the barricade on Bielańska Street on our right flank. At the beginning of the Uprising, during action next to the post office, soldiers of *Kiliński* Battalion had captured one and destroyed another of these turretless tank destroyers. They were Jagdpanzer 38 *Hetzers* (baiters) armed with a 75mm gun and a four-man crew. When the tanks were spotted, Nałęcz sent me to all our positions to repeat his order: not to waste ammunition shooting at tanks. When I returned, the leading tank had approached Bielańska Street. An anti-tank grenade blew off its track. A few Molotov cocktails finished the job by setting it on fire. Three of the crew, one on fire, jumped from the tank and were immediately killed by a few single shots from the top floors. The fourth crewman never got out. The remaining two tanks moved back to the ruins of the opera house. From there, they started to shell us. Several machine guns from the opera building were pouring heavy fire into the windows of the town hall. We all took cover, apart from a few observers, who moved around.

Then the shooting stopped. A group of about 200 civilians – mostly woman with children and a few older men – emerged from the opera house. Amongst them were a few Germans followed by a larger concentration of Germans behind. Again, on Nałęcz's order, I ran to all the riflemen telling them to hold their fire until the signal from Nałęcz. I continued downstairs to the main gate and told the detachment there to unlock the small door in the main gate and be ready to open it to allow the civilians to escape to us. When I returned to the top floor, the slowly moving group had covered about two-thirds of the distance. The cries of the civilians – and the Germans' shouts and swearing – were clearly audible as the tanks and their machine guns stopped firing.

When they were within 50ft, Nałęcz leaned out of the window and yelled 'Poles to us, run, run to the barricade, run to the gate!' On that signal, our machine guns started to bark very short bursts at the Germans' flanks; at the same time, the rifleman carefully picked off the Germans in the crowd of civilians. Some of the German soldiers removed their tunics to blend in better with the civilians. That did not help them. From that short distance our aim was very accurate and the Germans started to fall. They tried to return fire but it was not effective. The Polish civilians broke out and started to run towards us. They were shot at by the Germans, but some of them still made it. The square was covered with bodies, some in *feldgrau* but many other were civilians, including children. It was hard to look at this sight; most of our soldiers had tears running down their cheeks. Everybody was very subdued; there was no celebration.

Travelling in the tracks of the tanks, German ambulances slowly entered the square from Wierzbowa Street. They stopped and the German Army nurses started to pick up their wounded. Seeing this, our nurses ran out and started to remove wounded civilians. As the last German ambulance retreated, our nurses also left the square. There were still a lot of bodies. Polish civilians and Germans lay motionless. There was no movement on the square, and the two surviving *Hetzers* remained next to the opera house.

The relative quiet that descended after the removal of the wounded was interrupted by the sound of sustained machine gun fire coming from the ruins of the opera house. We realised that the Germans were executing civilians (that day, in the ruins of the opera house, they executed over 300 civilian men). After a prolonged silence, the Germans brought out another group of women and children to the middle of the square in front of the two tanks. Expecting to be executed, the woman knelt and started to sing '*Boże coś Polskę*'.

Two more *Hetzers* emerged from Wierzbowa Street, followed by infantry. The tanks were very cautious and it was obvious that they did not want to come close to our positions. The infantry behind could not deploy because of crossfire from our two machine guns. Again the tanks started to shell us and the machine guns from the opera house started to rake our walls. Nevertheless, their attack stalled and they withdrew. The same tactic was repeated twice more without success. Finally, around 5 p.m., all fighting ceased. When the first attack started, some women scattered and managed to escape, but many were killed. When all the fighting stopped, standing on the top floor of the town hall, Nałęcz and I counted thirty-four German corpses lying in different contorted positions on Theatre Square. The Germans who attacked us were from the SS Dirlewanger Brigade.

That evening we buried our five dead. We also had several wounded. Later that night, a few of our men crawled into the square to salvage weapons and ammunition from among the dead Germans. This was a dangerous task as German troops would light the square with flares and spray it with machine guns at any sign of movement.

The next morning, 9 August, was all quiet in our sector. We heard constant explosions from the centre of the old town. Stukas were flying and dropping their bombs there non-stop; at one point, I saw four planes over the old town at the same time. The planes were based at Okęcie Airport, on the outskirts of Warsaw, so it took no time to fly, bomb, return to the airport, rearm and return over the city. There was a constant sound of screeching from the diving plane and the whistle of a falling bomb followed by an explosion with its clouds of dust and smoke. We on the front line were lucky; the Germans did not bomb us due to the proximity of their own lines. In most cases, the enemy line was just on the other side of the same street.

In the early afternoon the Germans again entered Theatre Square shielded by Polish women. After a while they withdrew without attacking us. We continued to receive machine gun fire from the opera house. Our losses that day were only one killed.

In the late afternoon a runner arrived with an order from Lt. Col. Kuba, commanding officer of the sector, to turn over our position to the company from the Łukasiński Battalion. We were to become Reserve of the Group and were assigned new quarters at Hotel Polski, No 29 Długa Street. I accompanied Lt. Nałęcz to Group HQ on Barokowa Street, where I overheard a heated discussion between Nałęcz and Lt. Col. Kuba. Nałęcz tried to convince the colonel to rescind his order and allow our battalion to stay in its current position. He argued that our soldiers were very familiar with the position and would be able to react better and more quickly to attacks, and find cover, thus avoiding unnecessary losses. Newly arrived troops, on the other hand, would be at a disadvantage and would suffer larger casualties and could even lose the defensive positions. The colonel curtly said that he had made his decision to have troops frequently change positions. Further arguments from Lt. Nałęcz resulted in the terse command, 'Lieutenant, acknowledge and execute!' Coming to attention, Lt. Nałęcz saluted, 'Yes, Colonel, sir!'

The following morning, 10 August, our men turned over their positions to the new unit and moved to new quarters. P-20 Company moved with us and the platoons of Lt. Leszek, integrated into our battalion, remained with us. This created bad blood between Lt. Nałęcz and Cpt. Barry, who had commanded them before. Since Barry's unit had become military police, Leszek preferred to be in the front line unit.

Later that afternoon, after our officers had briefed the new replacements, Nałęcz was relaxing, sitting with some of our officers around the table in the prison guards' mess hall in the rear of the town hall. There were still a few bottles of the old wine from the cellars left. Nałęcz decided that they all should have a 'stirrup cup' before leaving our old positions. Well, after a few cups somebody checked the calendar and discovered that 10 August was my name day. Nałęcz proposed a toast to me and decided that I would have to drink it with them. A demitasse was filled with the old wine and I drank it while they sang '100 years, 100 years ...', the Polish equivalent of 'Happy Birthday'. The wine was very tasty, sweet and syrupy. I was also given a bottle as a name day present. After a while I tried to get up and couldn't. I had problems moving my arms and legs. After a couple of hours a very merry, but not very steady, group made its way to the Hotel Polski. Andrzej was there and he had a place for me to sleep. The next day I got up not knowing how I ever got there.

The day of 11 August was devoted to clean-up, resupply and reorganisation. The battalion had grown to over 200 men by absorbing volunteers wanting to join a unit that became famous for its defence of the town hall. The battalion was formed into two companies. The first was commanded by Lt. Poróg with lieutenants Skóra, 'Orwid' and Leszek as platoon commanders and the second by Lt. Holski with lieutenants Jur, Bar and Zew. The squads were commanded by cadet officers from the KB Officer's School. More girls and young women joined and increased the ranks of our nurses, commanded by Baśka. Other women became auxiliaries, doing the cooking and other chores.

The men started to change into uniforms that Jur and Andrzej brought from Stawki. The uniforms were reversible SS camouflage smocks, with summer green and autumn brown shades in a spotted 'panther' pattern. They were called *panterki*. We all wore them brown side out, which blended better with the city landscape. Andrzej kept the smallest one for me and one of the new women shortened the sleeves. Andrzej also gave me a 'parade' type German helmet made of a light-gauge steel. It was considerably lighter than a regular helmet. He had already scratched off the SS insignia and painted red and white Polish pennants on it. It was in effect a 'safety helmet' that protected my head from falling debris and banging when passing through small wall openings.

That afternoon a man came to Nałęcz wanting to show him where he had been hiding thirteen Jews for the last couple of years. We followed him to his workshop in the basement of a nearby building down Długa Street. We entered a low basement housing a typical mechanical shop with an array of metalworking machines. A workbench against an internal wall was moved to reveal an opening in the floor. Crawling through a short tunnel, we emerged on the other side of the wall. There was a candle burning on the table. In the light of our torches we realised that we were in a space created by a false wall. The space created was about 16ft long and trapezoidal in shape. At one end, about 3ft wide, were a water closet and a slop sink. At the other, about 5ft wide, were three wooden platforms, one above the other, with bedding on them. The space, like the basement, was only about six and a half feet high. There was a narrow table and a couple of benches against the long wall. Thirteen people had lived in this space for two years, without daylight, receiving food passed through the tunnel every two or three days. They could only flush the toilet at night. If they were ever found out, or betrayed, then not only they but also most of the inhabitants of the building would have been killed.

That night I had the luxury of sleeping on an actual, relatively clean, bed, with my shoes and uniform off. I did not know that I would not be able to remove either my uniform or shoes for the next two and a half weeks.

Plan of Old Town around Telephone Exchange Building and Radziwill Palace

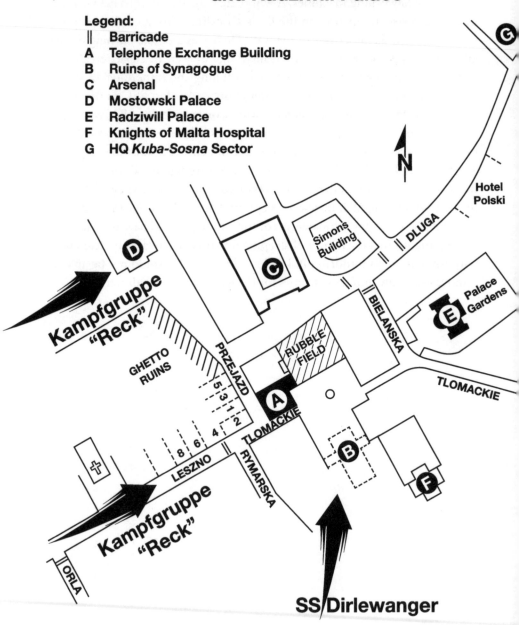

Legend:
- ‖ Barricade
- A Telephone Exchange Building
- B Ruins of Synagogue
- C Arsenal
- D Mostowski Palace
- E Radziwill Palace
- F Knights of Malta Hospital
- G HQ *Kuba-Sosna* Sector

N

Hotel Polski

DLUGA

Simons Building

Palace Gardens

BIELANSKA

E

Kampfgruppe "Reck"

D

GHETTO RUINS

PRZEJAZD

5 3 1
1 2
8 6 4

RUBBLE FIELD

TLOMACKIE

TLOMACKIE

A

B

F

LESZNO

RYMARSKA

Kampfgruppe "Reck"

ORLA

SS Dirlewanger

Old Town – Telephone Exchange Building, 12–20 August 1944

The next morning, 12 August, the Germans recommenced their aerial bombardment of the old town, as well as heavy artillery and mortar fire. For the first time, the Germans used the *Nebelwerfer*, a six-barrel rocket launcher which fired 8in high-explosive or incendiary rockets. It made a very specific, loud howling noise, nicknamed 'mooing cows'.

Unbeknownst to us, a very serious situation had developed that morning. The barricade at the beginning of Leszno Street, defending the principal access to the old town from the west, had been captured, opening the way into the rear of the Polish defences. A counter-attack by an assault group from the elite *Parasol* Battalion temporarily recaptured the barricade. However, a second German attack once again occupied the barricade, though only after Lt. 'Ryszard's' replacement unit faltered after he was severely wounded. The way to the soft underbelly of the old town was open once again. A small garrison in the five-storey telephone exchange building was still holding on. This building was on the corner of Przejazd and Tłomacka streets opposite the beginning of Leszno Street.

A second counter-attack by P-20 Company, ordered by Lt. Col. Kuba, broke under concentrated mortar and machine gun fire on Tłomacka Street before reaching the barricade. Lt. Col. Kuba requested and received permission to engage our battalion, the only reserve of the group. Early that afternoon, Lt. Nałęcz received orders to recapture the lost intersection.

Przygoński described our action as follows:

The 12th of August ... Col. Wachnowski conducted the successful action of recapturing ... the position on the confluence of Rymarska-Tłomacka-Leszno streets. The action was audaciously executed by the detached units from KB *Nałęcz* Battalion, cutting through Długa Street from the

Arsenal side, making their way through the cellars of the buildings on Przejazd Street and into the rear of the German-occupied barricade on Leszno Street, relying on surprise, they attacked them, achieving complete success. The Hitlerites running away in panic were pushed to the crossing of Leszno and Orla streets. The KB Battalion secured the barricade, closing the exits of Leszno and Rymarska streets, organising their key defensive position in the reinforced-concrete building of the telephone exchange on Tłomacka Street at the intersection with Przejazd Street.

*Powstanie warszawskie w sier-
pniu 1944 r.*, vol. 2, pp. 17–18

Two assault groups were formed under the command of Pobóg and Holski. The sapper's section, two machine gun crews and battle nurses followed both groups. Nałęcz, as always, was at the head and I was 'glued' to him. We departed from the Hotel Polski walking west on both sides of Długa Street towards the Arsenal, where the two groups split. Pobóg and his group with the machine gun crews left to capture the east (even) side of Przejazd Street and take control of the telephone exchange. Nałęcz, Holski's group and the sappers were to capture the west (odd) side of the street and the intersection with Leszno Street.

From the Arsenal we reached the courtyard of 5 Przejazd Street, the last building standing next to the ruins of the ghetto. We expected all the cellars to be interconnected. As we entered the cellars Nałęcz asked me to take the lead: he relied on my sense of direction. The cellars were almost empty; most of the civilians had already left as this had been the front line for some time. There were flickering candles here and there were small groups of people near them. We made our way under numbers 5, 3 and 1, and then entered what I estimated to be the cellars of the corner building with Leszno Street. Our immediate objective was the barricade closing Leszno Street, which adjoined this building.

We quietly reached the staircase. There was light from an open door upstairs and we heard German voices. Nałęcz and I flattened ourselves against the stairwell to make room for the assault vanguard. On his signal, the attack started. We ran after the vanguard, followed by the rest of the group. Grenades where exploding in the courtyard, machine pistols were barking, long bursts by the Germans and short ones by us. We could hear the sound of single shots, running and the screams of the wounded. Bodies were lying on the courtyard cobblestones. Some were still; others moving and moaning. Even though we managed complete surprise, the fight to clear the

Germans from the courtyard and ground floor, where there had been a restaurant, was very brutal. Eventually, the surviving Germans escaped through a staircase to the upper floors.

At the same time, Pobóg and his group recaptured the other side of Przejazd Street and connected with the few remaining defenders of the telephone exchange building. Nałęcz sent me to Pobóg to tell him to place his machine guns on the top floor of the telephone exchange in order to cover us when we continued our attack down Leszno Street. The attack moved forward. We found that the buildings on the even side of Leszno were all interconnected by wall openings on the top floor. We pressed forward, clearing the buildings along the way. We reached the barricade on Orla Street supported by our machine guns on top of the telephone exchange. The blocking fire of German machine guns from Orla Street and the assault guns from Leszno Street made it impossible to capture that barricade. We retreated after repeated unsuccessful attacks. The attempt of Pobóg's group to capture Rymarska Street barricade was also unsuccessful.

As we consolidated our defences at the Leszno Street barricade and telephone exchange, the Germans commenced heavy fire with mortars and artillery in preparation for a new attack. In the meantime, the nurses were taking care of and evacuating our wounded. Our soldiers were stripping German corpses of their weapons and ammunition.

Within a short time we saw a large group of Polish men being pushed out into Leszno Street from the Protestant church about a block away. They were followed and flanked on both pavements by German soldiers. Two assault guns, their engines and the clanking of their threads clearly audible, kept their distance behind. Nałęcz ordered the sapper section and sharpshooters to the top floors. We took positions on the second floor of 2, 4 and 6 Leszno Street. All these buildings, and those further down the street, were interconnected by holes in the party walls. The sappers had the 'bombs' made for our ill-fated catapult. The rest of the men were on the ground floor to deal with any German breakthrough from the street. Nałęcz sent me to the top floor of the telephone exchange to tell Lt. Zew to fire his machine guns only on the opposite side of the street in order to keep the Germans on our side. He was to wait until he heard our bombs go off before commencing fire at will.

I ran back to Nałęcz. He was on the second floor of No. 4, the building next to the barricade. He was holding a periscope fashioned from a broomstick with a mirror taped to it. We saw Polish civilians walking in the middle of the street, slowly approaching our barricade. We heard our machine gun firing short bursts and saw Germans moving against the buildings on our side to avoid its fire. We were absolutely quiet and kept away from the windows. I went down the line again quietly repeating the order to hold fire until the signal was given by Nałęcz. I returned to No. 4, where Nałęcz and 'Abczyc' were standing next to the window. 'Edek', 'Łuniewski', 'Adam' and the other sappers were further down the line in the next buildings. They were standing next to the open, glassless windows, holding bombs in one hand and lit cigarettes in the other.

The civilians reached the barricade and started to dismantle it. Directly under us we heard German voices, the rattling of equipment and sporadic firing. Still not a single shot was fired by us, the sporadic short burst of our machine gun was no longer heard. From time to time, using his periscope, Nałęcz observed the Germans below us. They were all leaning against the walls directly beneath us. After one last long look, Nałęcz turned to Abczyc and whispered, 'Ready?' Abczyc nodded.

Nałęcz leaned out of the window and yelled, 'Poles, run behind the barricade, run, run!' He turned to us: 'Fire!' Abczyc touched his glowing cigarette to the priming cord of his bomb and started to count 'one hundred and one, one hundred and two ...' I ran along the buildings unnecessarily repeating 'Fire, fire ...' as all the sappers had already activated their bombs. There was a tremendous explosion as the first bomb went off, followed by others down the line. I leaned out of the window and saw complete carnage below. German bodies were lying around in all directions torn and bleeding; the survivors were running back along the wall. Unfortunately, there were also bodies of Polish civilians. We heard the sound of a firefight in the courtyard of the corner building below us. The explosion had blown open the gates of the courtyard from Leszno Street and a few Germans had managed to escape there. They did not last long; they were all killed by our soldiers on the ground floor. Unfortunately, we also had casualties.

When the fighting stopped we counted over thirty Germans killed and severely wounded. We managed to recover a lot of weapons and ammunition. A great prize was a Russian *Tokariev* ten-shot repeating sniper rifle, a German Mauser rifle with grenade launcher and a signal pistol with flares and explosive projectiles.

After a while the Germans made a second attempt. Another attack emerged from Orla Street covered by the assault guns from Leszno Street. The assault guns did not want to come close and the infantry advancing behind was kept at bay by our machine guns from the telephone exchange. This attack was simultaneously supported by a German sortie from Rymarska Street. It too was repulsed. By 8 o'clock all fighting had died out.

We estimated that about fifty Germans had been killed and many more wounded. Our losses were relatively light: one officer and seven other ranks killed and several more wounded. In addition, the remnants of the other Polish units taking part in this fight suffered one officer killed and two wounded, and several other ranks killed and wounded.

Once the fighting died down, we needed to reorganise all the fragmented units into permanent defences. Col. Wachnowski, the CO of the old town, decided to retain our battalion in its current position. He appointed Nałęcz to overall command of this position, later called the *Reduta Nałęcz* (Nałęcz Redoubt). P-20 Company was integrated into our battalion. Twenty men with a flamethrower joined our battalion from the remnants of Lt. 'Nowina''s 'Tigers of Wola' unit, which had suffered heavy casualties. The remnants of Lt. Ryszard's platoon were withdrawn from the front line. Headquarters sent a detachment from a work battalion to repair the barricades. They worked all night and left in the morning.

Nałęcz consolidated our defences in the area. Our southern perimeter was closed off by the barricade on Rymarska Street. The eastern, against the axis of the Germans' main thrust, by the barricade at the beginning of Leszno Street anchored against the building next to the corner with Przejazd Street. All the buildings on both sides of Przejazd Street, on the block between Długa and Tłomacka streets, were in our hands. The main defensive position was the five-storey, reinforced-concrete telephone exchange on the corner of Przejazd and Tłomacka streets. Leszno Street terminated at the intersection with Przejazd Street (from where it continued as Tłomacka Street) but it was offset by about 8ft. From the projecting part of the telephone exchange, there was a clear view down both sides of Leszno Street. Our observation post was on top of the building, manned by a sharpshooter and a machine gun.

Our weakness was our flanks. On the right flank, the last building was 5 Przejazd Street, opposite the end of Długa Street. Beyond that, towards the north lay the levelled ruins of the ghetto destroyed in 1943; it was no-man's-land. Further along to the north along Przejazd Street was Mostowski Palace, which was in Polish hands. On our left flank along Tłomacka Street, there were no buildings standing beyond the telephone exchange. The block between Tłomacka and Długa streets had been reduced to a 300ft long field of rubble after the siege of Warsaw in 1939. The facades of the destroyed buildings had been knocked down to one storey high and the window openings bricked up. The remaining ruins of the buildings between the two streets had been levelled. On the other side of the rubble field, the buildings facing Bielanska Street were still standing. The buildings on both sides of that street were defended by the *Łukasiński* Battalion. Opposite the rubble field, on the other (south) side of Tłomacka Street, was the ruin of the Great Synagogue of Warsaw, dynamited after the 1943 Ghetto Uprising. That ruin, and the Hospital of the Knights of Malta behind it, was also no-man's-land.

The hospital was overflowing with Polish and German wounded. By tacit agreement neither side occupied the hospital, but this situation could have changed at any moment as the area further south was solidly in German hands. The Germans held a large magazine of spirits at the hospital, which some civilians now began looting then returning to the old town through our positions. We received an order to stop the looters, confiscate the liquor and allow each person to keep one bottle. In this way we acquired a few cases of *Hine* cognac, some champagne and red wine.

That night an assault group led by Pobóg reached the Germans' rear positions by moving across the roofs on Rymarska Street. In a surprise attack they recaptured the barricade closing Rymarska Street. Throughout the night German medics picked up their wounded and dead from in front of the Leszno Street barricade. We did not interfere. I spent most of the night following Nałęcz around as he organised defences, in this way becoming familiar with the locations of all our units. As we made our rounds German AA batteries across Warsaw opened up. We heard the heavy drone of multi-engine planes. Traces of AA fire and searchlights lit up the night sky. The long-awaited Allied airdrops were finally coming! The planes arrived singly, at very low altitude; we saw several white parachutes floating down from the direction of Kraśinski Square in the centre of the old town defence area.

At daybreak we returned to the ground floor of the building on Przejazd Street adjoining the telephone exchange, where Nałęcz had located his command post. Our first aid station was already there. After I summoned some of the officers for a meeting he told me to go and get some sleep. I could not find a suitable sleeping place as they were all taken. Then I spotted a very large pram with all the bedding. I squashed into it in a sitting position with my legs hanging over the edge and immediately passed out. Renewed artillery and mortar fire woke me up. It was the morning of 13 August. I got out of the pram and collapsed in pain. I had cut off the circulation to my legs and couldn't get up.

Stukas had arrived, strafing our position and dropping bombs behind us. Before noon the Germans renewed their attack on Leszno Street. Groups of infantry advanced under cover of two assault guns. At the same time, the Germans occupied the Knights of Malta Hospital and attacked the Rymarska Street barricade. After an hour of heavy fighting we withdrew from that barricade and concentrated our defences on the barricade that closed off Leszno Street.

When the fighting subsided, I followed Nałęcz as he made the rounds of our positions. We moved through the ground floor of 1, 3 and into 5 Przejazd Street. Coming to a staircase adjoining the common wall with the entrance gateway we noticed the interconnecting passage was not protected. The two-man outpost that was supposed to be there was missing. Nałęcz chambered his machine pistol and I took out my grenade. As we cautiously approached the opening we heard German voices on the other side. We pressed ourselves to the wall on both sides of the opening. I slipped the finger of my left hand into the ring of the grenade pin ready to lob it. There were more voices, then footsteps, which subsided. We stood still and listened for a few minutes; no more sounds came from the other side. Nałęcz told me to stay by the opening and to throw the grenade and run if I heard any more German voices; he immediately left to get a replacement.

I was standing by the opening, straining to listen. 'Sten' arrived about five minutes later. He was only two years older than me and had also been in the Underground Boy Scouts before joining the battalion. He was armed with a 7mm Belgian FN pistol. We took positions on both sides of the opening. Nothing was happening and the sounds of fighting died down. Sten asked me if I knew how to strip an FN pistol. I said no, that I was familiar only with the VIS, *Parabellum*, P-38 and *Nagant* revolvers. 'Come over and I'll show you how.' I crossed to his side of the opening. He removed the slide from the top of the pistol, exposing the barrel and the cocked firing pin on its spring. 'You have to be very careful removing the firing pin,' he said as the pin and the spring flew off, landing several feet away on the rubble-covered floor. 'Guard the opening,' he ordered as he frantically searched for the missing parts. We spent the next half hour taking turns standing guard, with the remaining armament of my solitary grenade, and systematically searching the floor on our hands and knees. Finally Sten found his missing parts. As he finished reassembling his pistol, a properly armed, two-man detachment took over.

Later that afternoon, an assault group counter-attacked, cleared the pocket of Germans on the other side of the Leszno Street barricade and recaptured the Rymarska Street barricade. We took a few prisoners and since they were Wehrmacht, not SS, they were escorted to headquarters rather than being shot out of hand. We suffered more dead and wounded that day.

Nałęcz prepared a situation report, which I delivered to sector headquarters on Barokowa Street. Maj. 'Sosna', a new commanding officer, had taken command after Lt. Col. Kuba had been severely wounded. He called me in and asked several questions about the disposition of our forces, our losses and the status of our ammunition.

Returning around 6 p.m., I heard a tremendous explosion behind me from the direction of the old town. There were clouds of dust. It was definitely more powerful than a Stuka bomb or artillery shell. Later I learned what had happened. A German armoured vehicle was captured after its crew abandoned it close to Polish positions and it was brought to Kiliński Street in the centre of the old town. A jubilant crowd surrounded the vehicle when it exploded. It had been booby-trapped by the Germans. Over 300 people were killed. The most severe losses were suffered by the Boy Scout Company *Orląt*, which lost eighty. The carnage was so great that when I visited the site the following day, there were still pieces of human flesh stuck to the walls of the adjoining buildings.

When I returned I learned that there was no more water. The Germans had cut off the water supply. Electricity had long since disappeared. The only water we had access to was what we could find in bathtubs. As part of the air raid protection, the Germans had required all tubs to be filled with water at all times, although not everyone complied. The few full tubs we found were secured for drinking and cooking only. It didn't make any difference to our hygiene as most of us had not had a bath since the Uprising began.

That night, once again, AA guns opened up and the skies were lit by searchlights and tracers from AA guns of all calibres. There were many more planes. From the top floor of the telephone exchange we watched parachutes floating down, some over Kraśinski Square. Unfortunately, none of them came down within our positions. There was great celebration – the long-expected resupplies were coming. However, what we did not know at that time was the high cost paid by the aircrews. That night three Liberator bombers were lost; eight the next night. Before the flights were abandoned two days later on 15 August by the British High Command, the overall losses of Liberator and Halifax bombers flying from Italy to supply Warsaw were fifteen Polish Air Force, twelve Royal Air Force, nine South African Air Force. Russia refused the Allies' requests to allow Allied planes to land in the territories captured by the Russians. This would have significantly reduced losses since the majority occurred over Germany while the planes returned to their Italian bases in daylight.

During the night Pobóg led a sortie to collect weapons abandoned by retreating Germans. They ventured along Leszno Street, past the Protestant church, into the ruins of the ghetto. They recovered some weapons and equipment. Pobóg gave me a German military torch that was better than mine; it could change white light to green or red. They also returned with five Greek Jews who had been hiding in the ghetto. The Jews had escaped from a small concentration camp in the old ghetto called *Gęsia* when it was captured by the *Zośka* Battalion a few days before. Three of them stayed with the battalion, helping wherever they could. One of them was a baker and helped with the cooking. Another had a great voice and was always singing Italian arias and love songs. After the capitulation, one of them managed to survive for over three months, hiding in the cellars of Warsaw, until January the following year, when Warsaw was liberated. He returned to Greece.

Very early on the morning of 14 August we received a case of 9mm ammunition and a PIAT (Projector Infantry Anti-Tank). This was our share of the supplies dropped the previous night on Krasiński Square. The PIAT was a British-made, very portable hand-held weapon, about 3ft long and weighing only 30lb. A PIAT could fire an anti-tank projectile an effective distance, about 100yd. The projectile was launched by the force of a spring and a propellant charge in its finned tail. It required considerable strength to cock it and, as we found out later, it had a recoil like the kick of a mule. The projectiles came in cardboard tubes in sets of three; unfortunately, we only got two packs, giving us a total of six projectiles.

That same early morning a wounded boy, about two years older than me, was carried in on a stretcher. He had joined only a few days before and had been accepted, despite not having a weapon, because he was a distant nephew of Holski. Early that morning, when it was still dark, he had gone over the barricade in search of an abandoned German weapon. He was shot, managed to crawl to the barricade and was picked up. Since I had gotten to know him I went over to him, and as I leaned over the stretcher he grabbed my hand. The nurse cut open his shirt. Under his left collarbone was a small entry hole, a typical rifle wound with no blood. A nice clean wound, I thought. When the nurses turned him over there was a lot of blood on the stretcher. When the rest of his shirt was cut off there was a huge, jagged bleeding hole, the size of a saucer. Baśka attending him shook her head and mouthed, 'Dum-Dum'. I kneeled holding his hand as his grip slowly loosened and he died. I never knew his name and have forgotten his code name. He was one of many who joined our battalion and are now referred to only as 'NN', not known.

Ryszard Budzianowski included a list of soldiers who went through the battalion during the Uprising in his book *Battalion KB 'Nałęcz' in the Warsaw Uprising* (pp. 111–27). There are 378 entries: 340 men and thirty-eight women, mostly nurses (the equivalent of 'medics' in the United States Army). Of the first 302 entries, forty-eight have code names only, no family names, including eleven killed and nineteen wounded. Entries 303 to 378 are 'NN': these seventy-five soldiers, forty of whom were killed in action, are listed with neither family nor code name.

From the morning onwards, heavy artillery and mortar fire fell on our positions. The Stukas were bombing around us. The building on the south side of Leszno Street in front of the barricade took a direct hit and caught fire. Fires were impossible to put out as there had been no water since the previous day. The wind carried the heavy smoke and the stench of the bodies decomposing in front of our positions. The men in the front positions protected themselves with handkerchiefs across their noses and mouths.

Later in the morning the Germans renewed their attack along Leszno Street. Again, their infantry was supported by two assault guns, 75mm StuG IIIs. From a short distance the guns opened fire directly on our barricade and the telephone exchange. We were forced out of our forward positions and away from the barricade. We retreated to the telephone exchange. Finally the guns came close enough to test our new PIAT. I led Nałęcz and the PIAT crew up the back stairs to the fourth floor of the telephone exchange. That floor, like the two below, had a 'forest' of steel angles bolted to concrete slabs from floor to ceiling. The steel angles supported a labyrinth of wires and switching equipment, and provided additional support for the building, and cover for us.

The PIAT crew loaded the weapon and fired. The sound was no louder than a rifle shot and there was no telltale smoke. I looked in disbelief as the projectile hit the first assault gun and bounced off without exploding. The gunner let out a string of obscenities, realising that he had not armed the projectile. Checking the carrying tube, he found the fuse still in the container attached to the lid. Even though the projectile did not explode the German crew immediately started backing out, realising that we had an anti-tank weapon. Our second shot was much more satisfying. It exploded, immobilising the gun. The second assault gun pulled the disabled one out. The Germans abandoned their attack. Later that day we destroyed two other assault guns.

During the attack there was another new and very dangerous development on our left flank. The Hospital of the Knights of Malta, which had been a no-man's-land, was evacuated by the Germans. The hospital and the ruins of the Great Synagogue were occupied by the SS Dirlewanger Brigade. The newly placed machine guns in the ruins had a clear field of fire along the whole of Tłomacka Street and the rubble field behind our positions. We were cut off.

Late in the evening our counter-attack regained most of the positions, securing the barricade, the corner building and 1 and 3 Przejazd Street. The Germans retained control of the buildings on Leszno Street behind the barricade.

During the night an equally dangerous situation developed on our right flank. Past 5 Przejazd Street, towards Mostowski Palace, were the ruins of the ghetto. The Germans occupied this area and made firing positions for machine guns that controlled the square in front of the Arsenal, Długa Street and part of the rubble field behind us. We were now boxed in.

Throughout the night we witnessed the largest Allied airdrops to date. The huge four-engine planes were coming singly from different directions towards Krasiński Square, the designated drop point. The sky was illuminated by searchlights and traces of AA guns firing from all directions. The falling parachutes were only visible for a brief moment as the drops were made from very low altitudes. There was an explosion and a ball of fire. Some time later, a second explosion and a fireball came from the same direction. Two planes were shot down during the drop and crashed on Miodowa Street. The feeling of euphoria upon seeing the airdrop left us as we watched the fires from the downed planes. The total losses that night were eight planes (one Polish, three South African and four RAF). The other six planes were lost over Germany in daylight, while returning to their bases in Italy.

The day of 15 August began with the customary mortar fire at 8 a.m. The Germans were very punctual. Later that morning one of our soldiers ventured from Przejazd Street towards the Arsenal and was shot, falling face down. As I watched, one of the nurses ran out from the first aid station, brushing past me. As she reached the fallen soldier she was shot herself and fell on top of him. A few minutes later, another of our soldiers ran out; as he tried to pick up the girl he was shot and fell down with her. After a few more minutes our only male medic, 'Pigularz', stepped out with a Red Cross flag and slowly moved towards them. When he reached them and leaned over, a shot was fired and he too toppled onto the others. As I continued to watch there was an explosion and all four bodies were lifted about 3ft in the air, landing spread out. 'Ninka' and 'Pigularz' were the first two medics from our unit to be killed in action. We later speculated that the first man had a grenade under him, which somehow exploded.

Later that morning the Germans renewed their attack, shifting the axis of attack north from Leszno Street (where we were) to Nowolipki Street, about 380yd away. They were trying to capture Mostowski Palace, shelling the whole area heavily and setting 5 Przejazd Street on fire.

Around noon, I followed Nałęcz to Długa Street on the edge of the rubble field, to the last building still in our hands. On the east side of the interior courtyard there was a wall about 10ft high abutting the rubble field. There was a two-man post there. One of them reported that earlier that day a civilian man had tried to run to the other side; he was cut down by machine gun fire, his legs literally cut off. The German machine guns on top of the ruins of the synagogue had a commanding view. Later on that morning a boy of about 12 also tried to make it across and he too was killed. We could see both bodies ahead, the man about a third of the way across and the boy closer. I recognised the boy. I had spoken to him before; he had lived in this building and his father was a POW in an *oflag*.

As we stood on two adjoining ladders Nałęcz asked me, 'Do you think you can make it?' 'Yes, Capitan, sir!' (Nałęcz had been promoted captain). He took a small notebook from his pocket and scribbled a note. 'Deliver this to Maj. Sosna and report that we urgently need a surgeon as we cannot evacuate our wounded; we are critically low on ammunition and we have run out of PIAT projectiles; we are holding and will not abandon our position.'

I had been through this rubble field several times before the Germans occupied the ruins of the synagogue. It was about 300ft from where we were standing to the opposite side and the buildings on Bielańska Street. There was an opening in the wall of one of them. The field was not perfectly level; it had high and low points. I looked, trying to locate the sunken areas. I spotted one close to the boy's body and made a run for it. As I was diving into it the machine guns on the synagogue opened up. When they stopped, I inched forward and touched the body; it was cold. After a few minutes I crawled about 20ft to the next depression. From there, with a series of crawls and zigzag runs, accompanied by bursts of machine gun fire and explosions from a rifle grenade, I reached the other side, jumping through the opening. As I landed on a stair platform below, a stream of bullets poured through the opening and ricocheted all over. The stairs were in the back of the building. I walked all the way down to the basement. As I walked through the cellars, I was suddenly hit by the suffering of the civilian population. In the darkness, small groups, mostly women and children, huddled around flickering candles. There were many wounded amongst them. They all looked gaunt and very tired, yet they all smiled and asked how the fight was going.

Through the cellars I emerged in the courtyard of the corner building on Bielańska and Długa streets. There was a barricade closing Bielańska Street that was always manned. As I emerged from the gate and turned left towards the barricade I saw three badly mangled bodies with blood and pieces of flesh splattered all over. They must have just received a direct hit from a mortar.

From the barricade I looked at the ruins of the ghetto. Machine gun fire sporadically sprayed Długa Street in front of me. I sprinted over to the other side, which was shielded from the gun. It was a short distance down to Group Headquarters on Barokowa Street. I reported to the duty officer: 'Runner from Capt. Nałęcz', and was immediately taken to Maj. Sosna. I saluted, gave him the note and repeated my verbal instructions. I never actually read this note, but Rejmund Szubański quoted it as follows:

15.8.44 11:45 Report to headquarters of Kuba Group. Request send-ing a doctor with instruments to the redoubt. We have a large number of wounded we cannot evacuate under fire. Urgently request a surgeon. Receiving heavy fire from mortars. We are holding steady, we will perse-vere. Surgeon! Nałęcz Cpt.

1 Batalion Szturmowy KB 'Nałęcz' W
Powstaniu Warszawskim, p. 88

Maj. Sosna asked several questions and I gave detailed answers. I was told to wait outside and sat down on the floor of the long corridor (the building was a school), leaned against the wall and dozed off. I was woken and taken back to Sosna. Standing next to him was Col. Wachnowski, overall commander of the old town defences. I was asked more questions by the colonel, about our losses in manpower and terrain, and the state of our ammunition. I was told that I would have to wait until darkness before I could return. I was escorted out, given some food and told to wait. I laid down on the stairs and immedi-ately fell asleep.

Someone had shaken me awake and in the dim light I saw Sgt. 'Mocny' from our battalion. He told me that since I had not returned Nałęcz assumed that I had not made it. He asked for volunteers to try again and Mocny had volunteered. He started in early evening, through Arsenal Square as there was a lot of smoke. 5 Przejazd Street and the building next to the Arsenal, on the corner of Przejazd and Długa streets, were on fire.

We were called to Maj. Sosna, who gave us the following instructions: we were to carry back the ammunition that he could spare us; we were to tell Nałęcz that the Work Battalion had already started digging a trench across the field con-necting to the redoubt; he could not send a surgeon, they were all needed in the field hospitals; the new trench would allow us to evacuate our wounded. He gave us a handwritten note expressing his approval of our defence.

We were shown the ammunition we had to carry back: a large cardboard box of German rifle cartridges, a smaller one of 9mm ammunition, a small sack of English grenades (Mills Bombs) and two containers (six tubes) of PIAT projectiles. We decided to split the load equally in case one of us did not make it. I carried a backpack with half of the rifles, the 9mm ammo and about ten grenades. Mocny had a backpack with the other half of the cartridges and more grenades than me since they were quite heavy. We both carried one container of PIAT projectiles. The three tubes in each container were flexibly interconnected by webbing straps and had a carrying handle.

We decided to go to the Arsenal before deciding which way to take. We reached the Arsenal and from its gate we could see that the rubble field was constantly being lit by flares and sprayed with machine gun fire. The Germans were trying to obstruct the digging of the trench. We looked to the right and noticed that the fires that had started that morning had died out and were now smouldering and still smoking. There was sporadic machine gun fire on the square in front of us coming from the ruins of the ghetto. No flares were being fired over the square, but there was some light from the smouldering fires. We decided to go that way. We moved along the wall of the Arsenal towards Przejazd Street, taking advantage of the cover provided by the smouldering building on the corner that protruded into the square. Reaching the end of the cover I signalled with my new German torch, alternating green and red. It was acknowledged from the gate on other side of the square.

We decided to crawl through the square. It was awkward and difficult for me because of the weight of the backpack and the PIAT container in my hand. Halfway there, I indicated to Mocny that I wanted to sprint the rest of the way. He agreed and on his signal we both got up and ran. As a flare went up and illuminated the square, the machine guns from the ghetto opened up, blindly spraying the square. By the time they found us we had reached our target, an open door in the gate of the corner building. I saw a grinning Nałęcz and others waiting for us. Mocny was wounded during the final sprint. Luckily, it was only a flesh wound and he was taken away to have it taken care of. I reported to Nałęcz and answered his questions. He told me that the work on the trench had begun as darkness fell and had encouraged him to think that at least one of us had made it. There was much jubilation over the ammunition that we brought.

* * *

There is a Polish saying: 'he knew that the bells were ringing but he did not know in which church.'

While he was a POW in Germany, Stanislaw Podlewski, a lieutenant in the Uprising, started interviewing his colleagues and keeping notes. Based on those and subsequent interviews, in 1957 he published his first, very popular, book, *March through Hell*, about the fighting in the old town. He related several stories about our battalion. In one of them, 'Redoubt "*Nałęcz*" Cut-off', he had this to say:

> For the last few days 1st Assault Battalion '*Nałęcz*' under the command of Cpt. '*Nałęcz*' (Stefan Kaniewski) has been defending barricades on Leszno-Przejazd and the building of the PAST telephone exchange on the corner of Przejazd and Leszno, called the '*Nałęcz*' Redoubt.
>
> The enemy is keeping the building under relentless fire. From Leszno Street and the ghetto ruins there are constant attacks by infantry supported by tanks. From the ruins of the synagogue heavy machine gun and mortar fire. The Redoubt is cut off from the rest of the old town. For two days it has been impossible to establish communications with headquarters. The situation is tragic: lack of ammunition and grenades, no water and food … Incoming fire is so strong that the runners cannot get through the streets … Runners undertake constant attempts to establish communications with headquarters. Ignoring incoming fire, runner Andrzej (Andrzej Hryniewicz) crawls from the redoubt. Halfway, the boy contorts in pain and calls for help. A burst of machine gun fire cuts off both of his legs. This scene takes place in front of the men. They are helpless. Before anybody can assess the situation, runner Bohdan (Bohdan Hryniewicz), a 14-year-old boy runs out without an order. Reaching his prostrate brother, confirming that he is dead, he takes the message from his hand, crawls further through the ruins and happily reaches headquarters …
>
> 'Redoubt "*Nałęcz*" Cut-off', pp. 323–4

This fictitious version of events was repeated in several other books about the Uprising. There's always someone who would like to do 'one better'. There was a cadet officer in our battalion, a very brave man who was always in the midst of the heavy fighting. After the war he published several articles as 'Memories of an officer of KB AK, Janusz Wisniewski ("Sternik"), who fought in the Warsaw Uprising in the ranks of 1st Assault Battalion "*Nałęcz*"'. In the Polish weekly *Za i Przeciw* of 24 September 1972, he 'recollected' as follows:

> There is nothing left to do but renew attempts to re-establish communications with headquarters. They [implying Cpt. '*Nałęcz*' and Wisniewski himself] are sending the 13-year-old runner 'Tarzan' [Andrzej Hryniewicz].

He leaves. Somewhere halfway through the rubble he receives a long burst of machine gun fire. He contorts in a paroxysm of pain and calls for help. The next burst of machine gun fire cuts off both his legs. 'Sternik' is watching this with 'Nałęcz'. Nearby stands Private 'Bohdan', the 14-year-old brother of the runner. Without any command, he runs away from them and crawls to his brother lying in a pool of blood. He bends over him, takes his head in his small hands, trying to bring him to the conscious-ness yelling: 'Andrzej! Andrzej!' After a while he realises that his brother is dead. He kisses him, takes the message from his hand and crawls forward. The Germans from the synagogue spot him. The staccato of machine gun fire commences again. But Bohdan pays no attention to it; he crawls for-ward metre after metre. From the ladder, with bated breath, his comrades at arms follow his movements. Will he make it or not? The future of the redoubt and its defenders depends on it. The Germans spare no one.

Bohdan has already crawled around 80yd in the direction of the build-ing adjoining the rubble field. Before him is the most dangerous part: a wide incline leading to the opening in the wall. We can see how the boy is concentrating before making the jump. In the meantime, the Germans are sending bursts of machine gun fire right next to the opening. For fif-teen minutes he makes no forward movement. We wait full of expectation. All of a sudden he runs ahead and on the run covers the dangerous sector. We do not know if he made it through the hole; from our positions we see machine gun fire biting into the wall next to the opening and red dust obscuring the hole.

Za i Przeciw, 24 September 1972, p. 20

In the above 'recollection', he stretched his *licentia poetica* past the breaking point. Because father read those two stories he never wanted to believe me when I told him the true circumstances of Andrzej's death. I guess he pre-ferred this more 'heroic' version.

During the night there was heavy fighting on our right flank. Mostowski Palace, captured the previous day by the Germans, was retaken at night by the Boy Scout Battalion *Wigry*. As before, heavy shelling of our posi-tions started again in the morning, but there was no German activity in our sector. That same night our outpost in 3 Przejazd Street reported a hammering noise coming from the cellars. A patrol under Lt. Skóra was sent to investigate. After a short firefight, they pushed out a few Germans. Surprisingly, the Germans did not try to fight but withdrew quickly. Lt. Skóra found an opening leading to the cellar in the building behind ours, which he barricaded as well as he could. The patrol also found an enclosure with two piglets in it. Nałęcz ordered the evacuation of the building. As soon as the communication trench was completed he sent a runner with a report to Maj. Sosna. The runner returned with a direct order to defend all positions. The evacuation was stopped but most of the civilians who had been there had already left that morning.

Meanwhile, I attached myself to 'Pantera' and one other man and we left in search of the two piglets. We had no problem locating the pen as the piglets, most likely very hungry, were making loud honking noises. We entered the enclosure and in the dim light from a small, high window we spotted the piglets. The other man claimed he knew how to slaughter and butcher pigs. The 'butcher' pulled out a bayonet and tried to grab one. After a few unsuccessful runs behind the squealing piglets, Pantera killed the pigs with two short burst from his machine pistol. The pigs were butchered in the courtyard. We all looked forward to a good meal as food was very short in supply. The pigs were sent off to be cooked in the kitchen of the ground-floor apartment in the back of the courtyard.

Around noon Nałęcz sent me to find out how the piglets were progressing. All of us were already licking our chops in anticipation of fresh meat for the first time since 1 August. I walked into the entryway of 3 Przejazd Street looking towards the ground-floor window on the other side of the courtyard. I saw an open window and two of our girls leaning over the stove. I waved and shouted to them. One of them turned from the stove and waved back. Then, as I was still looking at them, the building, in front of my eyes, rose up a couple of feet. A pressure wave hit me, followed by a cloud of choking dust from pulverised plaster. A surrealistic picture unfolded: in almost complete silence, the building crumbled down, as if in a slow-motion film. There was no loud noise as with a typical explosion, only a deep rumble, as the five-storey building collapsed in a heap of rubble and a cloud of heavy grey dust on the other side of the courtyard. Then there was silence, except for the ringing in my ears.

The immediate rescue effort was in vain. The whole back part of the building had collapsed into a huge mountain of rubble. The losses, estimated at around forty people, were severe. Our battalion lost fourteen soldiers and several were wounded. Equally large losses were suffered by the remnants of other units and civilians.

We were baffled by the explosion; it was so different from those caused by conventional explosive materials such as TNT. Abczyc, the head of the sapper section, speculated that this explosion was similar to ones in coal mines.

It turned out that he was right. The explosion was made by *Taifun-Gerät*, an experimental weapon that mixed coal dust with air. The mixture was pumped into the cellar and then ignited. The Germans were developing the weapon in the hopes of destroying American bombers by directing powerful explosions upwards. This was the first and only confirmed use in the Uprising.

The German follow-up attacks, expected immediately after the explosion, never materialised. Much later, they resumed their two-pronged attack, along Leszno Street, and from the ruins of the ghetto towards Przejazd Street. By that time new defensive positions had been established in the ruins of No. 3 Przejazd. Those attacks failed after the Germans suffered losses. In the meantime, the few remaining civilians in our area left through the new trench to the old town.

Later that day there were a lot of celebrations. Since our communications were re-established, we received order No. 40 from our headquarters: 'for heroism during the battle for Warsaw from 1 to 13 August 1944, officers, non-commissioned officers and privates from the 1st Assault Battalion KB are awarded, for the first time, the Cross of Valour.' Captain Nałęcz, several lieutenants and other ranks, including nurses and myself, were awarded. The last bottles of champagne and cognac from the Knights of Malta Hospital were drunk. Nurses prepared 'ribbons' handmade from red material stretched over cardboard, cut in the regulation size of 1 x 5cm, with two stripes made from white tape. I was very proud when Nałęcz pinned the ribbon on my uniform.

That night, heavy artillery shelling started a fire in the telephone exchange. It was put out with difficulty. The next morning, 17 August, the artillery fire intensified. From the depths of Leszno Street two large assault guns emerged. Delfin identified them as *Sturmpanzer IV Brummbär*s. They had a 15cm (6in) short-barrel howitzer designed to provide direct fire support to infantry attacking in urban areas. The guns opened fire on the barricade and the telephone exchange, causing severe damage. When the firing stopped the expected follow-up infantry attack did not materialise. Instead an armoured vehicle came forward with a PA system and started transmitting in Polish. First, in German-accented Polish, a man's voice told us to lay down our arms or we would be annihilated. If we surrendered, we would be recognised as regular soldiers and treated with honour. He told us that many soldiers had already surrendered and many civilians had crossed over the lines. This introduction was followed by 'testimonials' from Polish women. They introduced themselves as mothers and wives of insurgents. They told us how well they were being treated, that they had received medical care and food. They were waiting for us. This was repeated several times. After the last transmission there was an hour or two of quiet. The Germans suspended all fire on our positions.

Nałęcz decided to return the favour. We did not have a PA system, but someone found a large horn from an old gramophone that perfectly amplified and projected a human voice. Delfin was called and Nałęcz briefed him on what to say. Alternating with 'Kmita', the other Wehrmacht deserter, they started our transmission in perfect German along the lines of:

> Soldiers of the Wehrmacht! You are fighting us when the Allied Air Force is pulverising German towns and villages, killing and maiming your wives, children and parents. On the eastern front the huge Russian Army, helped by the Polish, is slowly moving forward and will invade your homeland. They will take revenge for the atrocities you have committed. On the western front the large armies of Britain and America will soon reach the German border. The whole world is against Hitler. Give up now! Come over to us and you will live and see your families.

Our transmission was overpowered by the high volume of the German PA: 'You Polish bandits, you will not escape us. We will kill you all!' And then one of the 'Polish mothers' pleaded with us, saying that if we continued to fight they would be shot by the Germans. After those words the euphoria that we had felt when we had turned the tables on the Germans quietly disappeared.

The German PA vehicle retired and the assault guns renewed their fire. Our conditions inside the redoubt were deteriorating. The lack of food, particularly water, was very troublesome. The only water we had was from the two remaining bathtubs and a shallow well dug in one of the courtyards. There had been no water to flush toilets for quite some time, which created the problem of spreading dysentery. The plague of big, green-black flies was troublesome, particularly to the wounded. Luckily I had a cast-iron stomach and was not affected.

There were more and more casualties. Staff Sgt. Mama, who enlisted us, was severely wounded by shrapnel. It became more and more difficult to evacuate the wounded who were rapidly filling the first aid station, which had been moved into the basement. We had no doctor and medical supplies were running out. There were no more painkillers, so the wounded suffered in silence. The nurses were doing everything they could but were completely worn out. Nevertheless they kept going.

Word came that 'Jaga' had been killed evacuating one of the wounded. Both Andrzej and I had got to know her. She was the youngest nurse, only three years older than Andrzej. She had been in the Underground Girl Guides for a long time and we had the common bond of being scouts. Insurgent nurse and journalist Danuta Kaczyńska wrote:

On this day (17 August) a nurse from the 1st Company, my friend, 17-year-old Jaga, also perished. She was late arriving at the Parasol assembly point. The Uprising found her near the square by the 'Iron Gate'. She had joined the first unit she came across. It was Lieutenant 'Nałęcz''s unit from KB ...

Some time in the middle of August Jaga had come to see me in Krasiński Palace but did not find me as I was on the front line. She left news that she was in Lt. Nałęcz's unit on Długa Street. In a free moment I ran to her. I wanted her to return to us, to Parasol, as we were short of nurses and Jaga was a girl you could rely on. She replied:

– I want to return to you, but I know I am needed more here ...

During this short visit I noticed how well liked she was by the soldiers. I understood her: several days of fighting had bonded her to this unit ...

... I managed to find the person present at her death. Dr Barbara Zylewicz [Baśka] was commandant of the battle nurses in Nałęcz during the Uprising. She knew Jaga and talked of her attitude and bravery with admiration:

'On 17 August Jaga and I were carrying a wounded to the hospital. We stopped to rest in the entrance of the Arsenal building on Długa Street. Jaga was standing close to the entrance talking with an insurgent. At that moment a shell struck, shredding them both.' From Jaga's pocket Barbara Zylewicz took a photograph of her and on the back noted the date and place of her death. I have this photograph ...

Dziewczęta z "Parasola" [The Girls from Parasol], p. 245

The day of 18 August was relatively calm. There were no armoured or infantry attacks on our positions, just constant shelling from artillery and rocket launchers, while Stukas pounded our rear positions, causing widespread destruction and fires. We had the feeling that this might be the 'calm before the storm', and that the Germans were preparing a major attack on our positions – the only positions left from the original defence against the Germans' main assault on the old town from the west. We were a projecting salient with exposed flanks.

That night we looked in vain for Allied airdrops, there hadn't been any for the last three nights. The next morning an artillery barrage of unprecedented intensity began at precisely 9 a.m., not only on our positions but all over the old town. The Germans employed everything in their armoury: artillery, mortars, *Nebelwerfer* rockets and assault guns. In the middle of August a *Karl-Gerät*, the largest existing siege mortar, previously used in the siege of Sevastopol, had been brought to the outskirts of Warsaw. It fired a 24in shell weighing over 2 tons, causing more destruction than anything previously fired or dropped on Warsaw.

A big building on Rymarska Street close to the Leszno Street barricade was burning and blowing smoke towards our positions. The smoke reduced visibility on Leszno Street, the Germans' main avenue of attack. The back of the telephone exchange received a direct hit from a Stuka bomb. Luckily, the front part facing Leszno Street had not been hit. We were sure that the attack would start soon. At that point there were no more than fifty men capable of fighting, including wounded. The only positive thing was that they were all very well armed, but ammunition was running out.

The anticipated attack deployed from Leszno Street. Through the thinning smoke we saw one assault gun followed by two others further away. Three Goliaths, tracked mines, slowly advanced in front. They looked like miniature turretless tanks, about 2ft high by 3ft wide and 5ft long, and carried about 220lb of explosives. The Goliaths were propelled by a small gas engine and controlled from an assault gun following behind it, connected to the Goliath by a cable that unfurled as it moved forward.

The assault guns stopped just outside the range of our PIAT and started to fire directly at the telephone exchange. Our men, including the machine gun crew, moved to a part of the building not visible from Leszno Street. We were still holding the corner building of Przejazd and Leszno streets adjoining our main barricade. The other buildings on Leszno Street, numbers 4 and 6, were no-man's-land. A small team moved along the top floors of those buildings and with a lucky drop of a grenade managed to cut the cable to one of the Goliaths, immobilising it. The other two continued forward. As Nałęcz and I watched from the telephone exchange, one exploded in front of the barricade. The building on the corner of Leszno and Przejazd streets collapsed. A few minutes later the last one exploded next to the barricade, damaging it even further.

After the two explosions, another attack deployed from Leszno Street. The Germans again used Polish civilians as a shield. This time almost all of them were women and children. Like the last time, Nałęcz again ordered us to hold our fire. The women reached the barricade and started to take it apart. Not hearing or seeing any fire, the Germans assumed we had abandoned our positions. They started to be careless and expose themselves. Some had even crossed over the barricade when Nałęcz yelled to the Poles to escape. Our sharpshooters started to pick off individual Germans while our machine guns let off several short bursts. The Germans retreated in panic. Again there were bodies lying around mostly in *feldgrau,* but sadly women and children too.

Soon after, another attack deployed. Under the suppressing fire of *Brummbärs,* German infantry attacking from Leszno Street and the ghetto managed to capture the odd side of Przejazd Street. We had now fallen onto the block of the even (east) side of Przejazd Street, between the telephone exchange on the corner of Tłomacka and Długa streets. Our back was a very vulnerable field of rubble.

From behind the motionless assault guns there emerged a tracked armoured vehicle without a turret or a gun. As it moved towards our barricade, Holski picked up a PIAT and yelled, 'Bohdan, grab the ammo and show me to the top.' We were on the second floor of the telephone exchange. I took the lead running, carrying a canister with projectiles, and Holski followed with the PIAT. We ran up the interior staircase to the fourth floor. The front wall was practically non-existent from having received so many hits. To our right, hidden from Leszno Street, was the position of our machine gun. The Mirowski brothers were manning it from behind sandbags, where they had a good view of the barricade.

Holski put the PIAT butt down and cocked it with his foot. I took one of the two remaining projectiles, armed it and passed it to him to load the weapon. We crawled forward amid the rubble until we could see the barricade below us. The armoured vehicle, moving slowly, was only a few feet away from it. Holski fired, scoring a direct hit on the front glacis of the vehicle. The vehicle stopped but did not explode or burn. Nobody tried to get out. There was a strange moment of silence and the shooting stopped for a moment. As we picked ourselves up and ran downstairs, the floor above received more direct hits. After a while the assault guns retired and the Germans abandoned further attacks. During the night they towed away the damaged armoured vehicle.

Later on I followed Nałęcz as he made the rounds of our new, reduced defensive position. We counted less than thirty men capable of fighting. We were all hungry, tired and sleep-deprived. That night a runner from Maj. Sosna brought an order saying that we would be relieved the next morning. During the night we got help to evacuate our wounded.

The armoured vehicle we had immobilised was a Borgward BIV. The same type of vehicle as the one captured from the Germans that had exploded ten days earlier in the old town, killing over 300 people. These vehicles were used as ammunition or explosive carriers and could suspend a large explosive charge in front, to be placed before a target and fired remotely. If this vehicle had not been stopped, it could have climbed over the barricade and exploded its 1,000lb charge against the telephone building. The driver was probably killed by the explosion of the PIAT projectile, keeping him from placing and activating the mine it was carrying.

In the early hours of 20 August, a company from *Czarniecki* Battalion under Cpt. 'Jacek' started to relieve our positions. We were ordered to turn over our two machine guns but our crews refused to surrender the guns. They preferred to stay with them rather than leave them. Nałęcz reluctantly agreed and let the crews stay with their guns.

Once our men had briefed their replacements, they started to move to our quarters in the Spiess building at 5 Hipoteczna Street. By the time Nałęcz turned over command to Cpt. Jacek it was late morning. We left for the sector headquarters to report to Major Sosna. On the way there I mentioned that I hadn't seen Andrzej for quite some time. Nałęcz replied that we would see him in the duty room at headquarters when we got there (Andrzej was our battalion's runner at HQ). When we arrived at HQ on Barokowa Street we went directly to the second floor, where Maj. Sosna was based. I waited outside. After a short time Nałęcz came out and we walked down to the duty room, where he asked, 'Where is Tarzan from Battalion *Nałęcz*?' There was silence and then somebody said in a loud nonchalant voice: 'They made soup out of him.' Someone else whispered loudly, 'Shut your trap, you moron, that's his brother.' The nonchalant voice, a young runner, put his head down and quietly left the room without looking at us as I silently stared at him. I stood there not feeling anything. It was like an out-of-body-experience. I was there, I heard what was said, but I did not feel anything, I did not say anything. I just stood there.

We were told that 'Tarzan' had been wounded at the Arsenal a few days before and taken to the field hospital at 7 Długa. We walked down Długa Street. The devastation from Stukas and artillery fire over the previous eight days was very noticeable. Several buildings, including the Garrison Church, had collapsed under direct bomb hits.

The Field Hospital in the old Raczynski Palace was the largest in the old town. It housed over 500 wounded in very primitive conditions. We couldn't find any information as no one at that time kept records. We walked through the large rooms filled with beds and mattresses on the floor. There were wounded everywhere, including German soldiers, many amputees and people horribly burned by phosphorous from 'mooing cow' rockets.

We could not find Andrzej. A nurse finally told us there had been a priest who kept records of those who died, but he had been killed that morning. She handed us the priest's notebook, still sticky with his blood. It was a simple school notebook, folded in half. The very last entry read: 'Runner Tarzan, Andrzej Hryniewicz, died this morning after amputation of both legs and an arm'. The nurse then told us that several bodies from the hospital had been buried that morning, but she did not know where.

Nałęcz squeezed my shoulder and said 'let's go look'. We searched all the fresh graves in the pavements and courtyards of the adjoining buildings but could not find Andrzej. After a while I said, '*Panie Kapitanie*, (Captain, sir) you had better go back to the battalion.'

We returned to the battalion, or rather its survivors (in the previous eight days we had suffered forty-nine deaths and over 100 wounded, equivalent to 75 per cent of our strength). We learned that the Germans had renewed their attacks after our battalion left the telephone exchange. Early that afternoon Cpt. Jacek's relief unit abandoned our old positions under heavy attack, withdrawing without notifying our machine gun crews. The abandoned crews fought their way out, without losing the guns. Unfortunately, Kmita, our best and most experienced gunner, was killed.

The loss of our old position gave the Germans a good jump-off point for further attacks. Later that day they captured Radziwiłł Palace, creating a very dangerous salient into the Polish line of defence.

Capt. Ognisty, from *Czarniecki* Battalion, which held the sector adjoining ours, later wrote:

> in my opinion, had … Cpt. Nałęcz been relieved and reinforced by reserves earlier, then without question the Tlomackie-Przejazd line, anchored by the telephone exchange, this key position, would have been held until the end of the fighting in the old town … those units having superior military manpower would have provided resistance unbreakable by the enemy.
>
> Lucjan Fajer, *Zołnierze Starowki* [*The Soldiers of the Old Town*], p. 285

* * * * *

After the war my mother received a letter from the Polish Red Cross dated 27 October 1945:

> … With sorrow we inform … Andrzej Hryniewicz, son of Władyslaw – died in the period of September–October 1944 in Warsaw – was buried

provisionally near 15 Długa Street. From there the exhumed [body] was, on 23 April 1945, [moved to] Grave Nr. I in Krasiński Gardens, Burial # 3483.

A few months later we visited his grave. By then there were several mass graves of exhumed bodies reburied in Krasiński Gardens. On his grave lay a plaque listing seven names, including Andrzej's, plus fifty-three 'NN'. In April 1947, after our escape from Poland, father was notified that the grave was going to be exhumed and asked to collect my brother's body. He buried Andrzej in an individual grave in Warsaw's Powąski Military Cemetery. In the meantime, the rest of the bodies from temporary graves were moved to the Wola Cemetery, where over 50,000 bodies and ashes, mostly civilians, were buried. Somehow, Andrzej's death certificate was issued with the wrong date of death, 21 August. He died on 20 August.

It is a long tradition that on the anniversary of the Uprising, at 5 p.m. on 1 August, we all meet at the graves of our comrades in the Powąski Military Cemetery. A few years ago, while standing next to my brother's grave, one of my friends told me that Andrzej was not buried there but in Wola Cemetery. I was curious, so we went there. He showed me a grave with a monument listing the same seven names, including Andrzej's, and fifty-three unknown persons. My brother is one of the few people I know who is 'buried' in two places.

* * *

At the time of Andrzej's death all I knew was that he had been severely wounded. I speculated from the nature of his wounds that he had been hit by shrapnel a few days before the 20th. I also knew that Jaga was killed on the 17th, but didn't know how or where. Over fifty years later, I made contact with Dr Zylewicz, Baśka, and she told me what happened:

On 17 August, Jaga and I were taking a wounded soldier from our positions. Jaga was leading, carrying the 'legs' [lighter] end of the stretcher. We stopped in the gateway of the Arsenal to take a rest and put down the stretcher at the end of carriageway, close to the courtyard. Jaga saw Andrzej walking with an officer in the courtyard; he spotted her and ran towards her. There was an explosion. When I came too, lying on the ground, I saw Jaga's body, her chest ripped open, the wounded on the stretcher dead with the fin of the mortar shell embedded in his forehead and Andrzej lying on the ground with two nurses from *Parasol* tending to his wounds and carrying him off on a stretcher.

This is basically the same story told by Danuta Kaczynska in her book *The Girls from Parasol*. By the time I learned of this, my father had died. To his dying day he refused to believe me when I told him that the story in *March through Hell*, and subsequent articles and publications, was not true. He wanted to believe in the glorified description of Andrzej's death. He believed that Sternik, who wrote the article claiming that he witnessed the incident, was not making it up. Father's final argument was that he had seen my brother's exhumed body and knew that his legs had been cut off by machine gun fire. After all, he had seen enough bodies during the Polish-Bolshevik War to know …

13

Old Town – Radziwiłł Palace, 20–24 August 1944

T he following day, Nałęcz received orders to retake Radziwiłł Palace. Our 'rest' ended after a day, 21 August. We hardly had any rest as the area we were in was under constant Stuka attack. There were only about forty men fit for duty. Two assault groups were formed, one under Lt. Pobóg and the other under Lt. Orwid. Nałęcz and I were with the third, smallest group of sappers under C. Off. Abczyc. We made our way to the courtyard of Koloryt, a dye factory adjoining the back garden of the palace. The night was clear as we reached a hole in the wall which, to our surprise, was not protected on either side. We moved cautiously through the gardens to the palace. It was almost midnight as the assault groups entered, taking the German troops by complete surprise. They were busy plundering the palace and had not positioned guards anywhere. In a quick firefight, a few Germans were killed and the rest escaped, taking refuge in a guardhouse at the front of the palace. While our machine guns blocked their escape route, Molotov cocktails set the building on fire. The trapped men started to shoot blindly from the windows of the burning building. The ones who tried to escape were cut down and the rest perished in the fire. We had no casualties.

We took defensive positions at the windows of the first and second floors. The men were so exhausted that many fell asleep immediately. Those designated as guards tried very hard not to follow them. We captured weapons, ammunition and grenades. Among the dead we discovered that they were Azeris from the special 'Bergman' unit we called *Kalmuks*. I followed Nałęcz as he made the rounds of our defensive positions. Later, as we entered the palace cellars, we were met by Prince Janusz Radziwiłł and his butler. There were some other people, including a few members of his family. Wooden crates, trunks and luggage were stacked everywhere. The prince was a tall, handsome man approximately 65 years old. He invited us to sit down.

His butler had a chair ready for Nałęcz, while I sat on one of the trunks. After some small talk, Nałęcz asked the prince if he had any food or wine as we needed provisions. The prince replied that the Germans had taken everything but somehow this did not ring true as the cellar was in perfect order. If the Germans had in fact been there earlier, it would have been in shambles. 'In that case, you won't mind if we look and see if the Germans missed something?' The prince did not look very happy. Nałęcz nodded, and I went upstairs to get a few men. Needless to say, they found quite a large wine cellar with some canned food, so we confiscated what we needed. (Prince Radziwiłł was a cousin of Kaiser Wilhelm; it is very possible that the German officers protected him). Nałęcz and I went upstairs to the master bedroom, which overlooked the garden, and crashed on the largest bed I had ever seen.

The next day, 22 August, was again sunny and warm. In the morning, we twice attempted to continue our attack across Bielańska Street. Both attempts were fruitless as heavy machine gun crossfire blocked the street. Later, I walked through the rooms of the looted palace. Paintings on the wall were slashed or lay torn on the floor; furniture had been turned over and broken; drawers were pulled out, spilling their contents; the floor was covered with broken pottery, glass and plaster. In the upstairs library, books were scattered over the floor. The centre of the room held a row of museum tables, their glass tops smashed and their contents emptied. On the floor, amongst the broken glass and plaster, I noticed an ivory cross about 3in tall. The figure of Christ was beautifully carved and designed to hang from a cord of pleated horsehair. Attached to it was a small paper tag with elegant script in fading sepia ink: 'This cross was worn on her deathbed by Princess Izabela Czartoryska, mother of Prince Adam Czartoryski.' I picked it up and put it in my bag.

That afternoon we received an order from Maj. Sosna to recapture the group of buildings on the opposite side of Bielańska Street, between Tłomacka and Długa streets. The final objective was the recapture of the telephone exchange and the territory lost after our battalion was relieved from the Nałęcz Redoubt. Our action was to be reinforced: another group was to attack from the Simons commercial building on our right flank. Col. Wachnowski specifically ordered Nałęcz to take command of our group while Maj. Sosna was to appoint the CO of the other attacking group. The co-ordinated attack of both groups was scheduled to commence at midnight and the signal would be a shot from our anti-tank gun in the Simons building.

The promised reinforcements arrived towards evening. They included the remainder of P-20 Company under the command of Lt. 'Edward' as well as Lt. Nowina's unit. The third group was a partisan unit from Kampinos Forest, freshly arrived through sewers from Zoliborz. They were very well armed by the Allied airdrops; some of them even wore British battle dress. They were to provide supporting fire but we weren't sure of their urban fighting experience. Again assault groups were selected with lieutenants Pobóg and Orwid in command. Our immediate target was a building opposite the palace, 9 Bielańska Street. Abczyc's sappers were to blow up the entrance gate and neutralise the machine gun nest. We took the jump-off positions in the burned-out palace guardhouse. It was just an empty shell with walls as the roof had collapsed during the fire. I stood next to Nałęcz. We were checking our watches and straining to hear the gun shot. Midnight passed. A new day began, 23 August. Time kept on passing. Finally a runner came from Maj. Sosna – the attack was postponed until 3 a.m. The signal would be a white flare fired towards the Arsenal from the Simons building.

As we waited in the burned-out building, we started receiving mortar fire; the Germans must have been alerted. Three o'clock came and went, and still no signal. Finally, we saw a green flare from the indicated direction. There was a moment's hesitation as we were expecting a white flare. Then a fainter white flare became visible from the same direction and Nałęcz ordered us to attack. When Abczyc and his sappers sprinted forward, across the street, all hell broke loose. The explosion at the targeted building was drowned out by a barrage of German mortar and concentrated machine gun fire along Bilańska Street. To our left and across the street there were machine gun nests that had not been destroyed. The attack was stopped cold. The street in front was swept by machine gun fire, mortars exploded all over and illuminating flairs were fired by the Germans. The sappers retreated with Abczyc's lifeless body. Some mortar rounds exploded inside the roofless guardhouse and wounded Nałęcz, who was standing next to me. He received shrapnel wounds to his legs and falling masonry dislocated his left shoulder. We retreated to the palace. The other group, on our right flank, never left their jump-off positions. About twenty men from the attacking units in our group were killed, including six from our unit. Many more were wounded, including the majority of our officers. Our losses were about 50 per cent: of the approximately forty men who initially captured the palace, six had been killed and sixteen wounded.

Back in the palace, we manned defensive positions on the ground floor. The partisan unit remained on the second floor. Nurses tended to the wounded. Nałęcz wrote a situation report and sent me to deliver it to Maj. Sosna. I found him, delivered the report and answered all his questions.

When I returned, Lt. Orwid was in command. The wounded Nałęcz and Poboóg had been evacuated to get medical attention. Of the approximately twenty men left in our unit, some were also wounded.

While I was away, a grave had been dug in the palace garden for Abczyc's body. Most of the other dead were left where they fell: it was impossible to retrieve them. The remaining sappers invited me to be in the funeral honour guard. To save ammunition, only one volley was fired from three rifles and my pistol. A cross was made from packing crate boards, upon which his name and the date were scribbled in pencil. One of the sappers gave me the notebook Abczyc always carried on him. I used to watch him make sketches, in ink and pencil, of our soldiers and engagements; he was a very good illustrator. There were also descriptions of some of the actions, with situation sketches. The notebook was about 4 x 6in with a black oilcloth cover, about ¾in thick. There was a jagged hole in the middle made by the shrapnel fragment that killed him. It travelled through the book and his chest.

It was already dusk when Lt. Orwid, who had presided over the funeral service, and I returned to the palace. 'Go and get some rest,' he told me. I replied that I would be under the stairs in the entrance hall. I took off my bag and laid it on the floor, unbuckled my helmet, placed a brick under it and used it as a pillow. I curled up under the lowest part of the stairs and immediately fell asleep.

I dreamt I was flying in a plane. The noise of the engine got louder and louder. An explosion woke me up. I moved a few feet to the open door of the living room under the stair landing. Through the open doors, which were on the opposite side of the living room, I saw a smoking bomb crater in the middle of the garden. I got back under the stairs and lay down again. A few minutes later came the screeching noise of another diving Stuka, followed by the increasingly intense whistle of a falling bomb and the roar of an engine pulling out of a dive, then a thud and a slight shake of the building. A second or two passed and a thought crossed my mind: it's a dud ... then I blacked out. As I slowly came to, my ears were ringing and I was choking on dust. I could hear somebody faintly yelling: 'Bohdan! Bohdan!' Through the grey dust I saw the dim glow of torchlight. I yelled: 'Here! here!' Lt. Orwid's hand appeared through the dust, I grabbed it and he pulled me up. 'Are you okay?' he asked. I stood up, shaking off the pieces of plaster and dust. 'I am fine, sir!'

I tried to find my bag, which held all my keepsakes: my uncle's overseas cap, the set of city-of-Warsaw table silver, a bottle of 150-year-old wine from the cellars of the town hall, the ivory cross from the palace and Abczyc's notebook. I had laid it down on the floor close to me; it was now buried under rubble. The item I missed most was the notebook. It would have been a very valuable pictorial record of our soldiers and the actions of our battalion.

I gave up searching and went to join Lt. Orwid, who was calling me. I stayed with him as he surveyed the damage and established new defensive positions. The left wing of the palace had received a direct hit and was demolished. There were heavy losses in the partisans' unit on the second floor. The few men remaining from *Nałęcz* Battalion took positions around the windows of the ground floor of the main palace building. German infantry renewed their attacks from Bielańska Street but short bursts from our machine gun kept them at bay. The wounded were evacuated across the alleyway, through the hole in the wall of a building on Długa Street. The bursts from our machine gun were getting shorter and finally stopped. The only defensive fire was now from rifles.

Lt. Orwid scribbled a few words on a page of his notebook and told me to deliver it to Maj. Sosna. I was to report that we had received a direct hit from the bomb, had many casualties, were under attack and running out of ammunition. I was to stress that unless we received reinforcements immediately we would be forced to abandon the palace. I sprinted across the alleyway, which was already receiving German fire, to the hole on the other side. I found the major, already on his way to our position, in the courtyard of a building adjoining 29 Długa Street. He received my report and told me to tell Lt. Orwid he must hold as long as he could. I jumped back through the alleyway, which was receiving more and more fire, and reported to Lt. Orwid.

Our fire was slackening as we were running out of ammunition. The Germans were getting closer and were now using grenades. I followed Lt. Orwid to the open side door of the palace, opposite the hole. He told me to go to Sosna again and report that unless we received help in the next fifteen minutes we would have to abandon the palace. He looked at me: 'Get going!' I ran across the alleyway, which was now under heavy machine gun fire, and again found Sosna on the other side. He was organising the defence of what had become known as 'the Barricade of the Holy Mother' (because a picture of the Madonna remained hanging, intact, on the wall above a hole of the destroyed building). Shortly afterwards, our men started to withdraw across the alleyway. During the retreat, Lt. Orwid, one of the last across the alleyway, was wounded and Lt. Zew killed. We had three killed, including Nurse 'Jasia', and about ten wounded including, nurses 'Alicja' and 'Halina'.

The Germans reoccupied the palace, or what was left of it. We paid a high price: the battalion lost its fighting ability and was sent to rest in the Spiess building, where our wounded and sick were sheltered. The few remaining soldiers capable of fighting joined the defence of 'the Barricade of the Holy Mother'. Only twelve days before, a 200-man battalion had attacked the telephone exchange, later called the Nałęcz Redoubt. Only fifteen men capable of action remained.

From upper left clockwise: Zygmunt Rymszewicz, KIA 1 August 1944; 'Kot' Wiktor Rymszewicz, KIA 4 September 1944; 'Bohdan' Bohdan Hryniewicz; 'Tarzan' Andrzej Hryniewicz, DW 21 August 1944. Warsaw, June 1943. (Author's archive)

Mother and Andrzej, 1932. (Author's archive)

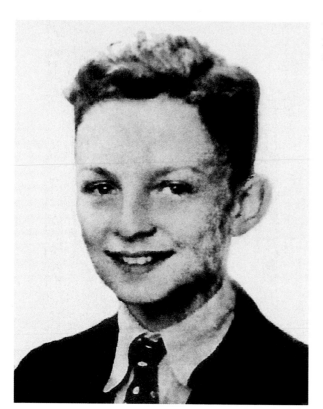

'Tarzan' Andrzej Hryniewicz, DW
21 August 1944. Warsaw, June 1943.
(Author's archive)

Bohdan Hryniewicz, Szczecin, February
1946. (Author's archive)

Number 35 Nowy Swiat, towards the intersection with Jerusalem Avenue. In the background, on the left, are the top floors of the BGK building that controlled the intersection. This is the first week of the Uprising. Note the Polish flag flying from the lamp post. (Warsaw Rising Museum, Braun)

Nowy Swiat 35 with a view to the west. The building with two shell holes is number 37, where the author lived with his family. (Warsaw Rising Museum, Braun)

A Jagdpanzer 38 *Hetzer* destroyed during the fighting for the post office on 3 August 1944. Used to strengthen the barricade on Szpitalna Street. (Warsaw Rising Museum, Braun)

German soldiers preparing a Goliath self-propelled mine on the outskirts of Warsaw, August 1944. (German State Archives)

A German police car captured during the first days of the Uprising on Swietokrzyska Street. Seated on the left fender is 'Kot', Wiktor Rymszewicz. (Author's archive)

Sanitary patrol in the old town. During the Uprising practically all medics were women. Second week of August 1944. (Warsaw Rising Museum, Chojnacki)

Old town, Raczyński Palace at 7 Długa, used as a field hospital. Second week of August 1944. (Warsaw Rising Museum, Chojnacki)

A group of soldiers with weapons received from Allied airdrops. The last man on the right is holding a PIAT antitank weapon. 23 August 1944. (Warsaw Rising Museum, Joachimczyk)

The *Karl-Gerät* siege mortar was the largest German mortar, firing 24in shells weighing 2 tons. It was transported to Warsaw in the middle of August 1944. (Wałkowski Z.)

A 'dud' from a 'flying coffer', a 2-ton 24in shell, landed in a restaurant in the centre of town. It was disarmed and the explosive material was used to make grenades. (Warsaw Rising Museum, Lokajski)

Prudential building hit by 2 ton shell from 24in *Karl-Gerät* siege mortar, 28 August 1944. (Warsaw Rising Museum, Braun)

Rocket launchers on the outskirts of Warsaw being prepared to fire. (German State Archives)

'Mooing cow' incendiary rockets in flight towards Polish positions in Warsaw. (German State Archives)

German infantry deploying towards the town hall on Theatre Square, with the opera house in the background, end of August 1944. (German State Archives)

A German gun next to the opera house, opposite the town hall, end of August 1944. (Wałkowski Z.)

The German crew of a Sturmpanzer IV *Brummbär* (Grizzly Bear) on the streets of Warsaw. The heaviest assault gun, with a 6in short-barrelled howitzer, it was specifically designed to support infantry in urban fighting. (Warsaw Rising Museum)

A view towards Theatre Square. This picture was taken after the fall of the old town in the first days of September 1944. It shows German superiority in heavy armament. (Wałkowski Z.)

Soldiers from *Radosław* Group in the centre following arrival from the old town via the sewers on 1 September 1944. (Warsaw Rising Museum, Braun)

Soldiers from *Parasol* Battalion. *Radosław* Group in the centre, following their arrival from the old town. Left to right: medic 'NN', runner 'Kama' Maria Stypułkowska-Chojnacka, C.Off. 'Krzych' Krzysztof Palester. (Warsaw Rising Museum, Jochimczyk)

Caring for the wounded. (Warsaw Rising Museum, Joachimczyk)

Columns of Polish troops marching, with unloaded weapons, past the demarcation line to lay down their arms, 5 October 1944. (Warsaw Rising Museum, Chojnacki)

Female members of the AK, mostly medics and runners, follow columns of soldiers into captivity, 5 October 1944. (German State Archives)

Eisenhower amidst Warsaw ruins, old town market square, 21 September 1945. (CAF Warsaw)

The author in Germany, March 1947. (Author's archive)

REJON WALK
I-GO BATALIONU
SZTURMOWEGO
„NAŁĘCZ" WKSB-AK
POWSTANIE WARSZAWSKIE 1944

LEGENDA:

✳ MIEJSCA WALK POD DOWÓDZTWEM kpt. STEFANA KANIEWSKIEGO ps „NAŁĘCZ"

🚂 ŻYWE BARYKADY – LUDNOŚĆ PĘDZONA PRZED NIEMIECKIMI CZOŁGAMI

1 ARSENAŁ 2 GMACH PASTY 3 RATUSZ
4 PAŁAC RADZIWIŁŁÓW 5 BANK POLSKI
6 HOTEL POLSKI 7 PAŁAC MNISZKÓW
8 KLASZTOR KANONICZEK

Nałęcz Battalion plaque at the town hall. (Author's archive)

14

Evacuation to the Centre,
24–29 August 1944

2 4 August. I was with what remained of our battalion in the Spiess building behind the town hall. It was a large five-storey building belonging to a pharmaceutical company on the corner of Hipoteczna and Danielowiczowska streets. The day before, a German Stuka had been shot down during a dive and crashed into the roof of the building. The explosion broke a large glass demi-john of sulphuric acid, which splattered and burned some of our wounded and nurses. The worst affected, burnt on their faces and hands, were Gryf, the oldest of three Mirowski brothers, and nurse 'Baśka II' (thereafter known as 'Burned Baśka' to differentiate her from 'Baśka I'). I reported to Nałęcz, who was limping and had his left hand in a sling. His shrapnel wounds had been patched up and the dislocated shoulder reset. He told me to go rest and catch up on my sleep.

The next day, 25 August, Nałęcz formed two small assault groups from the men still capable of fighting, commanded by cadet officers since the few remaining officers had been wounded. The men were all very well armed as the weapons of injured soldiers had to be relinquished to other units. Some weapons were reluctantly surrendered but many others were hidden away. One assault group was sent to join in the attack that recaptured part of the town hall. The other reinforced the defence of the 'Holy Mother' barricade.

I requested and received permission from Nałęcz to go and look for Andrzej's grave. I walked, for hours, all around the hospital, checking pavements and courtyards in vain. Most of the graves were there; it was relatively easy to dig there since the paving stones had been removed from the pavements to construct barricades. The cobblestones of the courtyards were also easy to remove. While walking the streets of the old town I saw the destruction caused over the previous twenty days by constant air bombing, artillery and rocket fire. Almost all the buildings had been hit. Some were completely destroyed, nothing more than piles of rubble, others were severely damaged, full of holes, while still others were just burned-out walls with gaping holes in place of windows and doors. Masonry rubble spilled onto the streets and bomb craters were everywhere. On Miodowa Street I saw two burned-out piles of metal, Liberator bombers shot down while making airdrops over Krasiński Square. The streets were empty. From time to time a runner would go by, nurses carrying a stretcher with an wounded, a group of civilians with their meagre belongings looking for shelter.

The next couple of days were anticlimactic. As Nałęcz was recuperating from his wounds he was no longer directly commanding any unit. The two detached assault groups were integrated into other units. I followed him to meetings at the headquarters of Maj. Sosna, to our detached units and to the hospital to see some of our more severely wounded. Most of our lightly wounded were in the basement of the Spiess building.

In the late afternoon of the 28th a female runner arrived with two men. They all smelled rather bad. The men, called *kanalarz*, were employees of the municipal sewage department familiar with the extensive sewage system under Warsaw. The runner brought Nałęcz an order from KB HQ, to return to the centre of town immediately with the battalion. After a brief rest, the woman left with one of the men, leaving the other behind.

It was dark when I led Nałęcz to Col. Wachnowski's headquarters in the vestry of St Jacek church on Freta Street. After a short wait, the colonel's adjutant let us in. Nałęcz saluted as I stood at attention behind him. The colonel came forward, shook hands with Nałęcz, looked at me and asked: 'Are you the runner who came from the telephone exchange when your unit was cut off?' (He had also interrogated me on the 15th, in Maj. Sosna's headquarters when I arrived from our cut-off positions.) Standing at attention, I clicked my heels: 'Yes, sir! 'What is your name?' 'Runner Bohdan, sir!' 'Well done, Bohdan'. He nodded and sat behind his desk, indicating to Nałęcz to sit down in a chair opposite him. I sat down on the floor with my back against the wall. I heard the whole subsequent conversation.

Nałęcz stated that he had received a direct order from KB HQ to evacuate the battalion immediately to the centre of town, through the sewers. However, he said, he was under the tactical command of the colonel and would abide by his orders. The colonel replied that in recognition of the valour with which the battalion had fought, and the very heavy casualties it had suffered, he would allow the evacuation of the wounded only. Men capable of fighting would have to stay. Nałęcz acknowledged the order and asked for the pass to send the runner to KB headquarters. The colonel called in his adjutant and told him to prepare the pass to enter the sewers that night. He also told Nałęcz that the order allowing the evacuation of the wounded would be ready in the morning. We got up and saluted and left his office. Several minutes later, his adjutant gave us the pass. We returned to our quarters, where Nałęcz dictated his report. He called in C. Off. 'Czajka', who had almost recovered from his wounds, gave each of us one copy to deliver to HQ on Boduena Street.

Around midnight I led Nałęcz, Czajka and a sewer worker down to Krasiński Square, where the entrance to the sewer was. On the way over, I asked Nałęcz what I should tell my mother about Andrzej. After a while, Nałęcz said: 'Why don't you tell her that Andrzej was wounded and evacuated through the sewers to Zoliborz?' (This was a suburb of Warsaw on the north side of the old town.) After a pause, I quietly said: 'Yes, I will do that.' I took my diary, where I had made notes since the beginning of the Uprising, including the details of Andrzej's death. I tore out page after page, letting them drop as we walked through the ruined streets towards the sewer entrance.

I looked at my watch: it was after midnight, already 29 August. We reached the entrance to the sewer on the corner of Krasiński Square and Długa Street. The open manhole was guarded by military police. Cpt. Barry, CO of the military police was there himself. There was bad blood between him and Nałęcz after part of Barry's unit had decided to join us in the town hall. Nałęcz showed him the pass from Col. Wachnowski. Barry looked at it, then at us, and said: 'They are not going.' Nałęcz pulled out his 9mm Colt and said, 'They *are* going,' and to us, 'Start going down'. First the sewer worker, then me and then Czajka started to climb down the iron rungs of the manhole to a small, dimly lit chamber. The sewer worker gave us his instructions: he would be the only one to use the torch, we were not to turn ours on; when he stopped and turned off his torch I was to grab his belt and Czajka mine; we were to move when he moved and stop when he stopped; there would be no talking, absolute silence; altogether, we would cover over a mile, it should take about two hours; the first part would be easy, the sewer was large and we would almost be able to walk normally; the last part would be the most difficult, we would have to crawl using sticks. He gave us each a 20in length of broomstick.

From the little chamber we entered the sewer and proceeded south under Miodowa Street. As he said, this part was easy. This part of the sewer was the main collector, beautifully built of bricks, almost 8ft high by over 5ft wide. It had small walkways on both sides and a channel in the middle. A small amount of relatively clean sewage flowed through it. I have no recollection of any particular smell. We walked in single file at a relatively fast pace, easily following the light of the sewer worker's torch. After about fifteen minutes we stopped. We were near the end of Miodowa Street and soon would enter a different sewer under Krakowskie Przedmieście Street. The next part would be under German held territory so we would have to be very careful as there would be open manholes. He told us that if any Germans heard anything they would drop in grenades.

After a short time, we came to a junction and entered a sewer which led slightly to the right. This sewer was only about 5ft high and proportionately narrower. There were no separate walkways, only a concave bottom. We waded in 3 to 6in of sewage. I was able to walk straight with my helmet on. The other two had to bend forward. Czajka took his helmet off. This section, about two-thirds of a mile, took much longer. Every so often the torch was turned off; we stopped, grabbed each other's belts and then proceeded very carefully until we passed under an open manhole. Looking up, we could glimpse a clear sky full of stars. In a few places we heard German voices. Once, as a tank passed over us, the sewer worker whispered that we were next to the university. After about an hour and a half we stopped under a manhole. We were now within Polish lines, under Nowy Swiat Street at the intersection with Warecka Street. We couldn't exit here because this street was covered by machine gun fire from German positions nearby. From this manhole we crawled through the smallest sewer. With his torch the sewer worker showed us an egg-shaped pipe in the wall of the manhole. The pipe was about 3ft high and 2ft wide, the bottom was covered in a rather nasty looking and smelling slime (the sewers were combined, both domestic and storm). He took his stick and demonstrated how we would have to crawl: *grab the middle of the stick with two hands, push it forward as far as possible through the widest part of the pipe; jam it down against the walls of the pipe and pull yourself forward. Repeat the same motion until you reach the first manhole.* I would go first, he said, followed by Czajka, and he would go last. He would shine his torch over our heads from time to time; but most of the time we would be in darkness.

I started to crawl and found it to be quite easy. It was: one, stick forward; two, jam it down; three, pull myself forward. I heard Czajka behind me grunting from time to time, his wounds had not healed yet. Every so often, the sewer worker shone his light behind me; otherwise it was pitch dark. The unpleasant part was having my face so close to the smelly slime I was pulling myself through. I kept repeating the movements: one, two, three and again one, two, three ... It didn't take long before I saw a dim light ahead.

I reached the manhole and started climbing up the metal rungs. I yelled 'Starówka!' (old town).

A torch shone down and as I reached the top I grabbed an extended hand, which pulled me up. Czajka was next and the sewer worker last. There were questions, congratulations, slapping of backs. The sewer worker said that we had done very well. We were given some buckets of water and tried to clean ourselves up. We came out only three blocks away from where I lived. After thanking the sewer worker and saying goodbye, we walked to KB headquarters on Boduena Street, where we reported to the duty officer. Col. Doliwa, commanding officer of the KB, was woken and we gave him Nałęcz's report. Czajka was still answering questions when I was told to go and get some rest. I found a room on the ground floor with a few men sleeping on couches and the floor. I found a place near the wall, took my helmet off, and immediately fell asleep.

On the morning of the 29th I woke up late and reached for my helmet. It was gone and the room was empty. Over the previous few months my vocabulary had greatly expanded and I let out a stream of profanities that would make an old master sergeant proud. I found Czajka and we raised hell with the duty officer to no avail. Nobody knew anything; nobody saw anything. We were given some food and told to go to Chmielna Street, where a public bath was open for people coming through the sewers.

As we walked the short distance to the bathhouse we could not believe our eyes. In contrast to the old town, there was relatively little damage. This was particularly true on the smaller side streets. The principal streets suffered most damage in the first days of the Uprising. There were bombed and burned-out buildings, rubble and glass on the streets, overturned and burned-out cars and trams; but not the same degree of devastation as in the old town. There were barricades at most intersections. There was much more foot traffic. People were walking, not running. They congregated in building entrances and courtyards. Officers in clean uniforms and polished boots walked alongside pretty girls, medics and runners. The most striking thing was the relative quiet. There wasn't the constant whine of diving planes, whistle of falling bombs, rattle of machine guns, or noise of 'mooing cows', artillery and mortar fire. There was only the distant, subdued noise of explosions coming from the direction of the old town, under plumes of rising smoke.

Our *panterki*, the SS camouflage uniforms only worn by troops from the old town, made us stand out. We were constantly being stopped and asked about the situation in the old town. The bathhouse was only a couple of blocks away and the same distance from where I lived. It was called Orana and had been taken over by the German Army and used as a bath and brothel for soldiers during the occupation. After twenty-five days, I finally took all my clothes off and stepped into a shower. I stood under the warm water and luxuriated. I soaped and scrubbed myself until I was told to get out to save the warm water. When we arrived, a woman who noticed our *panterki* had offered to clean them as well as possible. She now returned with our clean uniforms, as well as a new shirt for me, too large but the smallest she had. We dressed and returned to headquarters. The duty officer told us that Col. Doliwa wanted to see us upon our return. When we reported to him, he asked us more about the battalion and its actions in the old town. He told us that he expected our wounded to start arriving that night. He asked me where I lived and when I answered that it was only two blocks away he told me to go home and check back daily. I saluted, shook hands with Czajka and walked out.

I had no more excuses not to go home. I wanted to see my mother very badly, but I also dreaded it. I had never lied to her before and I would now have to do so for the first time. I walked back the same way that, twenty-five days earlier, Andrzej and I had brought our mother to meet Nałęcz to give her permission to join the Uprising. As I entered our staircase and started up the stairs, I heard Zabcia frantically barking at the door. She knew I was coming up. When I reached the landing, I heard my mother's steps come to the door. She opened the door as I reached it. We both stood there for a moment as the dog frantically jumped on me. We embraced and then the question I dreaded but knew was coming, 'Where is Andrzej?'

Without hesitation, I gave an answer I had been rehearsing: 'He was wounded and evacuated through the sewers to Zoliborz.' The other anticipated questions came: 'How bad are his wounds, how did it happen, where and when?' And another rehearsed answer: 'I don't have much detail because I was with Capt. Nałęcz and we were cut off for a few days when it happened; Andrzej was our battalion runner at headquarters; when we were relieved, all we found out is what I've told you.' I tried to change the subject by asking about Wiktor, Zygmunt, my cousin Danuta and her husband.

My mother looked at me for a long time. I sensed that she wanted desperately to believe me, but I also knew that I had not really convinced her. She told me that Wiktor was alright, though he had been wounded and lost an ear. His unit was billeted nearby in the PKO building (the post office savings bank). I didn't say anything, but I thought of the prophecy he had heard from a fortune teller before he left Wilno. When Wiktor asked him, 'When will the war end?' the man replied: 'Before the war ends you will first be wounded and then killed.'

That night I slept in a clean bed in my own pyjamas. Zabcia jumped up and snuggled next to me, and my mother didn't make her get down. I slept non-stop until noon the next day.

15

Centre North, 29 August– 4 September 1944

I woke up to Zabcia licking my face. As soon as I opened my eyes she started jumping up and down. I got dressed in my own underwear; my mother had my *panterka* uniform ready, washed and pressed. I told her that I had to report to headquarters and would then try to find Wiktor. She told me that his code name was 'Kot' (cat). When I arrived at headquarters I learned that our wounded with the girl medics had arrived safely early that morning. Their journey was much longer and more difficult than ours. Carrying and supporting the wounded was hard and exhausting work. The hardest part was dragging the wounded through the small sewer pipe. They were now in the KB field hospital in the basement of 4 Boduena Street, in the same building as our headquarters. I saw both Gryf and Baśka II, badly burned by acid, as well as many others. I visited Sten. He and I had 'defended' our positions for a short time, armed with one grenade and a 7mm pistol. Sten was one of the few survivors pulled out of the blown up building on 3 Przejazd Street. He had suffered serious leg wounds. Before the Uprising was over he would be wounded twice more. I also ran into Baśka, the chief medic, who asked me if I'd seen my mother and what had I told her about Andrzej. Hearing my reply she agreed that for now it was for the best.

After a few hours, I left to find Wiktor. I wanted to see him alone, not in my mother's presence. The PKO building was only four blocks away. On my way there I realised the Germans had started to shell and bomb the centre of town, concentrating on the Powiśle district to the east. I saw Stukas diving and explosions in that direction. I could not get into the PKO building; General Monter, the Uprising's commanding officer, had his headquarters there and I did not have the necessary access pass. Wiktor was sent for. He appeared a few minutes later, wearing the same officer's boots and breeches and the same black beret that he was wearing over a month before, only now the beret had a Polish Army eagle on it. He had a bandage under his beret covering the left side of his head, where he had lost an ear. Since he outranked me I saluted him and tried to offer him my hand but he grabbed me and hugged me. He escorted me inside; we sat down and started to talk. His first question was about Andrzej. I repeated my story but I knew I had not convinced him. After a long uncomfortable silence, he started to ask me about my experiences. My mother had told him the name of our battalion, so he knew we were in the old town. I briefly told him my story. Noticing the ribbon on my uniform he congratulated me on my Cross of Valour. My *panterka* uniform was worn only by soldiers from the old town, which made me stand out; several officers from headquarters stopped to congratulate me and asked about the fighting in the old town. Wiktor introduced me to his CO, Lt. 'Kosa'. As soon as we were alone I asked him about Zygmunt, but he had no news and hadn't found out what unit he was in. All Wiktor knew was that following his escape that spring, Zygmunt had a new ID and had been hiding outside of Warsaw. Wiktor suspected that Zygmunt had been on his way to Warsaw just before the Uprising. (We found out many years later that Zygmunt had been killed on the first day of the Uprising; his body was never found.)

Wiktor told me that he was in Kedyw B, an elite unit for special action under direct orders of the high command. The unit also acted as security for headquarters. As we parted so he could return to his duties, Wiktor told me that he would try to come home the following day. Before he left he suggested that I go to the Palladium cinema, where newsreels from the Uprising were being shown. I stopped there on the way back; it was only four blocks away. There was a line in front waiting for the next showing. I went to the end of the line but was ushered to the front because of my uniform. The newsreel, titled 'Warsaw Fighting', had been taken by war correspondents and cameramen from the Polish Home Army. It looked very professional, with narration and background music, just like the German newsreels showing their 'glorious fighting' on the eastern front. The newsreel started by showing German POWs with big swastikas painted on the back of their uniforms, put to work clearing rubble from bombed-out buildings. There was a clip of a German POW disarming a dud projectile from a 24in *Karl-Gerat* siege mortar, removing the explosives. This was followed by scenes of manufacturing grenades using salvaged TNT. There was also a clip of a captured assault gun being prepared and painted with a big Polish white eagle. I recognised it as a *Hetzer*, the first armoured vehicle destroyed by us in front of the town hall. The most dramatic pictures were of the fighting for police headquarters. The whole show was about half an hour long and it was very enthusiastically received by a full-house audience. On the way back I stopped by headquarters and visited our wounded and nurses. That night I luxuriated once again in my own bed.

Next morning, the last day of August, Wiktor came home. I asked him about his unit and their combat. He said that on the first day of the Uprising his unit had been moving from their assembly point to the designated jump-off spot in Hotel Victoria on Jasna Street. They got into their first firefight half an hour before 5 p.m., the designated hour for the start of the Uprising. They came across two German cars, which they captured, killing the crews and collecting many weapons and ammunition. Later on that day, they encountered an armoured car, which escaped though they damaged it. Unfortunately, they also lost a few men. During the next two days they cleared Germans out of buildings in their area of operation, from the PKO building to the Saxon Gardens. On the third day, they engaged in clearing Germans from the Esplanade coffee house on the corner of Marszałkowska and Sienkiewicz streets. Wiktor's unit led the attack from Sienkiewicz and another unit from Marszałkowska. It was a long fight and moved from the ground floor to the cellars, where the remaining Germans gave themselves up. They took sixteen POWs and captured weapons including a machine gun. I told him, to his surprise, that the other attacking unit had been *Nałęcz* Battalion (this happened a day before Andrzej and I had joined). The next day (4 August), they went to Widok Street to clear out some reported Ukrainian forces. While in the building there was an air attack and a Stuka bomb destroyed it, killing one and wounding four, including Wiktor. He considered himself lucky the bomb fragment only took off his ear rather than splitting his skull. His unit's primary duty was to provide security and defence of the high command of the Uprising. They were also used as a 'fire brigade', to liquidate any reported pockets of Germans. During the last major action his unit took part in the successful attack on and capture of police headquarters and the Church of the Holy Cross on Krakowskie Przedmieście Street. The day before, I had watched the newsreel of this very action at the cinema.

Wiktor had to go back. We returned together and said our goodbyes in front of the PKO building. He entered the building, stopped, turned around and waved. I waved back at him and saluted. Wiktor returned the salute, smiled, turned and walked in. This was the last time I saw him.

When I awoke on 1 September 1944, I realised that it was the fifth anniversary of the German invasion that had started the War. I vividly remembered being in our living room in Wilno when my mother said simply, 'The war has started, the Germans attacked this morning.'

When I arrived at headquarters later that morning, I found most of the survivors of our battalion. They had arrived in the early hours. I was surprised to find new faces among them. After Czajka and I left the battalion late on the evening of the 28th, the wounded were evacuated the following day. On the 30th there was an attempt to break through the German lines and reach the centre of town. The right wing of this attack included the remnants of our battalion. The attack failed. The ambulatory wounded and unarmed soldiers of our battalion were ordered to evacuate on the afternoon of the 31st. As the news spread, several soldiers from different units volunteered to join us and some were accepted. Some of our soldiers tried to smuggle out their weapons, but were found out by our military police. Rather than give up their weapons, they stayed to continue fighting. The last of them entered the sewers the next morning, just before the entrance was covered by rubble from a newly bombed building. About eighty men and women had escaped from the old town.

I ran into Cpt. Nałęcz as he came out of a meeting with Col. Doliwa, and he asked about my mother. I said I thought she believed my story about Andrzej but I couldn't be sure.

Throughout that day everyone cleaned up, was fed and billeted in the adjoining buildings. The ambulatory wounded were attended to and some were hospitalised. Cpt. Nałęcz and the Battalion HQ staff took over an apartment on the top floor of 5 Boduena Street, in a five-storey apartment building opposite headquarters. During the officers' conference Nałęcz announced there would be a three- to four-day rest before the battalion returned to the front line, but we would not be assigned a sector of our own. The units currently defending the front line were already well acquainted with the terrain and their command structure; communications and supporting services were well established and functioning. The commander-in-chief, Gen. 'Bór', decided that the units from the old town would, after a short rest, gradually be placed in the line, assigned to different sectors to better take advantage of their battle experience. The men who had families nearby were allowed to visit them.

On the next day, 2 September, the old town fell. During the thirty-two days of fighting, about 7,000 soldiers lost their lives (German losses were around 4,000). Approximately 5,000 soldiers, including 3,000 wounded, were evacuated through the sewers, along with 6,000 civilians. There were nearly 35,000 people left in the old town when the Germans entered. There were 7,500 severely wounded, including 2,500 soldiers. The SS, with collaborating Russian, Azeri and Cossack units, went on a murderous rampage. Virtually all wounded fighters and doctors were brutally murdered, shot, blown up by grenades or burned alive. Nurses who stayed behind were raped and then murdered. About 8,000 to 10,000 civilians were also murdered.

In Poland we celebrated name days rather than birthdays. Each day of the liturgical calendar commemorates a particular saint and one of our officers celebrated his name day on 3 September. By early afternoon there was a rather lively party going on in Nałęcz's temporary quarters. At one time it had been a large, beautifully furnished apartment belonging to the well-known writer, Juljusz Kaden-Bandrowski. Now it was a shambles with windows blown out and covered in plaster and dust. Besides our officers and a few nurses also present was a special guest: the writer's son. He was a 2nd Lt. in the *Radosław* Group and like us had just arrived from the old town. He told us that his father had died when he was in the old town at the beginning of the Uprising. His twin brother had been in the Underground and was killed in action the year before. I learned later that he too was killed, two weeks later.

On this day, following the fall of the old town, the Germans switched their attention to our current position, the centre-north. The morning began with artillery shelling while Stukas dropped bombs nearby. No buildings were hit near our position on Boduena Street, but one block away, and visible from our windows, two buildings had been bombed. During this entire time, Nałęcz's party never stopped and a copious amount of alcohol was consumed. Midway through the party Nałęcz decided to have a shooting competition with side arms. The targets selected included small light bulbs on candelabras and wall sconces, eyes on portraits hanging on the walls and other such objects. Nałęcz gave me his 9mm Colt to take a turn. It turned out I was the best shot, probably because I was the only one sober. I had a great time.

Looking back, as I write this from the perspective many years later, that scenario must have looked like something from a great Russian novel: a room that at one time was grand but now lay in ruin; the noise of artillery shells exploding nearby; the screeching of a diving plane followed by the whistle of a falling bomb, a moment of silence and then a building one block away going up with debris flying high and a shockwave billowing the drapes on the blown-out windows; in the middle of all this a small group of men in uniform and young women on chairs around a large table, drinking vodka and shooting pistols at the candelabras and portraits …

16

Centre South,
4–17 September 1944

On the morning of 4 September, I reported to Nałęcz and was told that our battalion would be moving across Jerusalem Avenue to the centre-south district. Our new quarters would be on Krucza Street. Jerusalem Avenue was the main east–west artery through Warsaw. The Poniatowski Bridge connected Warsaw, on the left (west) bank of the Vistula, to the Praga district on the right bank. The Russian armies had already reached Praga when the Uprising broke out, but then stopped their advance and discontinued their aerial flights over Warsaw. It became clear that the Russians had given the Germans a free hand to finish us off. From the start of the Uprising the Germans had attempted to keep this thoroughfare open but with little success. They held the Poniatowski Bridge and the area near the roadway for most of its length. Our forces occupied only a small portion on both sides of the avenue between Nowy Swiat and Marszałkowska streets, a distance of about 440yd, while the Germans controlled strongpoints on both sides of those intersections, preventing us from crossing from one side to the other. That was the reason why Andrzej and I could not reach our original assembly point. During the second week of the Uprising a communication trench had been constructed, allowing for limited foot traffic. The trench was less than 3ft deep as there was a railway tunnel below Jerusalem Avenue. The barricades constructed on both sides of the trench allowed one to cross bent over. The German machine guns at their strongpoints on both corners with Nowy Swiat Street were only 270yd away and fired at any sign of movement. Access to the trench was strictly controlled by our military police and required a special pass.

Later that day our battalion crossed Jerusalem Avenue to new quarters in 42 Krucza Street and adjoining buildings. From that date on there was no more electricity; we assumed that the power station was either destroyed or captured by the Germans. The next day was spent working on administrative matters concerning the planned reorganisation. Our battalion was to be divided into two companies: Company number 1, under Lt. Pobóg, was scheduled to reinforce *Piorun-Zareba* Battalion; Company number 2, under Lt. Holski, the *Sokól* Battalion. Each company was to have about eighty men including officers. Both were to take their walking wounded. One half of the second company would include all soldiers from P-20 Company previously incorporated into our battalion.

Some time during the two days Nałęcz, who was an accomplished graphic artist in civilian life, found time to design our battalion shoulder patch. To my knowledge, we were one of the first, if not the first unit with shoulder patches. One of the Greek Jews who had come with us through the sewers from old town was a draftsman and eagerly worked making the patches. The material for the shields was cut from red pillowcases; the drawing and writing was done in black and white India ink. I managed to keep my patch through all the years and just recently donated it to the Warsaw Uprising Museum.

During these two days, German forces concentrated their massive firepower on the Powiśle district, an area east of Nowy Swiat Street extending to the River Vistula. Massive artillery barrages were followed by Stuka bombing. I observed, with growing concern, the explosions and fires to the east of our apartment building. In the afternoon I asked Nałęcz for permission to go and see my mother. He gave me a Priority Pass to cross Jerusalem Avenue, as a runner, without limitation. Late that afternoon, I arrived at the rear entrance to our building. As I ran up the stairs Zabcia was barking and whining behind the door to our apartment. When I opened the door, to my surprise, I did not find my mother in the entry hall. I stopped to listen: all was quiet inside. I picked up my dog and as she licked my face I entered the living room. In the falling dusk I saw my mother sitting motionless in an armchair. As I approached her, she lifted her head slightly without getting up, looked at me and said in a low, flat voice devoid of any emotion: *Wiktor nie żyje*, 'Wiktor is dead.'

I stopped a few feet away from her. A thought cross my mind: now both prophecies have been fulfilled and I knew that my mother had lost all hope that Andrzej was still alive. I sat down on a chair close to her with Zabcia on my lap. She turned her head towards me and told me that a man she knew, a friend of Wiktor who was in the same unit and lived nearby, had come to see her yesterday. He told her that on the morning of the 4th their unit returned from an all-night action and was going to stand down. He told Wiktor that he should go home for a few hours. Wiktor replied that he was very tired and needed to sleep for a few hours before going home. They parted company and Wiktor went down to their quarters in the bottom basement of the PKO building. Shortly after Wiktor's friend left the building an unlucky bomb dropped by a diving Stuka fell directly into an elevator shaft and exploded at the bottom level. Wiktor's body, together with others, including wounded from the field hospital sharing space in that basement, was never found.

I told my mother that I would be back the next morning to take her to our headquarters. We got up and she led me to the front door, held me close for a long time, turned around and walked to her room without looking back. I patted Zabcia, opened the door and walked out of our apartment for the last time.

* * * * *

Prophecies. The first was made in Wilno in 1942, when Wiktor asked a seer, 'When will the war end?' and the seer replied 'You should not worry because before the war ends you will be first wounded and then killed.' The second prophecy was made in Warsaw in the spring of 1944, when my mother went to see another famous seer, an old woman. When she asked her to tell the future, the woman refused, saying that she did not want to tell anybody their future any more because all she saw was 'death and fire, fire and death.' When my mother insisted – I was with her – the seer said, 'In a short time you will lose two very close members of your family; you will lose everything that you own; you will leave Warsaw, later you will cross a large body of water and never return to Poland.'

* * * * *

It was evening when I returned to Battalion Headquarters and reported to Nałęcz. Upon hearing of Wiktor's death, Nałęcz informed me, without hesitation, that my mother would be welcome with us and that tomorrow he would issue a pass for her. Next morning, the 8th, as he gave me the pass Nałęcz told me that the Germans had captured Powiśle district from Jerusalem Avenue to the university. The front line now ran through our street, Nowy Swiat. Walking towards the crossing and waiting for my turn, I saw Stukas dive bombing just ahead of me. The whole area north of Jerusalem Avenue between Nowy Swiat and Marszałkowska streets was under constant attack by the dive-bombers.

I approached our building from the rear and heard heavy fighting on our street. I entered the entrance hall through the back garden. I heard the sound of diving Stuka and made a run for the service staircase. As I jumped into the basement staircase the bomb exploded. The pressure wave hit me and also blew out all the candles in the cellar. In the darkness panicked voices were shouting: 'We're buried ... we will never get out ... God save us ...'

According to my mother I shouted: 'Shut up! Everybody shut up! We're not buried! The exit is still clear!' I turned on my torch and, seeing the people's faces in front of me, I burst out laughing. The explosion had blown open all the doors to the chimneys in the cellar, and covered everybody in soot. Everyone's face was black, with only the whites of their eyes showing.

The bomb demolished that part of the building that was a mirror image of our apartment on the opposite side of the courtyard. The other staircase from the basement was buried. The explosion had started a fire in that part of the building. People started streaming up the staircase. I went forward and found my mother calmly sitting against the cellar wall with Zabcia on her lap. The poor dog was terrified, she was whining and trembling. I told my mother we had better get going and picked up Zabcia. My mother grasped her handbag and we went towards the exit. We were among the last people leaving the cellar. It took some time since many people were carrying large heavy suitcases up the rather narrow stairs. As we started up the stairs Zabcia jumped out from my hands and ran up between the legs of the people in front of us. By this time the fire from the demolished section of the building was intensifying and smoke began drifting into the cellar. When we reached the courtyard I called out but could not find Zabcia. We looked in the back garden, but she was not there. I ran upstairs to our apartment, but again no luck. I went back into courtyard and waited another ten or fifteen minutes, calling her, and then we left without her.

Once we reached the military police checkpoint at the avenue crossing we were forced to wait a long time for our turn since my mother did not have a priority pass. By early afternoon we were back at battalion headquarters. It turned out that mother had left our apartment just in time. The next day, German forces again concentrated their bombing in the same area and managed to break through from Nowy Swiat Street along Chmielna and capture Gorski Street behind our building. After heavy fighting, the Germans were pushed out by a Polish counter-attack and the front line stabilised along Nowy Swiat Street.

While I was away, Pobóg and his men had left for their new positions. The *Piorun-Zareba* Group was defending a sector on Emili Plater Street between Hoża and Wspólna streets. Our men were assigned a position bordering on the Pomological Garden near the Church of St Barbara.

The first twenty men from the second company, under Lt. 'Patriota', joined *Sokół* Battalion, defending the front on Jerusalem Avenue between Nowy Swiat and Bracka streets. Our second company was assigned a position on the corner of Bracka Street and the avenue. It was very close to our present quarters.

The Battalion HQ moved to 44 Koszykowa Street. From then on, Nałęcz was CO in charge of only administrative and personal matters. The officers commanding the companies were in charge of the respective units under tactical command of the CO of the battalion they had reinforced. As a result of this new order, my life became boring. No longer was I taking an active part in any fighting, but managed only to be an 'observer'. I did, however, visit each company daily delivering the Battalion Order of the Day. Whenever I could, I would stay and hang around with the line units. I also accompanied Nałęcz when he visited our front line units, and to his meetings at KB headquarters, which was relocated from Boduena to Hoża, near Marszałkowska Street, on the south side of the avenue.

On 11 September, I accompanied Nałęcz and three of our officers to KB headquarters. The meeting was lengthy and after returning to our battalion headquarters I learned that our three officers would attempt to cross the River Vistula to Praga and get through the German–Russian front line. Contact was to be established with the communist Polish People's Army headquarters. Their mission was to brief Russian Army high command, via the headquarters of the LWP, of the situation in Warsaw and ask for help in the form of ammunition and weapon drops, and to establish radio communication to help co-ordinate artillery and aircraft support. This initiative was approved by the Polish Home Army high command. The three officers picked for this mission were Lt. Edward, 2nd Lt. 'Witold' and the newly promoted 2nd Lt. Czajka. Towards evening, Nałęcz and I accompanied the three officers to the edge of our positions on the corner of Nowy Swiat Street opposite Książęca Street. It was getting dark when we said our goodbyes and the men crossed Nowy Swiat and entered a building on Książęca. This street followed the hill down towards the Czerniaków district on the Vistula riverfront. This was the last area with river access still held by our troops. The elite *Radosław* Group, which had extensive combat experience from the old town, had been sent there to reinforce the area defence.

At the time, we didn't know if our three men had made it to their destination. There was no change in the Russian attitude. There still were no airdrops, no artillery support and no air activity over Warsaw. It was not until a year later that I learned part of their story. In the summer of 1946, after the war ended, I met Witold in Warsaw. He and his wife Marylka had a kiosk selling cigarettes and newspapers on Marszałkowska Street. He had recently been demobilised, having been severely wounded during the fight in front of Berlin. His leg was stiff and he walked with difficulty. He told me what had happened.

The three men arrived in Czerniaków without much trouble having only encountered fire from some high ground near the National Museum. They approached the waterfront at Mączna Street, where a lieutenant from a local unit supplied them with a two-man kayak. It was midnight when they all managed to squeeze aboard and started paddling across the river. They avoided being discovered by German searchlights and reached the Praga bank of the river. They ditched the kayak, overturned it and sent it floating down the river. After crossing the embankment, careful to avoid German patrols, Edward, Witold and Czajka made their way east through the once-affluent Saska Kempa district. They came across a stable, where contact was made with a local Polish woman. She informed them that the Germans had taken away all the local Polish men and large numbers of German troops, armour and actively patrolling military police were in the area. The building next door was full of German soldiers. The woman and a friend who joined her decided to move the three men, one by one, to a more secluded location. One of the women left with Czajka and Edward followed with the other. As Czajka reached the designated villa, Edward was spotted by German military police. He managed to hide in the osier willows along the riverbank, but was found by the Germans' police dog. Edward was taken back to the road, where Germans pretended to release him but as he started to walk away they sent the police dog after him. When Edward turned to look, the dog jumped on his chest and ripped out his throat. The Germans finished him off with a pistol shot to the head. All this took place in front of the two women, who were then told to bury him.

When Witold was told what had happened, he decided that Czajka and he should try to cross the front line separately that night. In the meantime, the woman had him hide inside a cold storage bin in the cellar of a nearby villa. That evening Russian heavy artillery fire covered the entire area and was followed by recurring air raids. German soldiers took cover in the cellar and made it impossible for Witold to leave. The next morning, 13 September, German troops began to evacuate the building and by noon the soldiers were gone, though some SS men remained. By nightfall a Russian artillery barrage commenced behind him while there was small arms fire in front. Witold left the building and saw a Russian soldier. He shouted to him in Russian, 'Do not shoot, I am Polish.' He was escorted to their battalion headquarters and next to regimental headquarters, where he was well received. The officers all wanted to know what the situation was in Warsaw. He was allowed to wash and shave and was fed. From there he was sent to divisional headquarters, where he was interrogated by three high-ranking staff officers. He gave them information as to the location of the front lines, areas for possible airdrops and the locations of German strongpoints as targets for aerial bombing. Witold described the situation on the waterfront and the best location to cross the river into Warsaw proper. A report of the meeting was prepared and signed. The following morning, after having breakfast in the general officers mess, Witold was taken to the headquarters of Gen. Rola-Zymirski, the commander-in-chief of the Polish People's Army. He finished the war as his adjutant.

I asked him about Czajka. He said that he had tried to find out what had happened to him, but could not obtain any information from the Russians. He assumed that Czajka didn't make it. A few months later, in August 1946, I visited Pobóg in Pomerania. To my great surprise and jubilation I found a very gaunt and emaciated Czajka there. He had also made it through the front line, but the Russian soldiers with whom he made contact delivered him immediately to Russian Army counterintelligence. It was the dreaded *Smersh* (death to spies). He was accused of being a spy collaborating with the Germans and sent to a Siberian Gulag. He had recently been released, after two years, without any explanation, and repatriated to Poland.

* * * * *

After Nałęcz and I watched the three officers slip away on their mission, we waited some time before returning to headquarters. It was quite late by then, most likely after midnight, when I entered the room I shared with my mother. She was lying on her back, in her clothes, on top of the bed, looking at the ceiling. There was a dim candle at her bedside. After a while, without changing her position or looking at me, she said in a low matter-of-fact voice, 'it is true,' she paused. 'Andrzej is dead.' This was not a question; it was a statement. 'Yes', I replied.

I felt immediate relief – relief that I would no longer have to lie to her or avoid her as I had been doing since arrival from the old town. I felt confident that she would never find out the horrible circumstances of his death. I did not know how wrong I was.

Nothing more was said by either of us. We both knew there was nothing more that could, or should, be said. She blew out the candle, I took off my shoes and belt, lay down in my uniform on the bed we shared and we both pretended to go to sleep.

*****

Battalion Order No. 28, from 11 September 1944:

II Promotions:

Private Bohdan from today's date is promoted to the rank of a corporal with seniority as of 11.IX.44. The above promotion was given in recognition of his services as line runner of the battalion. At the same time I commend Cpl. Bohdan.
    CO of 1st Assault Battalion Nałęcz
Nałęcz Cpt.

It was with great pride that I put on two stripes, signifying my new rank, on the shoulder boards of my uniform.

Around that time the front in the centre-north sector was stabilised. Our old street, Nowy Swiat, became the front line. The area to the east, Powiśle, was lost, together with the power station and access to the Vistula. Next to the centre-north and south there were three other separate districts in Polish hands: Czerniaków to the east, with its access to the Vistula; Mokotów to the south and Zoliborz to the north.

On the afternoon of the 13th, when I was at the command post of 2nd Company, we saw Russian planes again. They bombed the Poniatowski Bridge. Some time later there were more explosions from the direction of the bridge. I went with Lt. Holski to the top floor of a nearby building and we saw the bridge was down. The Germans blew it up after it was damaged by Russian bombing. We wondered if it were possible that our officers got through and this was the result of their mission. Later that day, all remaining bridges across the Vistula were dynamited by the Germans. The Russians now occupied the whole of the Praga district on the other side of the river. During the next few days German troops concentrated their assault on the separate remaining districts, starting with Czerniaków. During the night of 15–16 September, units of the Polish People's Army crossed the Vistula and reinforced the defences of Czerniaków. On the 15th, the KB hospital on Boduena Street was bombed, over a hundred wounded soldiers lost their lives. Our battalion was lucky; most of our wounded, with the exception of

Sten, were no longer there. Sten, first wounded in the old town, then again after arriving in the centre, was there and suffered wounds for a third time.

From the time that our two companies went to the front line, combat at their respective sectors was static. Both units were in defensive positions although there was one fierce action conducted in the same manner as we had fought in the old town. On the 15th, supported by tanks, the Germans captured a building on the corner of Bracka Street and Jerusalem Avenue. The Germans who occupied this corner building were separated from our positions by solid, thick party walls, which prevented them from further exploiting their breakthrough. The assault group from our 2nd Company under Lt. Patriota blasted a large opening in the party wall. Then, in a surprise attack, with machine pistols and grenades, they recaptured the building. Several German soldiers were killed within the building; more in the avenue when they tried to escape to the other side. The corner building was re-occupied by our 2nd Company. When I visited them next morning I saw about fifteen German bodies lying in front of their positions. During the next few nights, we salvaged most of the German weapons and ammunition.

We heard that more Polish People's Army troops had crossed the Vistula during the next couple of nights. Fighting there was very heavy as the Germans wanted to eliminate this bridgehead at all costs. After the Russians bombed the Poniatowski Bridge they launched night flights over Warsaw, dropping needed supplies. This action was more show rather than meaningful help. They flew outdated single-engine biplanes from the late 1920s. The planes were PO-2s, nicknamed *Kukuruznik* from the Russian word for maize, and used prior to the war for crop dusting, hence the name. The drops were made at night to points identified by signal fires. The plane usually turned off its engine to avoid AA fire and dropped the supplies during a shallow dive, restarting the engine when pulling up. The supplies were dropped from low altitudes without parachutes. The food was mostly hardtack and there was tobacco. Weapons were also dropped without parachutes in bundles together with ammunition in boxes, resulting in much damage to the supplies. The one anti-tank rifle the *Sokół* Battalion retrieved from a drop was so damaged that it became inoperative after being fired just once.

One evening, Nałęcz asked me if I knew of a tall building where we could look out for any airdrops. Just before midnight I brought him to the building where Holski and I had gone to see the recently destroyed Poniatowski Bridge. From the attic of the six-storey building we had a clear view all around because the roof was gone. The night was dark and all around us as far as the eye could see was a glow of fires and burning buildings. Flames were coming out of gaping open windows and from roofless attics. The whole of Warsaw was burning.

Beginning on the 15th, Cpt. Nałęcz was assigned to KB headquarters staff and from then on most of his time was spent there. His new assignment left me with even more free time, which I spent hanging around with one or the other of our two companies. I did, however, accompany Nałęcz on his inspection and visits to our companies.

The question of food was becoming very critical. Almost all of the reserves that our population had were exhausted. There was no meat as all the horses had been eaten during the first few days. Now the dogs started to disappear. Up until then I do not remember being really very hungry; somehow I always had something to eat. From time to time we would discover delicacies such as cans of pineapple, found hidden in an apartment in the old town, or boxes of Portuguese sardines, found recently behind a false wall in a cellar. From now on, our principal food was porridge made from un-husked barley. It was nicknamed *zapluwajka*. A rough translation is 'spit soup'. It was so named because after carefully chewing each mouthful one had to spit out the remaining husks. The barley came from one of the warehouses of the Haberbusch & Schile brewery, which remained in Polish hands. Each night the Army Work Battalions transported sacks of grain on their backs. It was hard and dangerous work. On many early mornings I saw caravans of men walking single file, carrying heavy sacks. Occasionally, civilians were allowed to join the work battalions and were permitted to keep a small part of the grain they brought back. Living conditions for the civilian population were becoming unbearable. No electricity or running water, food almost gone, constant bombing and shelling. People combined their meagre supplies to cook one daily communal meal on outdoor fires in their courtyards. Nevertheless, the civilian population was bearing these hardships with great determination and surprising fortitude. During all the time I spent walking through cellars and courtyards where people now lived and sheltered, I never came across any sign of anger or hostility towards our soldiers.

One day as I was savouring my daily *zapluwajka* from the field kitchen of 1st Company I found, to my great surprise, a small piece of meat. It tasted like any other overcooked meat but it turned out to be dog meat. That did not bother any of us and I would gladly have eaten some more. On another occasion, I was given a piece of sausage supposedly made from cat meat. I guess when you're really hungry you lose all inhibitions.

17

American Airdrop – Centre South, 18–29 September 1944

The Soviet government cannot of course object to English or American aircraft dropping arms in the region of Warsaw … But they decidedly object to American or British aircraft, after dropping arms in the region of Warsaw, landing on Soviet territory …

> *Andrey Y. Vyshinsky, message to Ambassador Harriman in Moscow, 15 August 1944, Foreign Relations of the United States, 1944, Vol. 3 (Washington, DC: United States Government Printing Office), pp. 1374–6*

Why should they not land on the refuelling ground which has been assigned to us behind the Russian lines … ?

> *Winston Churchill's telegram to F.D. Roosevelt, 25 August 1944*

I do not consider it advantageous to the long range general war prospect for me to join with you in the proposed message to U.J. (Uncle Joe).

> *Message from F.D. Roosevelt to Winston Churchill, 25 August 1944, Roosevelt Papers, Map Room Papers, Box 6*

On 18 September 1944, around 2 p.m., while returning to headquarters, I heard the sound of many aircraft engines. As the sound increased in intensity, many people, both soldiers and civilians, ran out into the streets. A huge armada of large bombers appeared flying from the north-west at great heights, trailing white contrails behind them. That was the first time I had ever seen a contrail; Polish, German and Russian planes never flew that high. German AA opened up with the greatest intensity that I'd ever witnessed. Above us, white parachutes began to appear, dropping from the planes. 'Polish paratroopers are coming,' people were shouting. We were all sure that the long-awaited arrival of the Polish Parachute Brigade had come.

Soon it became clear that containers, not paratroopers, were swinging under the parachutes. It was a supply drop. We all looked on in dismay as most of the containers drifted over our lines and into German hands. The planes continued in a south-easterly direction. The AA fire died down, leaving the sky full of puffs of black smoke. The white contrails slowly disappeared. The dejected population returned to their shelters. Our soldiers were seeking and recovering the dropped containers.

What we did not know then was that that same day the first elements of the Polish Parachute Brigade were landing at Arnhem. Three days later the rest of the brigade was dropped across the Rhine, on the German-held drop zone. They fought vainly in this faultily conceived, planned and executed last part of the operation known now as 'A Bridge Too Far'.

In the one and only large supply drop attempted by the Allies, 110 B-17 Flying Fortress bombers from the US Army 8th Air Force took off from England; 107 arrived over Warsaw and from a great height dropped 1,280 220lb containers. Because of the height only 380, less than a third, fell within Polish lines. Two planes were shot down and 104 landed at Poltava, a Russian airbase in Ukraine. The base had been assigned to and previously used by the USAAF United States Army Air Force for 'pendulum' bombing of the Ploesti oil fields in Romania. Until that day, Stalin had not allowed the United States use of this base for a mission to supply Warsaw. By the forty-ninth day of the Uprising, Stalin did not expect us to last much longer. He allowed this one and only Allied airdrop, simply for public relations.

* * *

After the war, I learned that Churchill had wanted Roosevelt to pressure Stalin to allow use of this base for supplying Warsaw. He wanted Roosevelt to threaten Stalin with stoppage of the Murmansk convoys, which were delivering supplies to Russia. Roosevelt declined his request. In February 2003, I attended an American Institute of Polish Culture function in Miami. One of the guests was Winston Spencer-Churchill (1940–2010), grandson of Winston Churchill. His mother, Pamela, was married to Averell Harriman. At lunch the next day, I was sitting next to him and our conversation turned to the Warsaw Uprising. I asked him if he knew anything about the Allied airdrops. He told me that his grandfather confirmed to him that Roosevelt had refused to threaten Stalin with stoppage of supplies to Russia in order to force help for the Warsaw Uprising. He added that later, when he asked his stepfather Averell Harriman (who had been Roosevelt's advisor and wartime

US Ambassador to Moscow), Spencer-Churchill said: 'Harriman gave me a dirty look and walked out of the room.'

Our conversation later moved on to the Katyń Memorial Monument in London. Winston Spencer-Churchill, as a Member of Parliament for a district near Manchester, represented a large constituency of Polish Second World War serviceman who settled there after the war. In 1975, he became a member of an Honorary Committee for the Katyń Memorial Fund. He intervened with the Foreign Office, trying to countermand an unpopular decision. Under pressure from the Soviet Union, the Foreign Office disallowed a description of the monument which stated that that Polish officers were murdered in 1940 by the NKVD. The government gave the committee two alternatives: the date of 1940 without the place (Katyń); or the place without the date. In the end, the description read:

> In remembrance of 14,500 Polish prisoners of war who disappeared in 1940 from camps in Kozielsk, Starobielsk and Ostaszkow of whom 4,500 were later identified in mass graves at Katyń near Smolensk.

* * * * *

The day following the US airdrop, The Russian Air Force appeared over Warsaw in strength. Their planes bombed several German positions, including the BGK building opposite our 2nd Company positions. We again speculated about whether our officers had managed to reach Russian headquarters, since this building was one of the designated targets. The Germans continued to concentrate their attacks on the Czerniaków district in order to eliminate the Vistula bridgehead. On the night of 19 September, Col. 'Radosław' evacuated his group through the sewers to the Mokotów district. On the 23rd, Czerniaków fell and the Germans repeated the same atrocities as after the fall of the old town. All surviving soldiers, including the wounded and nurses, were brutally killed.

The same day, our 2nd Company suffered the largest loss of life since evacuating from the old town. Heavy artillery and mortar fire on their position killed several officers and men, wounding many others. That same night, on the corner of Krucza and Nowogródek streets, in the courtyard of the buildings destroyed in 1939, a bonfire was lit to designate a drop point for an expected Russian airdrop. In addition to the designated soldiers, from our company and Sokół Battalion, a large group of other soldiers and civilians gathered there. Nałęcz and I arrived before midnight and left after a short visit. Shortly after there was a direct hit on the courtyard. In the resulting carnage our company had more killed and wounded that day. *Sokół* Battalion also lost four men and had several wounded. It has never been determined conclusively what happened. There are two speculations: one, a direct hit from a German mortar and two, a German plane with its engine cut out dropped a bomb. The next day's order of the day listed, by name, the following casualties:

Killed in action: two officers and six other ranks.
Wounded: one officer and seven other ranks.

Two days later, I joined our officers and men for a funeral mass for the fallen. Lt. 'Szczęsny' died that day of his wounds. Three other soldiers died over the next two days.

The Germans now concentrated their attacks on the Mokótow area. From the 26th to the 27th our forces started to evacuate this district through the sewers to the centre of town. For some of the soldiers from the *Radosław* Group this was the fifth time they had moved through the sewers. The remaining troops capitulated. By that time, the Germans had finally started to recognise combatant rights of the Polish Home Army under the Geneva Convention.

On the 26th, the HQ of the battalion moved across the street to 51 Koszykowa. We took over an apartment on the second floor overlooking the street. Two days later, as my mother was standing next to the open balcony door, a 2-ton shell from a *Karl-Gerät* siege mortar exploded on the street below. Luckily, it hit the street about two buildings to the side. Nevertheless, the explosion threw her clear across the room and ruptured an eardrum. (By that time, all the glass in the windows was long gone and there was no longer any danger of flying glass particles). Fortunately, she was only knocked about but, unfortunately, lost her hearing in that ear. We all knew that after each explosion you had about half an hour before the next one. It took a long time to reload this mortar. The shells were audible as they fell relatively slowly. They were nicknamed *latajace kufry*, 'flying coffers'.

During my daily visits to 2nd Company, I'd noticed that German bodies, lying in front of their position since the 16th, were decomposing and smelled rather bad. Also, there was a sack of supplies, recently dropped by a Russian plane, in the middle of the avenue.

Around the 24th, from their positions across the avenue, a German soldier who spoke Polish with a Silesian accent started up conversational banter. Our men replied, chiding him for not removing the corpses of his fallen comrades.

To this he said that they were afraid we would shoot them if they tried. On our assurances that we would not shoot, he replied that he would speak with his lieutenant. Next day, the conversation continued, but with a German officer. He proposed a brief ceasefire for them to remove the corpses and for us to retrieve the sack of supplies. During the proposed ceasefire an officer from each side would remain in the middle of the avenue. Following approval by our high command, since this involved other neighbouring Polish units, it was agreed that a ceasefire would begin at 4 p.m. the following day.

I was present the next day, when at 4 p.m. sharp the Germans waived a white flag. We responded and an officer from each side marched out. They met in the middle of the avenue, saluted each other and started a conversation. On a given sign from them both, German soldiers came out with stretchers and picked up the bodies, while a couple of our men dragged the sack of Russian supplies to our side. All of this was filmed by the Polish War Correspondent. Once the pickup was completed and soldiers returned to their positions, the two officers saluted each other and returned to their lines. A few minutes later the shooting resumed with increased intensity. The officer who represented us was 2nd Lt. 'Miki I'; he had lost an eye during the fighting in the telephone exchange in the old town.

This was not the end. The next day, the same German lieutenant contacted us across the avenue, saying that his battalion CO would like to personally thank our CO for this courtesy. He proposed that three Polish officers visit them, while three German officers remained with us as hostages. This proposal was again agreed to by our high command; hoping that we would be able to observe their positions and gauge the morale of their soldiers. Our delegation included Lt. 'Skała', 2nd Lt. Miki I and C. Off. 'Dębina', the last two from the *Nałęcz* Battalion. Dębina's recollections were included in Jan Lissowski, Jerzy Szanser and Marek Werner's book on the battalion's role in the Uprising:

At the designated hour, on a given signal, we and three Germans stepped out from our positions. Without stopping, we passed our German 'partners', in the middle of the avenue, saluting each other … In the ruins of the Cristal [a bar], a German officer with the rank of captain was awaiting us. He introduced himself very properly and was unusually pleasant and loquacious. He led us through a series of courtyards, across Nowy Swiat Street to the building at 13 Kopernika Street. Waiting for us in a second-floor apartment were several German Wehrmacht officers with an SS major in charge.

After introducing ourselves, we sat down at a large round table. I noticed there were flowers in the vases and some cakes on the sideboard. It was explained to us that the major had celebrated his Geburtstag [birthday] yesterday.

The glasses were filled with wine and cigarettes were passed around. A conversation began and was led by the major; the remaining Germans officers for the most part assisted the major and were supportive. The conversation was in German; though at the beginning our officers tried to converse in French, only one of the German officer continued in that language. The major first thanked us profusely for making it possible to remove the bodies of their dead soldiers, referring to the gesture as 'good military custom' ...

Next the major expressed his regret that we had to fight one another and under those conditions suffer unimaginable losses, when on the other side of the Vistula were the Russians, who had also invaded our country. He was talking more about European unity, that our common enemies were the Russians. Lt. Skała replied that we would always fight any enemy who invaded our country. It had always been that way throughout our history, and above all we were soldiers obeying our orders.

The conversation was very lively. The major was very well informed on the participation of communist units – he mentioned the AL (the 'People's Army' of the Polish Communist Party) – in the ranks of the Home Army. We replied saying they were our comrades in arms and their political beliefs should be considered a personal matter.

After an hour, concluding our visit, the major once more expressed his thanks and wished us good luck. The major clearly carried the entire conversation and we sensed that he was domineering and authoritative, the remaining Germans simply repeated his opinions. We conducted ourselves altogether differently – we each spoke and expressed our own opinions freely.

The same captain escorted us back. The sympathetic captain was the battalion's doctor. He mentioned that shots fired from our side were very rare, but always accurate. When his stretcher-bearers heard our shots, they would pick up their litters, without waiting for an order and go to the front line. He pleasantly bid us farewell. We left the ruins of the Cristal, passed the three German officers in the middle of the avenue and reported to Maj. Sokół on our 'visit'.

I would like to add that the recovered sack from the Russian drop contained, in equal parts, hardtack and tobacco. Both became quite useful. We were still smoking this tobacco in the Lamsdorf POW camp.

Lissowski, Szanser and Werner, *Batalion 'Sokół' w Powstaniu Warszawskim*,

pp. 152–3

18

Capitulation, 29 September–
4 October 1944

For sixty-three long days, the citizens of Warsaw heroically and bravely resisted the German occupier.

Chancellor Gerhard Schröder, Warsaw, 1 August 2004

It became apparent to us that neither the Russians nor the Allies were going to help us. A rumour began to circulate that capitulation talks had started. The Germans had already proposed capitulation on several occasions. Up to now, this had been refused by our high command. On 29 September the command communicated to Russian Marshal Konstantin Rokossovsky that unless the Russians gave us immediate artillery fire and air support and moved into Warsaw within three days, Warsaw would fall.

On the 29th Germans started a concentrated attack on Zoliborz, the last remaining district outside the centre. The attack, carried out by an armoured division with two supporting regiments of infantry, broke through our lines suffering substantial losses in tanks and men. Our losses were also heavy; the capitulation was negotiated. The remaining 2,500 AK soldiers laid down their arms on the evening of the 30th, and became POWs.

The same day, our battalion suffered its last fatalities. Cpt. Skóra and newly promoted 2nd Lt. 'Zadra' were killed. It was tragic and ironic, that after taking part in all of the battalion's heaviest fighting over sixty-one days, those two brave officers lost their lives in what turned out to be the final two days. Next day, in the afternoon I attended their funeral. As the ceremony ended, I realised there were no more sounds of fighting. On 1 October, the beginning of the third month and the sixty-second day of the Uprising, an agreement was reached for the evacuation of the civilian population. On that day the Germans were to hold their fire from 5 to 7 p.m., allowing civilians to leave Warsaw through two designated exit points.

When I returned, the son of the quartermaster was in our quarters. He told me that his father, Lt. 'Pelerynka', had just passed away in the hospital. A few days earlier, a mortar shell had exploded behind them as they were walking together. His father suffered more than twenty shrapnel wounds while he was not even scratched. He brought with him a German shepherd dog, found and adopted by them at the beginning of the fighting.

The temporary armistice was extended from the morning of the next day, 2 October. By then we realised that capitulation was inevitable. Most of our cadet-officers were promoted to the rank of second lieutenant; to be treated as officers while POWs. All of the soldiers were issued new ID cards. Up until then there were several variants of our ID. Besides the Home Army there were other units, tactically under command of the AK, including the communist AL (People's Army) and the ultra-nationalistic NSZ (National Armed Forces). They all had their own distinct IDs. The heading of the one I had originally been issued stated: *Armia Krajowa – Korpus Bezpieczeństwa* (Home Army – Security Corps). The new ID, which I have donated to the Warsaw Rising Museum, was headed *Armia Krajowa*, dated 28 July 1944 and stated: 'Cpl. Bohdan – Bohdan Hryniewicz is a soldier of the AK'.

Identity card issued by High Command of Home Army, before capitulation, to soldiers of all units fighting in the Uprising. (Author's archive)

Late that night Nałęcz returned from KB HQ, where he had spent that entire day. He told me that the capitulation had been signed that evening. It was an 'honourable capitulation' and he would brief us in the morning on its conditions. Next day, 3 October, after sixty-four days of fighting, the capitulation was announced. In the morning Nałęcz called the few remaining members of his staff and outlined the conditions of the capitulation agreement. They were:

Military action between 'Polish Military Units' and the Germans ceased as of 8 p.m. 2 October 1944.

'Polish military units' were defined as all units under the tactical command of the AK since 1 August 1944.

Polish units were to lay down their arms and march out in formation, under command of their officers.

The officers had the right to retain their 'white' side arms (meaning sabres) – that's what made it 'honourable', we all laughed when we heard that.

Our German POWs were to be handed over.

All soldiers would be granted their rights as prisoners of war under the Geneva Convention, including the members of auxiliary services, without any distinction, regardless of their sex.

No one recognised as a POW would be prosecuted for any military or political activities during and prior to the Uprising.

The civilian population would not be subjected to any reprisals.

All civilians must leave Warsaw; the German forces would not cause any unnecessary hardships.

The Germans guaranteed that only their armed forces, the Wehrmacht, will be used in handling POWs (this was a condition of the Polish high command in light of the crimes committed by the SS).

Nałęcz went on to say that our battalion would not be marching out as one unit to lay down our arms. Instead, each company would go with the battalion it had recently reinforced. 1st Company would go with the *Piorun-Zaręmba* Battalion and 2nd Company with *Sokół*. He gave each of us US$10 and 500 Polish occupational *złoty*. The army treasury was liquidated to prevent it falling into German hands. He proceeded to dispense the money and gave me double, one share for me and the other for Andrzej. He thanked and released us. As we were leaving, he asked my mother to stay. After a while he called me in. Mother was still in the room. He told me to sit down and told me he had decided not to allow me to go with our units and become a POW; instead, I would leave Warsaw as a civilian with my mother.

I felt as though I had been broadsided. I felt betrayed and angry. After all the events of the past two months I was to be abandoned. No longer was I to be a part of what we now call 'a band brothers', the people with whom I had formed such strong bonds, so many of them no longer with us. I was to be cast away. I sat there, biting my lip. Nałęcz then nodded to mother and she left the room. He turned to me and said: 'I know how you feel; I know you feel betrayed and disappointed by me; I made this decision not because of *you*, but your mother; after the death of Andrzej and Wiktor it is *your* responsibility to be with her.' He remained silent for a few minutes and I stood up, came to attention and said: 'As ordered, Capitan, sir!' Cpt. Nałęcz stood up, extended his hand, hugged me and said: 'I *will* see you after the war.'

Later that day I went with Nałęcz to say goodbye to both companies. The 2nd Company was going to march out the next day with *Sokół* Battalion, part of the 72nd Regiment of Infantry. After visiting Cpt. Holski and other friends, we moved on to Cpt. Pobóg and his 1st Company. Again, I said farewell to old friends. As I said goodbye to 'Borys', I felt jealous that he was going and I was not. It was difficult for me to keep my composure, but I did not let anyone know that I would soon be a 'civilian'.

Nałęcz went to KB Headquarters and I continued to ours. When I returned, mother mentioned that Adam (I believe that was his name), Pelerynka's son, would be coming with us since he was alone now. She said that we should leave tomorrow morning, if for no other reason than that we were almost out of food. She managed to get some warm civilian clothing for me. I very reluctantly took off my *panterka* uniform, removed the battalion shield from my left arm, one shoulder blade with its two stripes signifying the rank of corporal and the ribbon of the Cross of Valour. I secreted them in my wallet. I hid my military IDs in the binding of a book. My red and white armband, worn through sixty days, was too bulky to be hidden safely.

Early next morning, 4 October, we assembled in the kitchen and ate the last of our food: a very small bowl of *zapluwajka*, the watery barley porridge. There was nothing left, over the previous few days all the food had run out. We said our goodbyes to the remaining two members of the headquarters staff, Sgt. Mama and 'Maryla' (the wife of 2nd Lt. Witold), who were leaving to join 1st Company, which left only Nałęcz and us; he wished mother farewell then turned to me and extended his hand. I shook his hand without saluting; he smiled and left for KB headquarters.

The three of us, mother, Adam and I, remained in that empty apartment overlooking the ruined buildings across the cratered street. I told mother that I was going to watch the surrender of arms. Mother reluctantly agreed but wanted us back before noon. She wanted to leave Warsaw by then since we had nothing left to eat.

The German-designated point was next to the Warsaw Polytechnic, only a few blocks away. Adam, his dog and I arrived after 10 a.m. and stood watching as Polish troops arrived in columns of four, led by their officers. As each unit, marching in step, crossed the demarcation line, German officers initiated military salutes, which were returned by the Polish officers. Once over the line, units stopped and stood down. The Polish troops were to carry unloaded weapons, no ammunition or grenades. One by one, each soldier moved forward and handed his weapon to a German soldier, who then opened the breach, checked that it was not loaded and stacked it. The pistols and machine pistols had their magazines removed, checked and reinserted, then were placed in wooden boxes. The Polish soldiers re-formed and marched out in columns. The troops were making themselves as presentable as possible. They were wearing an assortment of uniforms and civilian clothing, but they were not allowed any part of the German uniform. They carried their personal luggage, mostly knapsacks.

As Adam and I were waiting to see the *Sokół* Battalion with our 2nd Company, we were approached by a German officer. He looked at Adam's emaciated dog and gave commands in German, which the dog immediately obeyed. He gestured and Adam surrendered the leash. As the officer was walking away he turned and said in German, 'Thank you for taking care of our dog.'

It was almost noon as we returned to the empty headquarters. Mother was already waiting. We put on our overcoats and knapsacks, she picked up her bag and we walked out. We joined the stream of dejected humanity making its way towards the nearby crossing point designated for civilians. Without any formality we crossed the demarcation line.

PART 4

UNDER GERMAN OCCUPATION

19

Transit Camp 'Dulag 121', 4–8 October 1944

We were back in German-occupied Poland. We started to walk on the designated road framed by sparsely stationed German soldiers. The German sentries were all elderly men from the Wehrmacht, clearly not front-line troops. There were no SS present along the way. Walking around us, people were sombre, dejected, sometimes crying; mostly women, children and elderly people. There were very few men or older boys. There were walking wounded with bandages, arms in slings and on crutches; there were sick and wounded on improvised stretchers or transported on small hand carts. Small children and infants were carried or sometimes pushed in prams. People carted their meagre belongings in backpacks, bags or suitcases. There were people carrying their belongings in sacks, pillowcases or tied in bed sheets. Adam and I carried only small backpacks and we helped others as much as we could. After walking for about half an hour, we saw several small vegetable gardens to our left. They looked pretty much trampled, but here and there were signs of growing vegetation. There was an elderly German Luftwaffe soldier standing by the road. We stopped near him, dropped our backpacks, and Adam and I slowly walked into the field. The soldier gave us a cursory look, but then turned around and pretended not to see us. We managed to find some carrots and onions and pulled them out of the ground. We returned, picked up our backpacks and continued walking, munching on the first fresh veggies we had seen in two months.

We must have walked for four hours and covered about 10 miles. Apart from our vegetables, there was no food or even water along the way. Luckily, it was an overcast day and rather cold, about 10°C. Finally, we entered the town of Pruszków and saw our destination. Behind a very high concrete wall mounted with watchtowers we saw the roofs of many large industrial workshop buildings. We entered through the large iron gate framed by concrete bunkers. We found ourselves in a sprawling yard of the Central Workshop of the Polish Railways. We were now in Durchgagslager 121, a transit camp known as 'Dulag 121'. Our group was directed to one of about ten workshop buildings. It was a cavernous industrial building with high concrete walls topped by metal windows and a steel construction roof. The windows were missing most of their glass; the floor was dirty concrete with railway tracks running through it. There were pieces of machinery and other industrial junk spread around. There was already a large group of people sitting and lying on the concrete floor, surrounded by luggage and crying children. Finally, there was some water from a few industrial taps surrounded by people trying to fill whatever containers they had. There were no sanitary facilities. We were pointed outside to hastily dug trench-cum-latrines. Screens separated the men's and women's sections. There were no seats, only a single long wooden pole over the stinking trench buzzing with flies. There were long lines of people in front waiting to use them.

We were there for three days. The conditions were subhuman. There was no electricity or heat. We slept crowded on the cold concrete floor in our clothes, covering ourselves with whatever we had. The smell of unwashed bodies, combined with that of the infected wounds and the excrement of the sick, was difficult to endure. Some preferred to brave the cold nights outside, huddled around small fires. The only food we received was one ladle of soup at midday and a cup of lukewarm 'coffee' with a small piece of bread in the morning and evening. Small children were given milky porridge. A few Polish, nurses wearing Red Cross armbands, nuns in their different habits and volunteer kitchen personnel in white aprons, were allowed to move freely between the different buildings. They tried to help but were overwhelmed by the multitude of people, the shortage of food and lack of medication. Each building held about 2–3,000 people and was isolated by barbed wire fence, becoming a separate camp. The buildings were guarded by Wehrmacht soldiers, but we also saw Gestapo and SS officers and men. On the second day I came across our old neighbour. He told me that he had returned to our building the day after it had been bombed and caught fire. He found one part of the building had collapsed but the fire had gone out. In the back garden he found the body of our dog lying on the grass. He speculated that she must have returned to the building and been overcome by the smoke and fumes. I was sad that we had lost her but glad that she probably did not suffer too much.

By snooping around I found out that, after a few days, everyone in the camp went through a selection process and was separated into different groups. Each group left the camp in separate trains. Men and boys over 15 were segregated and sent for forced labour in Germany. From the men's group, many, particularly the younger men who looked like they might have been in the Uprising or in the Underground, were further separated. It was suspected that they were sent to concentration camps. The women were likewise segregated and those between their late teens and their fifties were sent to Germany for forced labour. The rest, old men, women and children were sent to the Polish countryside and dispersed into villages. (It was determined, after the war, that from the more than 650,000 inhabitants of Warsaw who went through the camp, 200,000 were sent to Germany for forced labour; 50,000, including my father's brother, to concentration camps; and the rest resettled, spread throughout the countryside.)

On the morning of the fourth day came our turn for selection. A large group was taken from our building. There were very few men, mostly women, children and a few very old men. We were marched towards the siding and found ourselves on a platform between two railway tracks. On the left was a train of covered cattle wagons and on the right a train made of open cargo wagons of the type used for transporting coal. In front of us stood a Gestapo officer with a few SS men behind. Beside him stood an elegant woman in a black Persian lamb coat and black riding boots. As we moved forward it became clear that the younger women and few remaining men were being directed to the left, and the cattle cars. The others, older women, children and old men, were sent to the right. Mother told us to hold her arms, trying to look a small as possible. The Gestapo officer gave us a quick glance and pointed with his riding crop to the cattle cars. The woman behind, tapped his shoulder and quietly told him something we could not hear. He turned around, looked startled at her, waved his arm in resignation and pointed us to the open cars. My mother did not recognise her, but she thought that the woman was at one time a client of her beauty salon. Relieved, we entered the open car. Once the car was jammed full of people, the doors were locked. After an hour, the engine was coupled, the whistle blew a few times and the train slowly started to move.

As we passed through suburban stations we saw people standing on the platforms waving to us. About an hour into the ride the train stopped at a small station. There were people with baskets selling food. We realised that the German occupation money was still in circulation. We had some since, in addition to the cash my mother had, I had received 1,000 *zlotys* as part of my soldier's pay. We managed to buy a couple of loaves of bread and a kielbasa sausage. It was a quick transaction; we had no idea how long the train would be standing. I hung over the top of the car wall and the seller on the ground lifted the goods up in his outstretched hands. We were ravenously hungry, we had only had a small slice of bread the previous night and that morning, but we rationed the food to last two days. The train continued its slow journey, stopping from time to time to give priority to German military traffic. We passed larger stations without stopping. After a couple of hours locked in the car, the need for toilet facilities became urgent. One corner of the wagon was designated as a toilet. There was an advantage in being in an open car. My mother and I huddled together for warmth. The open coal wagon was not exactly a 'parlour' or 'sleeping' car. We noticed that Adam had decided to keep company with two middle aged 'ladies'. Actually, this had already started in the transit camp, when these women began to entice him into their company.

In the afternoon we passed through Piotrków and finally arrived on a siding at a small station. It was Rudniki, where people from two wagons, including ours, were disembarked. Awaiting us was a representative of the RGO (Rada Główna Opiekuńcza), a Polish civilian charity co-operating with the Swiss Red Cross and permitted to function by the German occupational government. Next to him were the elders of a few nearby villages ordered to accept the refugees. My mother and I were in a group of about thirty people selected to go to the village of Kościelec. We said goodbye to Adam, who had decided to go with the 'ladies' to another village. The *sołtys*, the elder of the village, was waiting with two other farmers and their horse-drawn carts. The luggage, some of the exhausted or sick people, and small children were loaded in. A procession of tired people followed the two carts, walking for about an hour. It was already getting dark when we reached the village. As we walked through it, the *sołtys* assigned people to different homes.

20

Kościelec, 8 October–November 1944

Finally it was our turn; we were among the last. Mother and I entered the yard of our assigned household. The door was open and a middle-aged woman appeared at the door when we were halfway across the yard. We entered a large room which served as a kitchen, living and dining room. It was obvious that the peasant family to whom we were assigned was poor. The room was dimly lit by a kerosene lamp. A large man got up from the table, came over and kissed my mother's hand, murmuring welcoming greetings but, unlike his wife, without any warmth.

We were invited to sit down at the table and were served a potato soup with bread and milk. I was ravenously hungry and stuffed myself to the obvious delight of our keeper. Following our meal, we were shown to an alcove off the kitchen which had a straw mattress on a wooden platform. There were two pillows and a couple of coarse blankets. We went to bed in our clothes and both slept like a rock.

When I woke up next morning, mother was sitting at the table talking with the woman. I ate a breakfast of fresh bread with butter and milk. After breakfast, the woman announced that the first day's business would be to have a bath and to wash our clothes. She noticed that I was scratching around my waist and surmised that we both had lice. She was right, as I had fully expected. When I scratched my waist, I found two of the creatures under my fingernails and they made a satisfying 'pop' when squeezed between my fingernails. A large cauldron of water was already heating on the stove. Our hostess prepared a wooden bathtub near the stove, where it was warm. We took turns to wash and scrub ourselves with homemade soap. It felt divine to have a bath, the first in over a month. As we sat next to the stove wrapped in blankets, our underwear and shirts were boiling in a cauldron of lye. In the meantime, the woman was ironing the inner seams of my trousers and my mother's skirt. We were lucky as the preventative action worked and we had no more problems. Most likely we had been infected, but only for a few days, while we were in the transit camp.

A couple of days later the village elder came and told me that I would need to be ready early the next day to work. The Germans had imposed a quota of about twenty-five men from the village for labour on their airfield. The next morning I joined a group of about fifteen men from our village and four elderly Warsovians. Led by a German Luftwaffe soldier, we walked a mile to the airfield. For the next three weeks I worked digging trenches or laying telephone and other wire. It was not particularly hard work; no one strained themselves and the elderly German who watched us did not show any particular zeal. Only when he saw his sergeant approaching did he yell at us and we pretended to work harder. But it was not all a picnic. Outside, it was cold, windy and there was quite a lot of rain. We were not given any food. We ate what we brought with us, which was very little.

While I was working, mother got to know our hostess well. She was not a local woman. Her family was from the village of Rzerzuśnia near Miechów, north of Kraków. Her family name was Tabak and her father was a very well-respected master builder of watermills. It was an old family trade he had learned from his father and grandfather. Her two brothers worked with him. She also had two younger sisters, both married, living near their parents. She told mother that some people from that area were smuggling tobacco grown near Miechów. They sold it on the black market in Częstochowa, where tobacco was not available. On the return trip they would buy women's cotton and woollen stockings made in clandestine workshops in Częstochowa. It was a good business but a dangerous one. The Germans had prohibited the black market, particularly in tobacco. If you were caught smuggling, you could easily wind up in a concentration camp.

Mother had already been to Częstochowa, where she had exchanged one of our two $10 bills for local money on the black market and purchased stockings. She showed me two sleeveless kaftans she had made by loosely stitching them together.

The next day, wearing our stocking kaftans, we walked in the early morning November chill to the railway station in Rudniki. We boarded the local train to the Częstochowa station, where we managed to squeeze into the Kraków-bound train. All the trains were overcrowded; people were standing wherever they could find space. A compartment designed for eight people held at least twice as many. The trains in occupied Poland designated for civilian use were the least important for the Germans. Each train had one first-class wagon,

Nur für Deutsche, for Germans only. Needless to say, the other cars were very old, some from the early 1900s. We changed trains at Kraków, where we had our IDs inspected. In the afternoon we arrived in Miechów and walked about 5 miles to Rzerzuśnia. It was a typical Polish village with houses strung out on both sides of the road. We found the house of the youngest Tabak sister, Cecilia (Czesia) Szczepka. A pretty young woman in her early twenties opened the door holding a 2-year-old boy. When mother explained who we were, she invited us in. She wanted to know all about her sister. I gathered that she was not very fond of her brother-in-law. She brought food to the table and invited us to spend the night and stay until we had finished our business. Towards evening her husband came in from working the fields. He was a quiet man, obviously devoted to his wife and son.

That evening we took apart our kaftans and assembled about fifty pairs of thick women's stockings. We gave 'Czesia' two pairs and she was very pleased. The next day she took us to meet her parents, who lived about a mile away. We met Mr Tabak and his wife and their older daughter, who had lost her husband in the 1939 campaign. She and her teenage daughter Tosia lived with them. The three Tabak women told us they would make sure that enough women came to buy our stockings. Sure enough, all of our stockings were sold by noon the next day. Later that afternoon, with our newly earned money we purchased about 13lb of tobacco. During the war, tobacco was very expensive and all of the tobacco grown in Poland had to be delivered to the Germans. Possession of even a small amount of tobacco and some designated foods was considered black marketeering and subject to draconian penalties.

Next morning, after leaving some stockings for her mother and sister, we said goodbye to Czesia. She invited us to come back. On our return trip we had to wait hours for a train at Miechów station. Along the way our train was sidetracked to let German Army trains pass by. As we approached Kraków it was already evening and very dark. I was very hungry and we had no more food. We were sitting on a hard bench, in a crowded third-class compartment and squeezed in next to a man at the window. I noticed that he had pulled some food out from his bag and was slowly and carefully eating. The wonderful smell of smoked sausage permeated the air. Even though it was pitch dark I saw him slowly take a bite of sausage from one hand and from the other a piece of fresh crusty bread. I was practically drooling as he slowly chewed each piece, clearly enjoying it. The train stopped at a small station. In the dim light from a nearby lamp post I saw him alternatively taking a bite from a clove of garlic in one hand and hardtack in the other. With the last swallow I stopped salivating.

It was already night by the time we returned to Kościelec. As we entered our quarters our hostess was very excited and wanted to hear all the news from her family. Mother spoke with her until her husband grumpily entered and sent her to bed. During the next few days, we made several trips to Częstochowa and sold all the tobacco without any difficulty. When we counted our money we had more than doubled our initial investment.

We decided to repeat our trip and first repurchased our $10 on the black market. Next we invested our profit in more stockings, and towards the end of November we returned to Rzerzuśnia. This time it took longer to sell the stockings since most of the women in the village had already purchased stockings from us earlier. We walked to nearby villages and sold stockings door-to-door. Mother approached Czesia about having us move in with her. She was very enthusiastic and it was agreed that after we got back to Kościelec and sold the tobacco, we would return and move in with her. The price for 'room and board' was agreed upon. The 'room' was a large bed in the corner of the kitchen with a straw mattress separated by a curtain.

While we were in Rzerzuśnia we learned that the Germans had intensified their searches of train passengers, looking for black marketeers. We decided to hide our tobacco in case we were searched. Mother made a small pillow with oil-cloth (to mask the odour of the tobacco) covered by a garish embroidered pillow cover. I had the idea of tying my trouser legs at the ankles and filling them with tobacco from the knees down. Though I thought it was a clever idea it turned into a torture. The tobacco irritated my skin and my legs started to itch; there was no way to scratch them. As the day progressed, there were innumerable stops and slow downs, and the tobacco started to feel very warm, further increasing my discomfort. The trip took longer than expected and when we arrived in Częstochowa it was already dark. Passengers disembarked and started to walk towards the exit; it was barred and guarded. As the train pulled out, we found ourselves surrounded by Germans. Everyone was herded into the large waiting room. After a long wait, people were taken, a few at a time, into the next room, where they were searched and interrogated; some were allowed to go while others were detained. We noticed quite a few people were walking towards the centre of the room and dropping packages of loose tobacco on the floor. The pile of tobacco on the floor was growing and from time to time a couple of Germans would come and remove it. We knew that we had no choice but to dump our tobacco too. We walked to the pile and my mother dumped her pillow and I, with great relief, untied my trousers and shook out all the tobacco. I spent the next few minutes gloriously scratching my legs. Finally, our turn came and we were told to go through to the controls. Men and women were separated. My backpack was searched. I was patted down and released. I had to wait about fifteen minutes and was beginning to worry that mother had been detained when finally she came out. She told me there was no problem with her bag, as it was practically empty, but that while a German woman had patted down her abdomen, she found a small bulge. 'What is this?' the German woman exclaimed. 'You know, it's that time of the month.' With obvious disgust, the German woman told her to move on. In fact, mother had sewn a pocket onto the inside of her garter belt, where all our money was hidden.

By the time we were released it was already near midnight and a German curfew was in force. We had no choice but to start walking. It was close to 10 miles. The night was very cold with a clear sky and bright moonlight. We carefully walked through the town, trying to keep to the shadows. Luckily, we did not come across any German patrols. Once, we heard the sound of someone running, what seemed to be two or three blocks away, then shouts of 'Halt! … Halt!' and the crack of shots being fired. We increased our pace and soon reached the road. More than three hours later we reached our house. Our host was not amused at being awoken at four in the morning.

A few days later we bought a smaller number of stockings and made only one kaftan. We packed our meagre belongings and early next morning said our goodbyes. We walked to Rudniki railway station to catch the early train to Częstochowa, where we were to change trains for Kraków. When the train arrived it was already full – there was no way all the people waiting would be able to board. While trying to push our way to the carriage entrance, I noticed that the flexible passageway between two cars was not locked on our side. I climbed on the bumpers and with my hands was able to separate the passageway between the cars enough for a person to squeeze in. I motioned to mother and helped her climb up. While I held the sides apart she squeezed through. I followed her but as soon as I was inside the two halves snapped together, behind me leaving my backpack on the outside. As I was trying to take my backpack off I heard German shouts and police whistles. Then I felt somebody pulling on my backpack and heard shouting in German to get out. I turned and saw a German railway policeman yelling, 'Get out!' At that moment, the engine whistle sounded shrilly and the train lurched forward, starting to move. The railway policeman was forced to jump off the bumpers where he had been standing. Without any more escapades we changed trains in Kraków, disembarked in Miechów and walked to Rzerzuśnia, arriving in the early evening.

21

Rzerzuśnia, November 1944– 16 January 1945

When we knocked and entered we were greeted warmly by Czesia. After a meal we unpacked and went to bed. Our new bed, which we shared, was much more comfortable. The straw mattress had clean linen sheets, two large pillows and an unexpected eiderdown. There was also warm water, soap and towels waiting for us. The next few weeks passed by very pleasantly. We managed to quickly sell the stockings we had brought with us. We moved to Rzerzuśnia for several reasons; most importantly, it was much closer to Warsaw, Czesia and her family were very friendly and the countryside, with rolling hills and streams, was more scenic than the flat countryside near Częstochowa.

We knew the Russians had stopped their offensive on the Praga side of the Vistula. We spoke with a man walking through the village selling second-hand flatware, who had just returned from Pruszków on the outskirts of Warsaw, where our transit camp had been. He confirmed that Warsaw had been completely destroyed by the Germans. Once the entire population was expelled following the Uprising, the Germans systematically looted the remaining buildings. The plunder, taken from Warsaw by truck, was sorted and shipped by train to Germany. Next the buildings were set on fire with flamethrowers, and any remaining walls of historically significant buildings were dynamited.

We decided to go to Konstancin and see what we could find out, and try to contact my aunt Barbara, who lived there. At the beginning of December we walked to Miechów railway station and managed to squeeze ourselves onto a train travelling north to Pruszków. We arrived in the late afternoon and found a place to spend the night. The next day we went to the largest flea market that I had ever seen. All the 'stuff' from the looting of Warsaw that had managed to slip past the Germans was displayed on the ground for sale. Talking with people we learned that there was no way we could reach Konstancin, which was about 15 miles to the east and too close to the front line on the Vistula. We were also warned not to linger anywhere because the Germans were arresting people whose ID cards were issued in Warsaw, as mother's was. We purchased some flatware and decided to return to Rzerzuśnia the next day. We were told that there was an express train to Kraków but it was very difficult to get on as there were not enough wagons for Poles.

The next day, an hour before our departure, we arrived at the station and purchased our tickets. When we reached the platform we found a multitude of people already waiting. After an hour, at the sound of a whistle, the train slowly pulled into the station. Through the windows of the first wagon we saw several German soldiers and officers. The following three coaches were empty. They were immediately surrounded by a mob of people pushing and shoving, manoeuvring to be closer to the doors. There was no way all those people could ever fit into the three wagons. The forward wagon was first class with the sign *Nur für Deutsche*. It was reserved for the Germans but also allowed the citizens of Axis countries: Hungary, Finland and Romania. After assessing the situation, mother said, 'We are going to be Lithuanians,' and we proceeded to enter the wagon. Walking through the corridor, we bypassed the first compartments of German soldiers and officers until we came to one with two civilians. They were sitting opposite each other at the window. There were two large suitcases on the luggage racks above them. We sat on the opposite side, next to the corridor. Everyone was silent, pretending not to see one another. Ten minutes later our train started to slowly move out, to the shouts of disappointed people who had not managed to squeeze in.

About thirty minutes into our journey, the morbid silence of our compartment was abruptly broken by our door being loudly pushed opened. There were two men: one in the dark navy blue of the German Railway Security Police, the other in the *feldgrau* of the German Army wearing a military police gorget. The two civilians sitting across from us were asked for their ID and they provided a pass and some other IDs. The railway policeman then turned to us. And mother gave him a pleasant smile and her Lithuanian ID, issued when Wilno was annexed in the autumn of 1939. The ID was in Lithuanian with a photograph and an appropriate amount of stamps and signatures. It was obvious that he had no idea what it was. He looked at her questioningly and she said in German, 'Lithuanian'. She looked at me and I babbled something in Lithuanian. The railway policeman looked to the military policeman, who shrugged his shoulders. It was clear he had no interest in civilians. When the corridor door closed we all looked at each other. The two men opposite us started talking to each other in Russian. Mother, a fluent Russian speaker, joined in. It turned out that they were anti-communist Russians co-operating with Germans involved in the Committee for the Liberation of the Peoples of Russia. Soon after, when they opened one of the large suitcases, it became obvious that they were smuggling *spritus*, 198 proof vodka. The suitcases were full of the stuff. They opened one bottle, took a swig each, and passed the bottle to my mother. She took a small sip and managed to swallow it. Years later, I learned how painfully that high-est proof alcohol burns your mouth and throat. The Russians continued to drink and fall asleep.

It was evening when our train finally arrived in Kraków. There was a long wait for our local train to Miechów so we entered a large, crowed, dimly lit waiting room. We squeezed in and sat down at the end of a wooden bench, resigning ourselves to a long wait. It was quite cold, the room was barely heated – just sufficient to prevent the pipes from freezing. After an hour we heard a commotion at the front door: voices shouting in German and the metallic stomping of military boots. Two Gestapo officers entered followed by SS guards, who positioned themselves at the entrances. An announce-ment was made in German that everyone's identity papers were to be checked. We were ordered to stay in place. Anyone who tried to escape would be shot. The waiting room was very large. In the middle of a short side there was a wide entrance guarded by SS. One of the long sides, along the platform, had windows; the other was blank with a few closed doors. The short back wall had no openings. The walking aisles were parallel to the long walls: there were three aisles between four rows of benches. They were full of people sitting facing the door. There were also people standing and sitting around the walls. As soon as the Germans appeared at the door the whole room quieted down. There was some occasional coughing and the sound of babies crying.

The two Gestapo men, each with a civilian interpreter and an SS guard, began checking papers. Each started at the beginning of one of the two out-side aisles and proceeded methodically. It became clear that a few Poles were allowed to remain, most were released and permitted to leave the room, and the rest were escorted out by armed guards. It was murmured that all Warsovians were being arrested. Mother's ID, a German *kannekarte*, was issued in Warsaw. We were sitting three-quarters of the way down the aisle and it took about an hour for the Gestapo to work their way to us. The one on our side checked two to three rows of benches on the opposite side of the aisle before turning around and doing the same on our side. Mother was sitting beside me on the end of the bench. She quietly said: 'Get ready, when I get up, get up with me, take me under my arm and on my signal we will walk out.' She moved her bag to the outside and held her *kannekarte* in her right hand. I slowly put on my backpack.

As the Gestapo officer finished checking the row before us he turned and moved to the other side of the aisle together with his interpreter and SS guard. When he began to question someone else, mother said 'Now', and we stood up and slowly started walking. She held her *kannekarte* in her hand while the second Gestapo officer, on the other side, looked at us questioningly. Mother smiled and waved her ID at him. He looked at the other officer who had his back turned, hesitated for a moment and then continued checking people on his side. We kept walking towards the door, where one of the SS guards opened it and we just walked out, leaving the station.

Nearby we saw the people who had been arrested held in two trucks guarded by the SS. It was late, well past curfew. Kraków was a large city and the seat of the occupational government. There were Germans everywhere; it was dangerous to be out during police curfew hours. The neighbourhood around the railway was mainly commercial. We hugged the walls of the buildings on the main street and turned into the next intersection. There was a small light visible in a service door. We knocked and were admitted into the small apartment of the building's watchmen. We explained our predicament. He and his wife made a place for us to sleep on the floor. We covered ourselves in a blanket and immediately fell asleep.

We were glad to be back in Rzerzuśnia. There was no longer any German presence nearby except for in Miechów. There were Polish partisan units operating in the surrounding countryside. One night, shortly after our return, we heard a commotion at the end of the village. It was another raid by the partisans, which had destroyed a clandestine still that had been making *bimber*, moonshine vodka. The Polish underground government wanted to eradicate clandestine stills since they consumed scarce food grains and contributed to alcoholism.

For quite some time now everyone had expected the war to end soon. We were all waiting for the Russian offensive to begin. Christmas of 1944 and New Year's Day 1945 arrived and were celebrated with the certainty that the war would soon be over.

One night in early January, I was awakened by the sounds of movement on the village road below us. I stepped outside and in the moonlight saw a long column of partisans, including mounted scouts and a wagon train, moving west. They were units of the NSZ, the military arm of an ultra-nationalist party that did not recognise the authority of the AK and fought against Germans, Russians and Polish communist partisans. They were withdrawing ahead of the Russian advance. Two days later a squad of front-line German soldiers arrived in our village. Four soldiers were billeted in Szczepka's house. Prior to our arrival the Germans had built a line of fortifications across the valley on the east side of our village. By now, we were sure this was the beginning of the end. On the evening of the second day the corporal in charge, a Silesian, told us in Polish: 'We will be gone early in the morning and the "Ruskis" will be here later in the day.'

I woke up at daybreak to the sounds of German soldiers getting up and putting on their gear. Once they left, an eerie silence descended on the village; there were none of the usual morning sounds, everyone stayed inside. I sat next to a window looking eastward. A solitary horseman appeared around noon. As he entered the village I recognised that he was a Russian soldier, with a PPSha (Russian machine pistol) hanging from his neck, mounted on a shaggy pony. Ten minutes later, more Russian troops walked through the village.

We were free of the Germans. It was 15 January 1945.

PART 5

RUSSIAN RETURN

Return to Warsaw, January 1945

The departure of the German troops and arrival of the Russians was very anticlimactic. There was celebration and joy knowing that the Germans were gone and the war would soon be over. For us, who had previously been under Russian occupation in Wilno, there was a feeling of unease. Nevertheless, we all were very happy that after five and a half years the worst was over, and the war would end.

We decided to go to Miechów and find a way to return to Warsaw. During our hour-and-a-half walk we did not see any signs of fighting until we came across a Russian plane that had been shot down. The two dead crewmen were still in their seats and as I walked on the wing I realised that one was definitely a woman while the other was burned beyond recognition (the plane was an IL-2 Sturmovik, the famous 'flying tank').

Miechów, a county town established in the twelfth century, was situated at the main highway and rail line between Warsaw and Kraków. It was full of Russian troops. I was impressed by the amount of equipment: tanks, the famous T-32, and American trucks and jeeps, which we saw there for the first time. The Russian soldiers all had good winter clothing: fur hats, padded jackets and trousers, overcoats or sheep skin coats and *valenki*, thick high felt boots with rubberised soles. To my surprise, the soldiers and officers all sported shoulder boards of the old Imperial Russian Army. There was a large volume of military traffic moving both ways through the town.

Mother started a conversation with some soldiers resting near a large Studebaker truck. She learned from them that the road to Warsaw was open. It was possible to get rides on army trucks especially if 'something' was offered. It became clear that a small bottle of vodka was the surest way to hitch a ride. The soldiers were eating dark Russian bread spread with copious amounts of *tushonka* (a canned stewed pork meat more than half fat). They offered us some. The can was painted in the same green as the American trucks and had English lettering. I asked one of the soldiers where it was made. 'In Russia', he replied proudly. 'Why then is the can labelled in English?' 'Because we send them to America.'

Next day we purchased a dozen quarter litre bottles of moonshine. The village still that had earlier been destroyed by partisans was back in production. That evening we packed our luggage. Mother's small bag held half of the vodka and my backpack the rest. At daybreak, after tearful goodbyes with the Szczepkas, we walked to Miechów. When we reached the road leading to Warsaw, mother held out one of the bottles and the first truck stopped for us immediately. The soldier sitting next to the driver moved over and we squeezed into the Studebaker. Soon we reached Jędrzejów, the next town. Now we were 30 miles closer to Warsaw. The driver had us get off at the outskirts and we walked into town. In the centre of Jędrzejów's market square we noticed a group of people surrounding a body lying on the ground. The body was in a German soldier's uniform and tied to a wooden board. Its legs were flat and the trousers were soaked in blood. The Russians had captured a RONA (Russian National Liberation Army) soldier, tied him to a board and slowly rolled a T-32 tank over his legs. We left, walked across town and were immediately picked up by another truck. The Russian drivers slammed on their brakes at the sight of vodka. Two days later we reached Raszyn on the outskirts of Warsaw. We found a place to sleep in exchange for one of our last bottles of vodka. Next day, probably 25 January, we walked for two hours and entered what had been Warsaw.

How do you describe a dead city? As we walked along the Kraków highway we had not seen all that much destruction in the Ochota suburbs. Once we passed through, the enormity of Warsaw's destruction was before us. There were no buildings left standing. Every district was a sea of rubble punctuated by skeletons of black burned-out fragments of standing walls. There were hardly any people to be seen except for on Jerusalem Avenue, which we walked along. The avenue was cleared for traffic, but all the side streets were canyons filled with rubble from collapsed buildings. There were footprints visible in this moonscape. Here and there were signs: *Uwaga Miny* (caution mines). Closer to the city centre, there were more people; civilians like us wandering through, soldiers of the LWP Polish People's Army and a sprinkling of Russian military. I spotted a couple of officers in NKVD uniforms. Mother and I looked at each other and she murmured, 'Back to 1939'.

At the Marszałkowska Street intersection we found a makeshift wooden kiosk with a fire burning in a metal barrel and selling hot food. We bought some and while eating and warming ourselves up, we listened to the nearby conversations. We overheard one man recall a parade he had watched a week earlier on 19 January, two days after Polish soldiers entered Warsaw. He said there had been a 'liberation' parade right on this avenue. The reviewing stand was nearby and visible from where we were. The entire Provisional Polish Communist Government was present together with Polish Marshal Rola-Zymirski and Russian Marshall Zhukov. 'Liberation', the man repeated sarcastically: 'What is liberation to one is just another occupation to the other.' There was a murmur of approval.

It was time to see our apartment. We walked further down the avenue and passed Krucza Street. It had only been four months earlier that I stood wearing my uniform and had watched the brief ceasefire that took place just farther down the street. I thought of Cpt. Skóra and Lt. Zadra, who were killed nearby on the last day of the Uprising. When we reached Nowy Swiat Street we turned left and walked the block and a half to our apartment. Since the entire area was destroyed it was impossible to get there from the street. Walking around the block we reached the back garden. The rear section of our building, including our apartment, was in ruins. As we looked at each other, mother shrugged her shoulders and said, 'Let's go see if we can find aunt Barbara.' Retracing our steps to Nowy Swiat, we began walking eastward.

Walking and catching a ride on a horse-drawn wagon, we finally reached Konstancin and found aunt Barbara's home. It was late and we had been on the road for five hours; we were hungry, tired and chilled to the bone. When we started our journey to aunt Barbara's we had no idea what we would find. We knew there had been no fighting in the area during the Uprising and the Russians' offensive. My aunt's family, on the other hand, had feared the worst for us in Warsaw.

After some hot tea and food I went to sleep in the kids' room as my mother and aunt continued to talk in the kitchen. I woke up in the morning with 5-year-old Maciej climbing all over me and his younger sister, 3-year-old Małgorzata, looking at me with her large child's eyes. We stayed with them for a few days. They had had no news of Barbara's brother Jerzy Emir-Hassan, my godfather, since his disappearance during the 1939 campaign.

Three days later, we left early in the morning and headed west. At the intersection with the Warsaw–Kraków highway we found three parked trucks with Polish soldiers. There was an unusual number of women present. It was the LWP Theatre, travelling to Kraków to perform there. When they learned that we were in Warsaw during the Uprising, and were trying to get back to Miechów, we were immediately invited to join them. The people in the truck were mostly actors, men and women, wearing Polish Army uniforms, identical to the pre-war uniform with one exception: the eagle on their headgear insignia did not have a crown and was of a different design. No one liked it and derisively called it a *wrona* (crow). During the long ride we learned more of what had happened since the Uprising. A Provisional Polish Communist Government had been formed in July 1944 and controlled the civil administration. The army had a large number of Russian officers and political officers and the NKVD was everywhere. It was obvious that none of these people were communists or sympathisers. During one of the stops the director of the theatre group came out of the cab and joined us. He invited us to see their performance in Kraków, which was to be given few days later. We reached Miechów by early evening and on the way back to Rzerzuśnia we learned that train connections had been re-established with Kraków. An hour later we were warmly greeted by the Szczepkas, who wanted to know all about our trip.

Miechów and the End of the Second World War, February–9 May 1945

The following Sunday we were on our way to Kraków and the theatre. In the evening we picked up our tickets and were directed to the second floor. We followed the usher down the right-hand corridor to the last door. When he opened the door we found ourselves in the presidential box. It was the first time since the war started that I had been to the theatre (during the war all theatres were closed). I remembered the last time we had sat in the same box, when as children we had watched a performance of *Puss in Boots* in Wilno. A few more people arrived before the performance started. It seemed obvious they were local dignitaries from the new communist administration and they looked surprised to see us there. A play by Wyspiański had premiered in 1901 in this same theatre. Written during the time of lost independence, it had a lot of national symbolism. The play was enthusiastically received by the audience as it was the first play performed in Polish to a Polish audience since the beginning of the German occupation.

On our arrival from Kraków we heard that the secondary school in Miechów, which had been closed during the occupation, had just reopened. It had been closed throughout the occupation. We went to register and after answering a few questions and completing a short exam, I was admitted to the second year of *gimnazium*. I joined my classmates and mother returned to Rzerzuśnia. When school ended around 4 p.m., I walked home. The next morning I got up at 6 a.m. to be in school before 8 a.m. For the following two months, I repeated my routine six days each week. When the weather was good I was able to get to school in just over an hour by taking short cuts through the fields. When the weather was poor, as when snow and rain turned the roadway to mud, it would take two hours.

In order for us to cover the required curriculum in the short time left, our school year was extended through July; two extra classes were added to the school day and Saturday was increased to a full day. During the occupation our school building had been used by the German Army. Once the Russians captured Miechów it became their field hospital. On my first day, one of the boys took me behind a building and showed me an open pit full of amputated legs and arms. The building still stank of formaldehyde.

I joined the school's Boy Scout troop and was named second in command. The local Underground Boy Scouts had been dissolved a few weeks earlier. Their members, including the troop commander, formed the nucleus of our new troop.

Towards the end of March I returned home to find father sitting and talking with mother. He had aged in the two years since I had seen him last, his face was gaunt and there was more grey hair at his temples. He had a short beard and a moustache that was also grey. He looked at me for a long time then hugged me. Mother was silently standing by. Father had travelled from Warsaw, where he found out our whereabouts and learned of Andrzej's death. He stayed with us two days. We learned that he had left Wilno weeks ago in one of the first repatriation trains of Poles. Being an expert in rail transportation, he had been assigned to a group that would eventually take over the German railways in Pomerania. The group was waiting for the OK from the Russian military as there was still heavy fighting in that area. After he left, mother told me that he wanted to get back together but she had said no.

A week later, when I returned home, I found a man in quiet conversation with mother. As I came closer the intense scrutiny of the man turned into a broad smile. Mother said, 'This is uncle Jurek.' It was my godfather, a captain in the Polish Army who had last been seen when the war broke out in 1939. In the evening, once the Szczepkas had left the kitchen, he began to talk quietly. He had been the CO of an infantry company during the September 1939 campaign and was wounded later that month. He avoided being taken prisoner. He had been arrested by Russians in November 1939, trying to cross into Hungary. After a stint in an NKVD prison he was sent to a Siberian gulag. Following Germany's invasion of Russia, Stalin released many of the Poles so they could join the Polish Army and uncle Jurek became commander of an officer's school. He had recently parachuted into Poland following some special training. While visiting his sister Barbara, she had given him our address. We talked until late and made arrangements to get together for Easter at aunt

Barbara's. Next morning, Jurek gave mother $300, a very significant amount of money at that time. I walked with him to Miechów, where he took a train for Kraków. We parted saying, 'See you at Easter.' Shortly after, during the Easter holiday, when we arrived at aunt Barbara's uncle Jurek was not there. When we left a few days later we still had no news from him. We were afraid that he had been arrested again by the NKVD.

During our stay with aunt Barbara we made our way into Warsaw. Some life was coming back into the city. All the major streets had been cleared of rubble and were again passable. Army engineers had replaced the bridges with two temporary wooden structures and a pontoon bridge. There was traffic on the streets, military trucks and horse-drawn wagons. Shops had re-opened in some of the ruined buildings. There were people living in heavily damaged buildings. We again visited our apartment building. Nothing had changed – it was still a ruin with part of the front wall standing and gaping holes where the windows had been.

Soon after returning home we received a letter from father, which included a document identifying me as the son of an employee of the Polish State Railways. On that basis, I was eligible for room and board at the local *bursa*, a government boarding house for students in an old police station located close to the school. There were about thirty boys living there, eight or ten to a room, sleeping on two-level bunks with wooden slats and straw mattresses. The food was bad; the school schedule, because of the shortened school year, was very demanding. Nevertheless, we were in good spirits and played all kinds of juvenile pranks on each other. The two most popular were partially cutting bunk boards so that beds collapsed, and placing a washbasin full of water in the straw of a mattress so when the target snuck in and carefully sat down he was in for a surprise. After a while a truce was declared.

Once the Russians had occupied Poland a new Polish communist administration was established. Nevertheless, Russian troops, now supplemented by special NKVD units, had been stationed in the area. The attitude of the Polish population towards the Russian soldiers, which had been friendly or luke-warm, was now hostile. The Russians were confiscating food and livestock, and committing rapes and robberies. There were armed encounters between Russian soldiers and Polish partisans, who were still active in the area. NKVD troops were brought in for the specific purpose of destroying what remained of the Polish Underground. According to findings made following the fall of Communism, in the time period starting with the Russian Army crossing Poland's pre-war frontier, the NKVD arrested more than 60,000 Polish Underground soldiers and sent 50,000 to Siberia. Occasionally during the night gunfire could be heard between the *Milicja*, Polish State Police and rampaging Russian soldiers. One night we heard an explosion from the direction of the jail. The next morning we learned that Polish partisans had attacked the prison during the night and liberated their comrades.

Towards the end of April we all knew that the war would be over in a matter of days. On 2 May, the Russians were shooting into the air. Berlin had fallen to the Russian Army. On 9 May, all hell broke loose. Russians were firing every weapon they had, from pistols to AA guns – Germany had capitulated. Actually, Germany capitulated to the Western Allies on 7 May; Stalin insisted that the capitulation be repeated, in Berlin in the headquarters of the Marshall Zhukov; it was signed shortly before midnight of the 8th Berlin time, when it was already the 9th in Moscow. To this day, the end of the Second World War is celebrated as VE Day on the 8th in the West and as the end of the Great Patriotic War on the 9th in Russia.

24

Second Visit to Warsaw, 9 May–August 1945

At the end of the Second World War, the Polish-German border had been moved west to the Oder–Neisse line. We decided to take a look at Silesia with the idea of settling there. There is no way that we could have returned to Warsaw. Not only was there nothing for us to return to, but at that time a special permit was required to live there and was very difficult to obtain.

We travelled by trains, as overcrowded now as they had been during the occupation. After changing in Kraków we arrived in Katowice. It was less than 20 miles to Gleiwitz, previously a German town and now renamed Gliwice. Once we were over the old Polish-German border the aftermath of Russian 'liberation' was plainly visible: mostly empty buildings, broken windows and dwellings completely ransacked. Apartments with broken furniture and floors covered in white down from emptied pillows, duvets and featherbeds. Russian soldiers greatly prized tightly woven pillowcases and sent them home to their families. A number of large pillows on a peasant's bed was a sign of prosperity in Russia.

After spending a couple of days in Gliwice and nearby areas we decided against staying. This industrial area of steel works and coalmines was depressing. We returned to Rzezuśnia. In the meantime, father reached Pomerania. His group was assigned to take over administration of the provincial railway. In his letters, he had strongly suggested that we consider moving to Szczecin. We decided that when the school year ended in July, we would first go to Warsaw and then Szczecin.

The accelerated school year ended in the last week of July. For the first time I had respectable results: rather than all Cs, I got mostly Bs. We said our goodbyes to the Szczepkas and their family, who had so very warmly welcomed us before.

We arrived in Warsaw and stayed with aunt Barbara. We learned that uncle Jurek and his wife had been arrested in March by the NKVD with several other high-ranking AK officers, and turned over to the Department of Security (*Urząd Bezpieczeństwa*, UB). A few weeks later he was sentenced to ten years and sent to Wronki, where political prisoners were incarcerated.

Two days later we ventured into the city. There were marked differences from six months before. In summer it looked less grim and desolate than in the dark days of winter. Most of the major streets were clear and traffic was flowing. There were no trams or buses, but rudimentary public transit was provided by trucks with wooden plank benches. Shops and restaurants were open. There were signs of people living in partially destroyed buildings, where some parts had been made habitable. Demolition and clearing was going on. The partially standing walls of burned-out buildings had been pulled down. Ropes had been attached to the top of the freestanding walls and teams of men were rhythmically pulling on them. The high walls oscillated as much as 6–8ft before collapsing in a cloud of red and grey dust.

Again we walked on our street. This time Nowy Swiat was completely clear. There was a lot of traffic because this street connected to the temporary bridges built over the Vistula. We passed the ruins of our old apartment building and continued towards the old town. A year ago, I had walked from the old town in the sewers below. When we passed the university, on our right was Karowa Street leading down to the new high wooden bridge built by Russian military engineers in 1945. We entered the old town. The air was heavy with the stench of decomposing bodies. The exhumation of temporary graves had started a few months before, when the thawed-out ground made digging possible.

For a long time, holding handkerchiefs to our noses, we watched bodies being dug out of graves, placed on stretchers and carried away for identification. After identification, if identification was possible, they were reburied in temporary communal graves in Krasiński Gardens. In the office of the Polish Red Cross we listed Andrzej's name. Unknown to us, his body had already been found, exhumed and reburied about three months before. Due to the sheer number of names, the paperwork was behind.

Over the next few days I spent most of my time in Warsaw. I went back to the old town and walked all over the places where we had fought a year before. In the garden of Radziwiłł Palace I found Abczyc's grave. The cross was leaning all the way down to the ground. I straightened it and carved out his code name, rank and date with a penknife. I saluted and left the old town.

In the centre of the city I came across some of the returning POWs. They were easy to spot by their English or American uniforms with Polish insignias. I was told of a new organisation that had formed for combatants. It was approved by the communist government after AK veterans' request for a separate organisation was denied. Its Polish acronym, 'ZUWZoWiN', stood for the pompous name of 'Association of Participants in the Armed Fight for Independence and Democracy'. In the Association's offices I found out that Nałęcz, Pobóg and Holski were already in Warsaw.

The first one I got in touch with was Holski. When he got the word he came immediately. He was wearing the uniform of a lieutenant colonel of the Polish People's Army. After capitulation he had escaped from the rail transport and rejoined the Underground. When the Russians came he joined the LWP. He knew that Nałęcz and Pobóg had returned. The next day we all had a reunion. Nałęcz and Pobóg had returned from an *oflag* that was liberated by the British in May, a few days before the war had ended. A couple of days after the war ended they found an abandoned Germany military car and started driving to Warsaw. Once they crossed into the Russian Zone they ran into trouble. They were arrested and held in detention. Several Polish ex-POW officers were detained there by the NKVD. They managed to bribe some Russian soldiers with American cigarettes and were smuggled out. Once they reached the part of Germany under Polish administration they made their way to Warsaw.

One day, Holski told me that he wanted to introduce me to somebody. When I met him next he was in the company of an American colonel to whom I was introduced. He was the military attaché in the just reopened American embassy (I believe his name was Clark). After some general conversation, translated by his Polish-speaking sergeant driver, we got into his car, a military green Hudson with American flag pennants on the fenders. I sat next to the driver and we drove all over Warsaw. The other two in the back seat were engaged in a quiet, long conversation in German.

I also met with the Mirowski brothers; they had made their way from the same POW camp. Towards the end of August, before I left for Szczecin, Nałęcz told me that I should join the Association. By that time the communist government had announced an amnesty and all members of the AK were asked to reveal themselves. Nałęcz verified my participation in the Uprising and I was issued a membership ID with my rank of corporal and the award of the Cross of Valour. I said goodbye to Nałęcz. He was leaving for the harbour town of Gdynia. He was promoted to major and appointed inspector general of the newly formed Harbour Guards, formed to protect the transports of UNRRA arriving by ship in Poland.

25

Szczecin, August 1945–July 1946

A fter two weeks in Warsaw it was time to continue on to Szczecin. The school year would be starting soon. While at the Warsaw train station we requested that father be notified of our departure from Warsaw and our scheduled arrival time at Szczecin. After an overnight journey in a crowded compartment, our train stopped in front of the bridge over the River Oder, a short distance before the city. The conductor announced that the bridge was not safe and that we needed to cross over on foot. All the bridges in this area had been destroyed by the retreating Germans. This bridge was a high wooden structure rebuilt by Russian Army engineers on top of the destroyed metal bridge. It was wide enough for two lanes of traffic. A single rail track ran through the middle. The bridge swayed noticeably as vehicular traffic passed by. Once everyone was across, the bridge was closed to vehicular traffic. Our train started to cross at a snail's speed while the bridge moved visibly. Once it had crossed we re-embarked and continued on to the recently reopened Szczecin station. Father was waiting with an official car and driver.

We drove to the apartment, which he had prepared for us. There was some food and we all had a meal together. After that we all talked. Father had heard from the Polish Red Cross that Andrzej's body had been buried temporarily in Krasiński Gardens. Towards evening, as our conversation wound down, he again repeated his desire to return to the family. Mother again declined.

Szczecin at the mouth of the River Oder had 270,000 inhabitants before the war. It was a harbour town with shipbuilding and other industries. It was carpet-bombed by Allied bombers in 1943 and August of 1944. The last raid created a 'firestorm' similar to those in Hamburg and Dresden. Thousands of people had died and 60 per cent of the city was destroyed. The old town next to the river ceased to exist. Eighty per cent of all harbour installations and 90 per cent of industrial buildings were destroyed. The retreating German Army destroyed over fifty bridges. As the Russian Army entered Szczecin on 24 April, only 6,000 Germans remained, most of the German population had already fled. Two weeks later, when the war ended, they started to return. The vanguard of the Polish administration arrived two days later, but, under pressure from both the American and British governments, who did not yet recognise Poland's new western borders, was withdrawn in mid-May. The Polish administration returned in early June. The Polish State Railway for Pomerania headquarters, and father with it, moved in July and began to transition from the German railway workers. There were only 1,000 Poles living there at that time. In July, the Polish People's Army took control over most of the city. The Russians, however, retained large parts of the city, including the harbour, shipyards and industrial areas.

The post-war agreement concluded in Potsdam on August 1945 by the Big Three, Stalin, Truman and Churchill, established the provisional western border of Poland on the Oder–Neisse line, which included Szczecin. The Potsdam Agreement provided for the expulsion of the German population from Poland, including from the newly acquired German lands, Czechoslovakia and Hungary.

From the day the Russian Army arrived, they raped much of the female population, sometimes without distinguishing between Germans or Poles. To Russians soldiers, rape was not a crime, but an act of revenge for German crimes committed in Russia. When we arrived in Szczecin the city was called The Wild West. Bands of AWOL Russian soldiers roamed around, German soldiers, mostly SS and RONA, were hiding from the Russian authorities and Polish criminals were busy looting and raping. During the daytime, the Polish military together with *Milicja* patrols managed to maintain control. Night-time was dangerous and filled with the sounds of shots being fired, feet running, calls for help and the glow of fires. The Russians brought three battalions of NKVD troops, who exterminated the gangs.

After searching for a few days, mother and I found a large abandoned second-floor apartment at 11 Piastów Avenue. It was perfect for mother. The apartment fronted onto a wide avenue and was within a block or two of other streets that were becoming desirable commercial streets. Damage was slight; there were feathers on the bedroom floors, some smashed furniture, broken china on the kitchen floor and a few 'calling cards' left on the floor by defecating Russian soldiers. Most of the window glass was intact. On the door we nailed a red and white postcard-sized cardboard notice showing a Polish eagle and the wording *Zajęte przez Polaka* (Occupied by a Pole). Mother registered our new home with the Polish City Administration and that completed the ownership process.

I started the third year of *gimnazium* on 2 September 1945. Only two Polish schools had opened; both were in the same building. The elementary school had about 250 children, the secondary school 250 co-ed students.

I located the recently opened Boy Scout headquarters. There I met Roman Jurgens, whose family had returned from Germany, where they had worked as forced labourers. Roman was already appointed to lead the first troop to be formed in the combined schools. I was appointed second in command. In a short time we organised a troop of forty Boy Scouts. At the same time, a group of girl guides was also formed.

Mother's salon was doing quite well. Our apartment was located in an upper-class residential area reminiscent of Paris. There were three consecutive multi-street intersections in the pattern of Haussmann's Paris. The first, half a block away, was referred to as Plac Sztywnych (Square of the Stiff Ones). The name mocked the Russian cemetery recently established in the garden section of the square. Only officers were buried there. All their graves were marked by wooden obelisks topped by red stars. Once, hearing martial music, I went there and saw a Russian funeral cortège preceded by a military band and followed by an honour guard. Once the coffin was lowered into the ground, and speeches were made, the command 'Fire' was given. A ragged volley sounded, followed by white torn newspaper confetti floating down over the honour guard. The salute was repeated twice more to increasing laughter and derision from the spectators. The Russians clearly had no blank ammunition and removed bullets from their cartridges, sealing the casings with wadding made from pieces of newspaper.

The period 1945–46 was a time of mass migration in Central Europe. When we arrived, in August, there had been 70,000 Germans and 12,000 Poles in Szczecin. Germans from all parts of Pomerania were directed to the border railway station of Szczecin-Gumience. The Allies approved the plan for the German expulsion from Polish territories. The newly formed 'Combined Repatriation Executive' was in charge. Under this arrangement two railway routes were opened to the British Zone of Occupation. A British military mission arrived. The transports were protected by Polish frontier guard troops to prevent the Russian soldiers' excesses. Father was in charge of rail transportation. He told me that more than a quarter of a million Germans left then.

Meanwhile, an influx of new Polish population arrived from several directions. First were the Poles from central Poland trying to find a new place to live. Most had lost all they had during the war. They were the largest group, over 50 per cent. Second were the Poles repatriated from eastern Poland, which had been given to Russia. Those arriving in Szczecin were predominantly from Wilno and north-eastern Poland; they represented a third of the new arrivals. Both groups came by train. The last group were Poles returning from Germany: forced labourers and prisoners of war. They arrived in British Army trucks. By the middle of November hundreds of thousands of repatriated Poles had arrived. In the spring of 1946 the British Army continued to bring Polish POWs from camps in Lübeck. Once a week, a convoy of twenty to thirty British Army trucks arrived. I was asked to be a guide and interpreter for the English captain in charge. He and I communicated in French. Once a week, for the following two months, I left school mid-morning and spent the rest of the day riding in his jeep. The convoy overnighted and returned empty the next day. After several trips the British captain asked me about the shootings and fires during the night. I explained the problems created by the Russian soldiers. I said that the situation had improved in the past few months, but I wasn't sure that he believed me. A few weeks later, with the arrival of a new convoy, a *Milicja* officer arrived at the *Państwowy Urząd Repatriacyjny* PUR office (State Office of Repatriation) and wanted the British captain to see what they had discovered that morning. I translated and the captain said, 'Let's go.' The police officer jumped into the jeep and directed us to the edge of a small park nearby. We stopped the jeep and walked over to where a few *Milicja* men were standing. On the ground we saw the bodies of two partially naked women, one young and pretty, the other in her fifties. Both had obviously been raped. The young one's throat had been cut and the other had been shot repeatedly. The captain did not say anything but was visibly shaken.

Nałęcz arrived in Szczecin some time in the autumn. As Inspector General of the Harbour Guards, he came to review the newly formed unit in Szczecin. At that time the Russians allowed Poles access to and control of the facilities on the west bank of the River Oder only. The main harbour and shipyards on the east side were held by the Russians. We spent the next couple of days together with a young lieutenant who commanded the Szczecin unit. We rode in the official car, a German VW *kuebelwagon*, and managed to access an area in Politz, where synthetic gasoline had been manufactured. This area had been given to Poland by the Potsdam Agreement, but it remained under Russian control for a year. The latter had dismantled all the machinery and removed all furniture and fixtures, even the railway rails. All this was trucked to Szczecin, loaded onto river barges and towed across the Baltic to Russia. The 10 miles between the plant and the harbour were littered with pieces of machinery.

The young lieutenant had been an AK partisan in Wilno. He was lucky to have avoided the fate of the Wilno AK brigade. In July 1944, this brigade helped the Russians liberate the city and was told by the Russians that it would be rearmed and would join the LWP. The brigade was surrounded by NKVD troops with tanks, and 6,000 soldiers were arrested and sent to Siberia. Most of the officers were executed but some managed to escape. The lieutenant and most of his men were from that group of escapees.

The political climate in Poland was very tense. The Allies recognised the Polish Provisional Communist Government and withdrew its recognition of the legitimate Polish government in London. We all felt betrayed. At the same time, we could not believe that the Allies would allow half of Europe to be taken over by Russia. Surely there would soon be another war between the Western Allies and the Russians.

The Allies recognised the Provisional Government on the condition that free elections would be held within a year. Stanisław Mikołajczyk, Prime Minister of the Polish Government in London, under pressure from Churchill, returned to Poland in July 1945. As the leader of the Peasant Party, the largest party in Poland, he thought he would win the elections. The underground civil government that had functioned during the occupation dissolved itself in the summer of 1945. The underground armed resistance continued against the NKVD and Polish communist forces. The government declared an amnesty in August 1945 and a large number of AK soldiers revealed themselves. Nevertheless, the armed resistance continued for the next two years.

Against this background of political turmoil, in April of 1946, the government organised a great manifestation in Szczecin. It was heralded as *Trzymamy Straż nad Odrą* (Keeping Watch over the River Oder). It brought an unprecedented number of participants, estimated at more than 23,000, from all over Poland. This was at a time when Szczecin's total population was slightly over 70,000 Germans, and only 30,000 Poles. The largest single group was the scouts, about 12,000 in their khaki uniforms for boys and grey for Girl Guides. There were also large contingents from the communist party *Zwiazek Walki Mlodych* or ZWM (Union of Youth Fighters) wearing white shirts with red kerchiefs modelled on the Russian *komsomol*. Equally large were the 'Wici', a Peasant Party youth group. There were other groups representing veterans, concentration camp inmates and trade organisations.

All these groups had arrived by special trains, trucks and buses. At that time there were only about 300 students in our secondary school. In our scout units there were less than thirty older boys and girls, who were put in charge of liaising with 12,000 incoming scouts. From then on, we were busy all the time. We met the rail transports and directed them to their places of bivouac. They camped in schools and parks, also next to buildings with bath and toilet facilities. The scouts all had camping equipment and the army provided field kitchens. The Organising Committees assigned us two trucks with drivers for food delivery. I was in charge of one. There were still problems with robberies at night, especially by Russian soldiers. The *Milicja* gave us weapons to protect ourselves and the Girl Scout camps. Fifteen of us were armed with First World War Austrian Mannlicher carbines. There was not much we could have done against the Russians and their PPSh machine pistols with their seventy-one bullet drum magazines. Luckily, we never had to find out.

Emotions were very high. Even before the ceremony started, there were clashes between the scouts and the communist ZWM. The opening ceremonies were officiated by Communist President Bolesław Bierut, his Prime Minister Osóbka-Morawski and Marshall Rola-Zymirski. Also present was the recently arrived Stanisław Mikołajczyk of the Peasant Party. President Bierut's speech was drowned out by shouts of 'Mikołajczyk, Mikołajczyk', which grew in intensity. They were started by the Wici youth of his Peasant Party, and immediately taken up by the scouts. The visibly angry president left.

The next day, the ceremonies commenced with a field mass and continued with a parade down the Avenue of the Polish Army. The political bosses were watching from the reviewing stand. Army units led the parade, followed by the Communist Party organisation and ZWM, their youth organisation. The scouts received orders that morning informing them that in punishment for yesterday's excesses, they would not be permitted to march. This order was ignored and about 12,000 scouts converged on the parade route, in perfect marching formation. The *Milicja*, army tanks and communist youth stopped them at several places. We organising scouts diverted the columns. They managed to join the tail of the parade in large compact units. I made my way forward (we local scouts did not march in the parade) opposite the reviewing stand. As soon as the first scout units arrived, the president and his whole communist entourage left the reviewing stand. Only Mikołajczyk stood reviewing the scouts as they marched to ever-growing chants of 'Mikołajczyk … Mikołajczyk …' That evening, there were several fights between the Boy Scouts and ZWM members.

Over the next few days special trains transported scouts home. On one of the trains, a scout hanging too far out of the window was killed when his head hit a pylon. Two days later, in an empty freight car, I and three other scouts escorted his coffin to Warsaw.

When I returned, Roman and I concentrated on completing plans for our camping trip scheduled for July. The campsite was on the shore of the Baltic Sea on the island of Wolin, a shore island located at the end of the River Oder between the Baltic Sea to the north and Szczecin Lagoon to the south, formed by two branches of the River Oder. The north coast was all wooded with pine and beech forest. It had wide pristine beaches with sand dunes. At that time the island was almost devoid of people. The Germans had left and Poles were just trickling in. The only town was Międzyzdroje, a typical resort. It had a small population as well as a few shops. Our camp was close to the *Leśniczówka Grodno*, the forester's house. The current Polish forester in residence was from an area near Grodno in eastern Poland, hence the name. The trucks dropped us off at his house, where the road ended. The forester led us to a clearing about half a mile away, close to the beach. That was our campsite. He warned us to be careful with fire as the forest was very dry.

There was a lot of game in the woods, mostly deer and wild boar. The forester, with whom I became friendly as we were from the same part of Poland, told me that there was an overabundance of game. During the last five years no one had been hunting. He had become concerned lately that the Russian soldiers stationed all over this area were 'hunting' using machine pistols and unnecessarily wiping out game just for fun. He invited me to return in the autumn and hunt with him; he promised to have a hunting rifle ready for me. July passed quickly as we engaged in typical Boy Scout activities.

At the beginning of our third week, a forest fire broke out nearby. There was no one in the area except for our troop and army units who were already working to contain the fire. We spent the next three days clearing and digging fire brake lanes. It was hard working in the glaring sun with the smoke and heat of the fire, but we managed to contain the fire.

I left a few days early, before the camping trip was over, at the end of July. Before I had left for the camp, Nałęcz told me I needed to be in Warsaw before 1 August. There was going to be a commemoration of the second anniversary of the Uprising that I should attend. I put on my pack, walked to town and took the 'bus', an army truck with wooden benches, back to Szczecin.

When I arrived mother was sitting alone in the living room. She looked at me and said, 'Please sit down. I need to talk to you,' indicating the chair opposite her. She looked very sad and sombre. She looked at me and said, 'I have to ask you something.' Looking down, she proceeded to tell me in a dead, toneless voice: 'A few days ago I was talking with one of my clients. It turned out that she was from Warsaw and was there during the Uprising. Commenting on the terrible human loss, she gave an example, an incident she had witnessed during the end of fighting in the old town.' She paused, looked at me and resumed: 'While in the Arsenal building she saw a young boy lying on the ground in the entrance gateway. He was about 15 or 16, handsome with wavy dark hair. Two nurses were bandaging his legs. As he lay on the ground he quietly repeated: "I will never be able to ski again … I will never be able to ski again."' Mother paused, looked up at me and asked: Was that Andrzej? I looked straight at her. Our eyes locked and I quietly said: 'Yes'.

As she slowly got up I did too. She came to me and hugged me close for a long time. Then, without a word, turned around, went to her bedroom and closed the door behind her. Once again, I felt relief. Relief that even though she learned that his death had not been a quick one, she had not discovered that he lingered on for another three days, in an overcrowded hospital, without painkillers.

26

Third Visit to Warsaw, 31 July– 11 November 1946

The following day I asked mother if she would come to Warsaw with me. She hesitated: 'No ... I will go in a few days.' It was obvious that she did not want to be there for the anniversary of the Uprising. The night train from Szczecin arrived in Warsaw the morning of 31 July. I met up with Nałęcz, Pobóg and Holski. Nałęcz told me that I would be one of several participants to be decorated during the next day's ceremonies. Witold was in Warsaw, I met up with him and his wife Maryla, and he filled me in on what happened two years before, when he, Edward and Czajka crossed the Vistula to establish contact with the LWP.

On 1 August, Nałęcz and I arrived at the Theatre Roma. I was shown to a special section where there were thirty to forty men and women already seated. I sat close to the stage, next to Pobóg and Witold. The usual military trappings were on stage: honour guard with colours and an orchestra. Members of the Provisional Communist Government and military brass took their places. Following the national anthem and the customary long-winded bombastic speeches, an announcement was made: 'The meeting of the Presidium of the Provisional Government, acting on the petition of the governing body of the ZUWZoNiD, has resolved on 30 July to decorate the following citizens of Warsaw province ...'

As names were called, we stepped forward, one by one, and had our decorations pinned on us. Our names were called alphabetically in the ranking order of our decoration. The first called were the eleven recipients of the Cross of Grunwald III class, followed by ten recipients of the Virtuti Militari V class, and the thirty-five recipients of the Cross of Valour. About one-third of the decorations were awarded posthumously. I was the third, and the youngest, to be decorated with the Cross of Grunwald. Before the capitulation, I had heard rumours that Nałęcz had recommended me for the Virtuti Militari award in recognition of re-establishing contact with our headquarters while we were cut off in the telephone exchange building.

The Order Virtuti Militari is Poland's highest and oldest military decoration awarded for 'heroism and courage in the face of the enemy in time of war'. Established by the last King of Poland during the War with Russia in 1792, it was awarded during the Napoleonic Wars and in the 1831 Uprising against Russia, reinstated in 1918, when Poland became independent and awarded during the Polish-Bolshevik War. During the Second World War, the Polish government in exile and the LWP formed in Russia continued to award the Virtuti Militari. Virtually all the recipients of this order, from 1792 to the Polish-Bolshevik War, had been decorated for warfare against the Russians. Needless to say, the communist underground did not like that and in 1943 decided to create its own military decoration. The Provisional Government confirmed the Cross of Grunwald as a state military decoration. The order was divided into three classes, so even though it was of a lower rank than the Order Virtuti Militari, its third class ranked higher than the fifth class of the Virtuti Militari.

I was happy and felt honoured to be decorated but, at the same time, I was disappointed and disenchanted because it was considered a communist decoration.

As I left the building I took off my decoration and put it in my breast pocket. After the ceremony, Nałęcz said that he did not know what had happened. He had nominated me for the Virtuti Militari and instead I was awarded the Cross of Grunwald. Seven of the eleven recipients of the Cross of Grunwald had fought in the ranks of the AK during the Uprising. To this day, no one knows why some nominees were awarded this order while others got the Virtuti Militari though, apparently, they were all nominated for the Virtuti Militari.

Pobóg invited me to visit him at his new home. As a 'military settler' he was granted a small abandoned farm near Kartuzy, close to Gdynia. I accepted, and we agreed that I would be there in a week. A few days later I was on my way to Gdańsk to visit Pobóg and Nałęcz. I needed to take the midnight express from Szczecin to Warsaw. Most trains were still overcrowded at that time. All express trains included one special car set aside for officials but getting a seat in that car required a pass. I obtained the necessary pass from father and, having arrived at the station an hour early, I entered the official passenger car. I sat down in an empty place in the only first-class compartment in the middle of the wagon. The rest of the wagon, before and after this compartment, was third class with wooden benches. I had been sitting by the window when, ten minutes before departure, an army lieutenant entered our full compartment and announced in a loud voice: 'Everybody out! This compartment is reserved for the colonel!' The compartment emptied as people stood up, grabbed their luggage and left. I took the Cross of Grunwald out of my pocket and pinned it on my Boy Scout uniform. When everyone left, the lieutenant looked at me and shouted: 'You, shithead, did I not tell you to get the hell out of here?'

Getting up, I slowly lowered my hands, and in a normal voice asked, 'Who is the citizen lieutenant calling a shithead?' (The communist government had tried unsuccessfully to change the customs of address. In place of *Pan*, meaning Mr or Sir, the official form was *obywatel* (citizen), as during the French Revolution. The Russian communist form of *towarzysz* (comrade) was used only between Communist Party members). He looked at my Cross, automatically came to attention and saluted. I calmly returned his salute. He apologised and explained that this compartment had been reserved for the colonel. After hearing him, and again addressing him as citizen lieutenant, I replied: 'We now live in a free, democratic Poland where everyone is equal. I have the necessary pass to be in this car and I have the same right as the colonel to be in this compartment. Anyway, there's enough room here for all of us.' At that moment the colonel entered the compartment, looked around and seeing my Cross, said, in Russian:

Malchyk wy gieroy? (Little boy, you are a brave one?)
Da, gieroy. (Yes, brave.)
Bili Germanca? (Were you fighting Germans?)
Bili Germanca. (I was fighting Germans.)
Harasho ostansia. (Ok. Stay there.)

He gestured to where I was standing. Turning to the lieutenant, and an orderly who had followed him in, he pointed to the two small single seats on the other side of the compartment. The colonel sat down on the long upholstered bench opposite me, removed his belt, unbuttoned his tunic, lay down and covered himself with his overcoat. He looked at me, sitting opposite him in my short trousers and called out to the lieutenant to cover me with his overcoat. The lieutenant looked unhappy but complied. I slept well that night, all warm and cosy covered by the lieutenant's military overcoat.

As our train arrived in Warsaw the following morning the colonel buttoned up his Polish uniform and put on his Polish military hat (which had the pre-war eagle with a crown). After they left, I removed the Cross of Grunwald and returned it to my pocket.

I changed trains in Warsaw and continued on to Gdańsk. The Harbour Guards headquarters were near Wrzeszcz station, where I got off the train and headed to Nałęcz's office. We spent the rest of the day together and after overnighting at his place we drove the 20 miles west to Pobóg's farm near Kartuzy.

Having heard our car, Pobóg was waiting outside when we arrived. Czajka was standing next to him although I didn't recognise him immediately; he looked older, gaunt and tired. He had just returned to Poland after being released from a Siberian gulag. He found Pobóg's address at the Association. Czajka was reluctant to talk about his time in Russia but he did confirm what I already knew from Witold of what happened to them. They crossed the Vistula; Edward was killed by a German police dog, while he and Witold decided to cross the front line separately. After making contact with some Russian soldiers he had been turned over to their military intelligence, accused of being a spy and deported to the gulag. Two years later he was released unexpectedly and without any explanation repatriated to Poland.

After a week I returned to Wrzeszcz and stayed with Nałęcz. Two days later we left in his car for Szczecin. Along the way he inspected the harbour at Koszalin. When we arrived in Szczecin, we paid a visit to mother. He made some excuse and did not accept her invitation to stay for dinner. That was the last time I saw him. He died in 1972 while I was in America.

Our new school year started. There were thirty students in our fourth and final year of *gimnazium*. This year we started *Przysposobienie Wojskowe*, paramilitary training. Our leader, a first lieutenant, was a political officer of the LWP and, no doubt, a member of the UB. On Saturdays we marched to the training grounds, formerly German Army property and drilled under his command. By that time the lawlessness of the Russian soldiers had finally been controlled. The remaining Russian troops kept to their barracks at the harbour, which was still under their control.

One Saturday in early October, while returning in marching formation from our drill, we came across a column of Russian soldiers marching in the opposite direction. They were lustily singing: '… *vychadyila na byereg Katyusha …*' (Katyusha went out to the banks). The song was the Russian soldier's equivalent of 'Lili Marleen'. As the columns passed each other, we began to parody the Russian style of marching while shouting the words of *Katyusha* loudly and out of tune. Once the Russian column passed, our lieutenant halted our column, ordered about face and marched us back to the training ground. On his command, we stopped and formed into double ranks facing him. He brought us to attention and began berating us: 'You shitheads! How dare you make fun of the Russian soldiers who shed their blood to bring us freedom, independence and democracy ... I will show you ... I will take you through this obstacle course until your swinging dicks scrape the ground.'

I took three steps forward, saluted and as he stopped rambling I said, 'Citizen lieutenant, Cadet Hryniewicz reporting. It is now twenty minutes past 3 p.m. The school day ended at 3 p.m. lieutenant, sir! You no longer have authority over us. I am going home.' I saluted, made a regulation about turn and started walking. The others followed me as the lieutenant yelled behind me: 'You will report to me tomorrow morning!'

The next morning, I knocked on his door with my Cross, entered, stood at attention in front of his desk and saluted. I held my salute while he was pretending to read some papers. After a pregnant pause lasting a few minutes he looked up and immediately stood to return my salute. He gestured to me to sit down. After an awkward moment he cleared his throat and said, 'You have a Cross of Grunwald.' (He used the plural form of 'you' typical of the Russian language. Obviously he was trained there.) I showed him the certificate of award. When asked, I informed him that I was in the Warsaw Uprising and saw action in the old town. Three months before, on the second anniversary, I had been one of the eleven participants so decorated.

A 'delicate' conversation followed. He asked me why I had not worn the ribbon of the Cross before. I answered that I didn't want to appear to be a show off. There are many others who deserved the award more than me. The Cross of Valour I had received during the Uprising was sufficient recognition for me.

About two weeks later; he called me to his office. '... So, you [again, the Russian plural] were not in the AL?' he asked. 'Where was the AL during the Uprising?' I replied. He gave me a menacing look and dismissed me.

27

Escape from Poland,
11 November–25 December 1946

Polish National Independence Day, the most important national holiday, is celebrated on 11 November, commemorating the anniversary of the restoration of the Polish state in 1918. The holiday was celebrated briefly until 1946, when the communist government substituted it with 22 July (when the communists established the provisional government of Poland).

A few days prior to 11 November 1946, it was announced publicly that this day would no longer be celebrated as a holiday. We were told that classes would be held and attendance would be mandatory. When I arrived at school, there was noticeable unease and the students were disgruntled. During the break following our first class, I met up with Roman, Zbyszek Cych and other members of our Sailing Scouts squad. I suggested that we declare this day a national holiday and disband our classroom. When the second class started, Roman and I stood up, declared a national holiday and said, 'Let's get the hell out of here and go celebrate.' The whole class stood up, left the classroom and went down the corridor banging on and opening doors to other classrooms. In a matter of minutes the entire school emptied. We divided into two groups. One headed to the girl's *gimnazium*, the other to the Commerce Gymnasium. Hundreds of secondary school boys and girls walked along the main avenues, arms locked, singing national military songs. Armed *Milicja* appeared and a tense situation developed. Fortunately for us the police did not intervene. We returned to school the next day and acted as though nothing had happened. But there was tension in the air. We started to relax over the next few weeks as it appeared clear that there would be no official reaction to our stunt.

However, one day in early December, our classroom door opened and a pompous, official-looking man walked in followed by a sombre-faced headmaster and our teacher, crocodile tears streaming down her cheeks. In the front of the classroom was a large platform with a podium and pulpit. We all stood up. The pompous fellow climbed the podium, stood behind the pulpit then slowly stared at us standing next to our desks. He paused for a moment, and then swept his hand across the classroom and in a slow but loud voice proclaimed: 'From this moment on ... this class does not exist!'

There was a moment of stunned silence. Someone at the back of the classroom shouted 'Z kurwy syn!' (You son of a whore!) We all stood motionless as the man shouted frantically, 'Who said that?! Who said that?! I'll have you arrested!' When he left, the headmaster announced that we were to take all of our belongings, leave the school building and not come back. We were all shaken by what had just transpired. A day or two later some parents of the expelled students met, formed a committee and sent a delegation to meet with the pompous man, who turned out to be in charge of all education in Szczecin. Two weeks later, he agreed to reinstate the class and to readmit all students, with the exception of the ringleaders – me and Roman. By then it was a week before Christmas. I decided to travel to Warsaw and try to enrol in a school there. Mother and I agreed that I would return no later than the 23rd, the day before Christmas Eve. My attempts to get into a school there were fruitless. First of all, I was not registered with the city administration as a resident of Warsaw, and second, I had been expelled for a serious disciplinary problem.

I returned on the morning of the 23rd. During breakfast, mother said that the day I left two UB officers had come to the apartment looking for me. She told them that I had gone to Miechów to enrol in school there. She assured them I would return for Christmas. I was to report to the Security Office immediately upon my return.

We had already been exploring different means of escaping Poland: crossing the border with the Russian Zone or on Swedish cargo ships loading coal in the harbour. While I was away in Warsaw, mother had found a route that seemed to be safe. She spoke with the Jurgens family and learned that they also wanted to return to the US Zone of Occupation in southern Germany. The plans had been already made. The next morning, together with Roman and his father, we would take a bus to Swinoujście. The Polish border with the Russian Zone of Occupation was only 3 miles west of there. We would then go to a pre-arranged restaurant, whose owner ran a smuggling ring and would lead us across the border. Roman's mother, his younger sister and two of his mother's sisters would follow separately a few days later. The Jurgenses decided to go separately; in the event that one party or the other were captured, at least a part of the family would be safe.

The next morning was 24 December. We left after breakfast, taking only one small bag and a backpack. Each contained several cartons of American cigarettes, a change of clothes and some food. Mother managed to obtain old German birth certificates for us. The certificates were authentic but both had different names. I was now Hans Maximillian Schmeling (Max Schmeling was a well-known German boxer who KO'd Joe Lewis).

My documents from the Uprising were very important to me and I insisted on bringing them. At first mother refused, but when I explained that if we were caught, the documents wouldn't make any difference; the authorities would find out who we were regardless, she agreed.

We reached the bus station and climbed into the bus, another truck with wooden benches. Roman and his father were already seated, but we pretended not to know each other. Two hours later we arrived at Swinoujście. Our bus had travelled the same route we had taken to our scout camp a few months earlier. Reaching the island of Wolin, we continued west crossing the Usetom River, the Oder's main branch and on to the harbour town of Swinoujście. We were now on the western barrier island, Usnam.

We walked over to our restaurant and sat down to order lunch. While ordering we asked our waiter for Mr X. As he served our meal, our waiter indicated a door behind us. After lunch we were to go through that door and wait there. While we were still eating, Roman and his father walked in and sat down at a different table. We finished our meal, paid the bill and stepped into the room indicated. Soon we were joined by the Jurgenses. The windowless storage room had a locked door to the outside. Inside it was cold and we kept our overcoats on as we sat there on cases of cold beer.

Our contact came by an hour later and explained that he would return at midnight with a guide. He and the guide would take us to the outskirts of town, where we would pay half of the agreed fee in US dollars. There would be another guide with some more people and both guides would take us to the border, less than 2 miles away. Our guide would show us where to cross the border. Then we would pay him the balance of his fee. While we were waiting, the sounds of merriment drifted in from the restaurant. It was Christmas Eve. The singing of Christmas carols had started. We wished each other Merry Christmas. Before midnight Mr X and another man came. We followed them outside and walked to the outskirts of town. The second guide, accompanied by eight men all carrying large backpacks, was waiting. The other group started out first and we followed. We overheard the men quietly speaking in German. Our guide explained that they were German smugglers carrying food, mostly meat products, into the Russian Zone, where food was scarce. We slipped into the woods and walked single file. The German smugglers and their guide were in the lead, followed by me and Roman, mother and Mr Jurgens with our guide bringing up the rear. We walked quietly heading west. The night was cold, around -5°C. Snow covered the forest floor while above us the sky was clear with bright stars and a half-moon. Walking was easy; bright light from the moon, reflected off the snow, providing us with sufficient illumination.

Less than an hour later our guide told us to be absolutely quiet: we were approaching the border. I was surprised when we reached it – it was not what I had expected. We stood at the edge of the forest; in front of us was a cleared strip of land, 50ft wide. The border was brightly lit by a powerful searchlight, which had been mounted on the guardhouse roof, 150ft to our left. A highway passed by the guardhouse. The entire area surrounding the checkpoint was floodlit. We didn't see a single guard but heard loud music, sounds of singing and slivers of conversation in Russian drifting from the guardhouse. A Russian Army truck drove in from the Polish side and two Russian soldiers stepped out to check papers. We heard them laughing and speaking Russian, finally the barrier was lifted and the truck proceeded into the Russian Zone. The two soldiers looked around, peered down along the border shielding their eyes, then turned around and walked back into the guardhouse. Once again we heard music, guards singing and laughing.

Our guide gathered us around and explained that the border further away, though not lit, was well patrolled by guards with trained dogs. Here the guards did not pay as much attention, assuming that no one would be so brazen as to pass right under their noses. His instructions were:

At my signal, one by one, run silently across the clearing. Once on the other side of the border, walk west perpendicular to it. Within 100 yards you will see a forest road. Turn right, walk another 200 yards to the railway track. This track is not in use. Turn left and follow it, away from the border, for 3 miles. There will be a small railway station. You will see only a few people; when the ticket booth opens, and no one is around, ask for tickets to Berlin and hand over two cartons of American cigarettes per person. Two trains depart every day from this station, once in the morning and once in the afternoon. It is a short ride, 28 miles, to a station at the other end of this island. The train does not continue on any further. All the bridges on the western side of the island are down. There is a military pontoon bridge that you will cross on foot. There will be a Russian-German checkpoint there and you need to be very careful. Once on the mainland continue to the nearby railway station. There take the train to Berlin.

We paid our guide the rest of the money and he wished us luck. Now we waited for our turn. The smugglers were the first to cross, then mother and me, followed by Roman and Mr Jurgens. Roman and I were watching the smugglers as they ran silently across the clearing one by one. The pines in the clearing were cut 2ft above the ground with stumps staggered at 3–4ft. The last smuggler to cross the clearing was an older man and he was carrying a heavy backpack. He stumbled midway and fell. The weight of his backpack prevented him from getting up quickly and he began calling out softly '*Hilfe! Hilfe!*' ('Help! Help!') The other smugglers had crossed and were nowhere to be seen. Instinctively, Roman and I ran out, picked up the poor fellow by his backpack and dragged him to the other side. We got him up, and with a '*Danke, danke,*' he disappeared.

We followed the guide's directions, found the railway tracks and in about an hour arrived at the station. It was Christmas morning, 25 December 1946, and we were now in the Soviet Zone of Occupation.

PART 6

GERMANY

28

Berlin, 25–31 December 1946

We waited at the edge of the woods close to the train station. In the grey light of dawn, we stepped inside a small waiting room. A few customers had already made their purchases from a woman behind the ticket agent's window. Mr Jurgens, who was fluent in German, approached the window when there was no one else in line. Roman stood nearby and blocked everyone's view as his father passed four cartons of cigarettes to the ticket agent. As Mr Jurgens completed his business, he turned around and nodded slightly to us. Mother went up to the counter and repeated the transaction as I shielded her. The train arrived in daylight. There were only two passenger cars and everyone boarded at the stationmaster's signal. The train moved along slowly, stopped at a few local stations and two hours later arrived at the end of the line. We got out and followed some of the other passengers along a highway leading to a pontoon bridge and the mainland. We had been warned to be particularly careful about a checkpoint at this crossing as the Communist German Security had been looking for escaping Poles. As we reached the bridge all foot traffic was funnelled into a narrow space where German security and Russian NKVD officers were stationed along with two Russian soldiers. The Germans were placed first in this security check; they carefully checked the papers and handed them over to a Russian, who did not bother with documents; instead, he scrutinised the person. We decided to split up, allowing a few people to move in line between each of us. When it was my turn, the German security guard noticed the name on my birth certificate and made a joking boxing gesture as I smiled back. He passed my 'German' birth certificate over to the Russian captain, who looked me over and he waved me across. We all passed through the security check and continued over the bridge, which bobbed as trucks drove across. We followed the road to Wolgast, where there was a larger train station. The waiting room was half-full. We found a corner to sit down and tried to look as inconspicuous as possible. We had been warned that the local population could be hostile towards escaping Poles and were sure to turn them over to the Russians.

We sat on the bench and pretended to be dozing. The waiting room gradually filled. Still there was no train. There was no schedule; apparently there were only two trains a day from Berlin. Noon came and passed, 1 p.m., 3 p.m., still no train. Mother indicated that we should eat. We hadn't eaten since the night before. She reached into her bag and pulled out a piece of smoked sausage and a roll. We started to eat slowly. Up until then, there had been a murmur of voices from the people packed into the room. That murmur started to fade until there was a silence around us. I lifted my eyes and realised that everyone was staring at the sausage and rolls, which we were eating. Fortunately, a whistle sounded and people started to stream out of the waiting room as the train pulled up to the platform. At that time there was a serious food shortage affecting Germans within the Russian Zone of Occupation. The train's arrival saved us; otherwise we would have been pointed out to German security.

We reunited with the Jurgenses when we reached the platform. They had been sitting in another part of waiting room. We walked then ran along the train until we found a relatively empty passenger car. It was old and had a series of separate compartments accessible from either side. Mother and Roman's father climbed up to one compartment and Roman and I into an adjoining one. Both compartments filled up immediately. We sat there and waited until finally, accompanied by shouts and steam whistles, our train pulled slowly out of the station. It was already dusk.

At some time around 8 p.m., after frequently stopping along the way, our train came to a halt just before Passewalk station, only 25 miles west of Szczecin. Thirty minutes later a train approached us then slowly came to a stop on the parallel track. At the same time the lights in our compartments were all switched off. Frightened voices were loudly whispering, 'Ruski! Ruski! Quiet!' There was absolute silence, then all hell broke loose. There were the sounds of men in heavy boots jumping from the other train, yelling and shouting in Russian, '*Padavay chumadany*' (Give us the luggage); moaning and crying, terrified people jumped down from the train. Everyone in our compartment got up and tried to escape through the opposite side door. One woman who had been sitting next to the door grabbed her large suitcase and in a panic tried to get out while carrying it in front of her. The suitcase was longer than the width of the door and stopped her cold. She panicked and pushed harder. The passengers behind her were pushing, making it impossible for her to back off. Somehow Roman and I managed to twist the suitcase and the woman literally catapulted out. Everyone jumped out before the Russian soldiers were able to get to them. People were running and rolling down the embankment. We found mother and Mr Jurgens. Mother had had a close call when a Russian soldier grabbed her by the hand yelling, 'Dievochka astain'sa' (Girlie, you stay behind). She managed to break loose and jump from the compartment.

Most of the passengers who were in the conventional wagons with entrances at each end only were less fortunate. Some managed to escape by jumping out of the windows. Others were robbed and some women were molested. Ten minutes later, several short engine whistles called the Russians back to their train. Soon, the Russian train disappeared and we all boarded our train once again. It was well known that Russians soldiers returning home often indulged themselves in some final act of robbery and rape. Our group boarded the nearest carriage.

Two hours later, we arrived in Berlin and got off the train at Stettiner Bahnhoff in the Russian sector. By then it was midnight and we made our way to an address provided by the smuggler. We were to stay there and wait for the rest of the Jurgens family. After a ride on the U-Bahn we walked through dimly lit, empty streets framed by bombed-out buildings covered in snow. I looked around – it looked like Warsaw. I do not know what I really felt. Was I glad to see this destruction? 'Well', I thought, 'they deserved it, didn't they? After all, it was they who started it all.' I guess I was immune to the sight of such destruction; I was just hungry and cold.

We finally arrived at our destination, an apartment building in a once well-to-do area of Berlin near the Tiergarten. We walked up to the third floor and rang the bell. The man who opened the door spoke Polish and showed us to a large room. It had once been elegant, but was now a dormitory furnished with eight cots. I woke up late that morning. It was Boxing Day, 26 December 1946. Over the course of the next few days it became clear that our apartment was a den of smuggling and black market operations. Mysterious and unsavoury characters and contraband goods came and went all day and night. After Christmas, Mr Jurgens and mother visited the office of a Polish organisation to learn if we could find help in getting out of the Russian Zone. They were told that no help could be given and that we would need to find our own way out of Berlin. Their advice was to attempt reaching Hannover in the British Zone. There were Polish displaced persons camps there in communication with Polish Army units on occupation duty. At that time Berlin had been divided into four sectors and there was still unrestricted travel between them. The city was policed jointly; patrolling jeeps had military policeman from the American, English, Russian and French armies together with a German policeman. Nevertheless, Berlin was deep in the Russian Zone.

The rest of the Jurgens family arrived the following day. There were now seven of us. Our host had a connection with a smuggler who could lead us across the border into the British Zone. The appropriate arrangements were made. On the evening of 31 December all seven of us were on a train. We were travelling westward to a town a few miles from the border. There we would be met by a guide. The train stopped at several locations. After midnight we alighted at a small station. The few passengers who left the train with us dispersed quickly. Our train left and we were left standing all alone. The guide was nowhere to be seen. We waited about 15 minutes, not knowing what to do. We then noticed a man looking at us from time to time and walking slowly along the station wall. Mr Jurgens approached him and they conversed for a while. He turned out to be a guide too and was willing to take us over the border. Not having much choice, we trusted him and made a deal. The hike to the border would take more than three hours.

We walked in single file across farmlands, avoiding roads and skirting around villages. The night was very cold, the snow was deep and it was tough going. There was sufficient light from the moon reflecting off the snow. Three hours later it was nearly dawn. We had been walking along a patch of shrubs and small trees and stopped on reaching the edge. A hundred yards ahead was a field posted with signs. Visible, about a mile away, was a small town. The guide said, 'This is the border, the town is in the British Zone. Russians patrol here every half hour. There should not be any for a while, so keep quiet and go now.' We gave him his money and started to walk quickly across the field. As we approached the frontier warning signs we saw a Russian soldier lying in the snow a couple of feet away from us. He was snoring loudly; obviously he had already celebrated the New Year. We passed him and a few minutes later approached a sign saying, 'Welcome to the British Zone of Occupation'. It was 1 January 1947.

29

British Zone of Occupation,
1 January–July 1947

We walked through the completely silent town. It was early morning on the new year. All the stores and restaurants were closed for the holiday. We did not come across a single person. The doors at the train station were open; we entered an empty waiting room. At least it was relatively warm. From the posted schedule we surmised that there should be a train to Hannover. Half an hour later the ticket window opened and a hungover man yawned as he busied himself behind the counter of the food stand. Soon we all had hot *ersatz* coffee and sandwiches. When the train arrived a few passengers boarded an almost empty train and several hours later we arrived in Hannover. At the station we found the address of 'Kosciuszko', a Polish displaced persons camp. It was a short ride by tram.

We registered, were assigned two rooms and were fed. The following day we met with the camp manager and explained that we just escaped from Poland. He confirmed that we should make our way to Meppen, to the headquarters of the 1st Polish Armoured Division, where there was a transit camp for recent escapees. He added that had we been here a few days earlier we could have gone directly to Meppen. The division's 10th Dragoon Regiment had been brought to Hannover to clean up the criminal element from the large air shelter near the station, which British military police and German police could not cope with.

He told us about the weekly Polish Army transport that would take us to Meppen. A few days later, a Polish Parachute Brigade truck drove us and several other recent escapees to their headquarters in Osnabrück. There, after lunch in the military mess, another truck took us to the transit camp in Meppen.

The division headquarters was located in Meppen and the division occupied the nearby area of north-western Germany as part of the BAOR (British Army of the Rhine). The transit camp was situated in a large three-storey brick school building in a park on the edge of the old town. The market square and the historical town hall were only a couple of blocks away. Nearby in a local *bier stube*, Roman and I enjoyed our first German beer.

Polish military intelligence *dwójka* had its offices nearby. We were all interrogated individually. When my turn came, I told my story and showed my documents, telling the captain interrogating me that I had been in the old town during the Uprising. The surprised captain mentioned that Col. Ziemski Wachnowski, CO of defence of the old town, was visiting the divisional headquarters. The colonel was then advised of my presence. When he walked in twenty minutes later, I stood at attention and reported: 'Colonel, sir! Runner Bohdan from *Nałęcz* Battalion reporting.' He looked surprised. 'Bohdan, what are you doing here?' 'I got out Colonel, sir!' 'Well done'. After a brief conversation, he left.

The colonel confirmed my service and Cross of Valour. He wrote, 'I confirm participation in the Underground and participation in the defence of the old town during the Uprising by the Battalion *Nałęcz* Runner, whom I knew personally and remember from the Uprising.' I was told that the British authorities clamped down on any further admission into the division. There was still a possibility of joining the Polish Armed Forces in Italy, where the Polish II Corps was on occupation duty. This large formation had close to 60,000 soldiers. At that time the very last transport was leaving in a week for Italy and we could join in. We decided to stay, under the illusion that we would be able to get into the US very quickly.

Even though I could not join the division, mother had been accepted into the ranks of the PWAS (Polish Women's Auxiliary Service). The division had joined the Allied invasion in July of 1944 and seen action in Normandy, Belgium, Holland and in Germany. In April of 1945 it had liberated from *Stalag Oberlangeni* over 1,700 women soldier POWs who had participated in the Uprising. It was from their ranks that the PWAS had been formed. As some of the PWAS enlistees left due to marriage or other circumstances, their places were taken by whomever divisional military intelligence chose to help.

On 4 February my service was verified and I received an AK Commemorative Badge. The next day, I was issued a Polish Armed Forces, Ex-Prisoner of War (PWX) ID card. PWX status gave me the right to wear a uniform and to receive basic pay, cigarettes and food rations. I was told to go to Maczków to enrol in the Polish secondary school and then proceed to the Polish Military Centre 104 in Wezuwe-Meppen.

Nº 90205

Polskie Siły Zbrojne
Polish Armed Forces

LEGITYMACJA

b. jeńca wojennego

IDENTITY-CARD

ex Prisoner of War

No. 3144

Nazwisko / Surname (drukiem—in capitals)	*Hryniewicz*
Imiona własne / Christian Names	*Bohdan*
Data i miejsce urodz. / Date and place of birth	*2. IV. 1931*
	Wilno
Wyznanie / Religion (option.)	*rz kat.*
Stopień wojskowy / Rank	*strz.*

Pieczęć Of. Kont. / Stamp Cont. Offic.

Podpis Ofic. Kont. / Signature Cont. Offic.

Data / Date *5. II. 1946* r.

If found this card should be forwarded to the nearest Military Government Detachment or Police Station.

Converted as an Allied Soldier from PWX to Civilian (DP) Status on *24. 6.* 1947
Signed *........* Rank
Assembly Centre No. *104*

Printed by PRINTING & DISTRIBUTION UNIT
Control Commission for Germany (B. E.)

CONTROL COMMISSION
FOR GERMANY
(BRITISH ZONE)

PWX/DP
Registration/Identity Card

Maczków had until recently been Haren, a small town near Meppen. At the end of the war Polish soldiers had been billeted in German homes while the former residents were resettled to nearby towns and villages. Five thousand Poles released from forced labour, concentration and POW camps took their place. A local order of nuns and their convent was an exception to this directive. The II Canadian Corps, which had included our division, came up with this idea and Field Marshal Montgomery approved it. Haren now had Polish administration, Polish schools and was renamed Maczków in honour of division CO, Gen. Maczek.

Maczków was 11 miles from Meppen and easy to reach by 'auto stop', hitchhiking. Roman and I were admitted to the school. We then proceeded to the military centre, which had been a *stalag* and still housed a small number of Polish PWX. It was situated 8 miles to the west, close to the Dutch border. There was no traffic on the road we walked along leading to the centre and a flat, windswept, snow-covered peat bog stretched as far as the eye could see. The camp was a collection of old wooden barracks; it still had barbed wire strung around it. Roman and I were issued uniforms and a food ration allotment. The following morning we made our way back to Maczków, wearing our newly issued British battle dress uniform beneath our warm overcoats and carrying two blankets and a change of underwear. The student body at our new secondary school was made up of some of our division's soldiers, ex-prisoners of war, and some family members.

About that time the Jurgens family had decided to move back to the American Zone of Occupation, where they had lived prior to returning to Poland. A couple of months later Roman left and I moved into a villa with four other Poles. Three of the men were in the Uprising and the fourth had been a displaced person. Time went by quickly during the next few months, there was a significant amount of schoolwork but we also had a lot of fun.

In the spring of 1947 the division began their re-deployment to England. Mother left in early May. Shortly thereafter, our secondary school announced that any serviceman of the division, or family member, who was scheduled to leave for England, could opt to take an accelerated exam and be dismissed from further classes. Though I was scheduled to go later, I took advantage of this offer. I passed all my subjects except for Latin, which I failed. I was issued a certificate of completion, excluding Latin, for the fourth year of *gimnazium*.

Just before mother left with the bulk of her battalion, she introduced me to Cpt. Halina Więckowska, CO of what remained of the battalion in Meppen. Her son Kazik had been in the Uprising and was a good friend of mine. I moved to Meppen and stayed there for the next two months.

I had a great time, living in the same large building with six young women. My only duty was to stop by division headquarters each morning and pick up the mail.

The fact that I did not smoke was a great advantage since my cigarette ration proved to be worth a small fortune. As a PWX I received my pay in occupational marks (Allied military currency), which were used as common currency throughout Germany at that time. However, there were also BAFSV (British Armed Forces Special Vouchers) pegged to the British pound. The armed forces were paid with these vouchers and military stores accepted BAFSVs. My cigarettes were easily convertible into BAFSVs to say nothing of the occupational marks.

At the end of June, I learned that I was scheduled to ship out within a few days. We left on a train to Hamburg, where we boarded a cargo vessel converted into a troop transport. Our berths were in the cargo hold, where steel pipes with bars welded between them made a ladder. Every few feet were hooks for hanging hammocks. We were each issued a hammock. Since I was the youngest I took the uppermost level. This turned out to be a blessing since soon after we left the harbour we ran into a very heavy storm. I did not get seasick, but most of the others did. Being at the top level proved a great advantage. Two days later, the storm subsided and we rounded the tip of Scotland, passed by the Hebrides Islands and anchored in the Firth of Clyde. We anchored near an aircraft carrier and watched in amazement as the admiral was piped aboard the carrier. A Rolls-Royce limousine drove him across the width of the deck to the point where he entered the superstructure.

The following day we disembarked in the port of Glasgow. We had arrived in the UK.

PART 7

ENGLAND

30

Nicholas Copernicus Polish College for Boys, July 1947–June 1949

L eaving Glasgow, we travelled the entire length of England by train and disembarked in Salisbury. We were taken by truck to the Hyde Park Polish Army Camp. I stayed there until the end of July, waiting for the beginning of the new school year at the Polish Lyceum.

In July 1945 the Western Allies had recognised the Provisional Communist Government that had been formed in Poland, nevertheless the British retained responsibility for the Polish Armed Forces who had fought under their command during the Second World War. More than 140,000 Polish service men from a total of 250,000 refused to return to a Poland now dominated by the communists. The British government then established a Polish Resettlement Corps (PRC) to facilitate their transfer to civilian life. This organisation continued to maintain the military camps.

During the war, the Ministry of Education of the Polish Government in London established numerous Polish educational facilities serving a quarter of a million military personnel and their families. On the university level, a Polish School of Medicine was established in Edinburgh, active from 1941 to 1949, there was a Polish Veterinarian School at the Royal Veterinarian College, the Polish Administration at the University of St Andrew's, the Polish School of Architecture located in Liverpool and the Polish School of Law in Oxford. Later in 1947, the Polish University College was established in London. There were secondary schools throughout the divisions of the Polish Army, Polish Air Force and Polish Navy, as well as cadet schools. By the time I arrived in England, only two Polish military secondary schools remained: one for women and one for men.

Towards the end of July, I collected my train voucher and food ration cards, and departed for the 3rd Polish Infantry Division secondary school, which had recently been relocated from Italy to England. All of the Polish military secondary schools for men were consolidated into this school. When my train arrived in Thetford, Norfolk, I went to the stationmaster and telephoned the Riddlesworth Camp, where the school was located. I was advised that there wasn't any available transport, nor was there any scheduled public transportation between the station and camp. I decided that I could get there on my own as the camp was only 6 miles away. I was about to pick up my kit bag when I noticed a Polish Army lieutenant standing nearby. I introduced myself and asked if he too was going to the same camp. Lt. Józef Bujnowski said yes, he had been assigned to the teaching staff at the school. He invited me to go with him by taxi. During our conversation I learned that he was from an area near Wilno and had studied there at the university.

During the war, the camp had been a USAAF base. The camp grounds straddled a country road leading to an airfield a few miles away. We lived in barracks that had been built in clearings between trees. Our classrooms, dining hall, kitchens and administration offices were all in 'Quonset' huts across the road from our living quarters. Our barracks were prefabricated huts of flimsy wood construction made in Canada. They were divided into halves and each room accommodated five of us.

The majority of the students were ex-service men of the Polish Armed Forces or members of their families; a few civilians were also enrolled. Many had missed several years of schooling due to the war, resulting in their average age being older than comparable levels in a more standard school. The academic programme was administered by the Committee of Education of Poles in Great Britain. Our teaching staff was excellent, very high calibre, mostly university lecturers; the curriculum was equally demanding. Daily life was spartan. Typically, five students shared a room, which had been furnished with narrow military beds, a small wardrobe and a table with chairs. In the middle of our room stood a potbelly stove and a single bulb hanging over the table was our only source of light. There were many shortages in England at that time and fuel was one of them. Hot water was available once a week on Saturdays, when the shower room boiler was fired up. Our coal allotment was insufficient. We used our stove only after 4 p.m., when we returned from class, and let the fire die down before we went to bed. Meals were unappetising and meagre. In the dining hall we sat six at a table. Breakfast consisted of half a stick (four tablespoons) of margarine, two tablespoons of orange marmalade and a piece of cheddar smaller than half a cigarette pack, for the six of us. In addition, there were two slices of sandwich bread for each of us. At noon, our main meal of the day consisted of soup and a platter with mashed potatoes, mystery meat and veggies. In the evening there was a small meal of porridge or farina with vanilla custard on top, referred to as 'revenge of the newborn'. Needless to say, we were all hungry most of the time. All food was rationed and we did not have ration cards. Our camp was very isolated; the nearest town was Thetford, 6 miles away. Anyway, most of us received only pocket money from the committee. The camp canteen, run by NAAFI, sold only small meatless sandwiches and sweet buns.

To assure equal distribution, each table rotated one man who divided the food into six portions and passed the platter to his right. Since he was the last one to take his portion, they were divided absolutely equally. The soup for the midday meal was served from a large kettle. Each table had a designated runner and a number two man. Their job was to sprint to the mess hall as soon as the bell rang and get in line. The technique for ladling the soup was to spin the contents clockwise, reverse the ladle, and scoop all of the solids as it was lifted up. By the time the first three or four tables had their dinner soup, only a thin watery liquid remained. Luckily, our classroom was one of the closest to the mess hall. To supplement our meagre rations of meat we would occasionally poach rabbits, which were abundant, by setting up snares. This was illegal, but a delicious rabbit cooked on top of the stove made the risk worthwhile. We were very careful to dispose of all the evidence. In the spring of 1948, bread was no longer rationed. We all biked to nearby bakeries to buy bread. It took me a long time to find a bakery where the bread was not already sold out. Finally my roommate Władek Miłkowski and I bought two loaves each. We sat down and each devoured a loaf of freshly baked bread.

We all had bicycles. Soon after my arrival at this school, I had been told to borrow a wrench, pliers and a bicycle pump and walk to the dump adjacent to the airfield. Home-bound American airmen dumped their bicycles there, literally hundreds of them in a large pile. What remained had been pretty well picked over. Nevertheless, I quickly managed to assemble a bike and ride back to camp. The bicycles were our principal means of transportation, whether we went to see a film in Thetford or to explore nearby villages.

The Polish Army 3rd Infantry Division administered the camp. Emergency medical services were provided by the camp's medic, and a Polish military hospital, 60 miles away in Diddington, served our camp. An army ambulance left the camp early in the morning and returned late in the afternoon on Mondays, Wednesdays and Fridays. Aunt Fela had been a nurse with this hospital during the war in Italy. She and uncle Richard were now living there and I decided to visit them. With an invented excuse I departed one Friday morning, 'missed' the return ambulance and returned on Monday. I had not seen them since they had been deported from Wilno to Russia in the summer of 1941. I had always liked them so I enjoyed the visit very much. I met my newborn cousin Andrew. They were very pleased to hear news of uncle Richard's mother and brother, whom they had not seen since the beginning of the war. When I repeated this 'visit' a few weeks later I was reprimanded.

Before leaving Germany I had been demobilised from the Polish Armed Forces. I had also been 'Converted as an Allied soldier from PWX to civilian DP status on 24.6.1947.' Though we were technically demobilised, we continued to wear our uniforms since they were the only clothing we had.

I had been conditionally accepted into the first year of the lyceum, subject to passing my Latin examination. Ours was the maths and sciences branch of lyceum and we no longer had Latin classes. After a couple of months, much to my surprise and discomfort, I was told to report to take my Latin exam. After a brief attempt on my part to answer some of his grammar questions, the examining professor smiled and said, 'Maybe you should just write an essay on the political situation in Rome at the time of Julius Caesar ... in Polish.' With this, once again, I breathed easier.

I had not seen mother since May of 1947, when she left Germany. We kept in touch by mail and I went to London to see her during the 1948 Easter break. Mother's first assignment when she arrived in England was in the PRC payroll department at Camp Willey near Guildford, south of London. In February she was released and went to work as a labourer in a London factory. She had stayed in a nearby Polish boarding house with several other demobilised Poles. Working in the factory was hard and monotonous. She and a co-worker fed large sheets of painted metal into a press to be stamped into lids for small metal boxes. Even though she was tired, mother had been in good spirits and was already making plans for a move into the centre of London to somehow start a business.

This trip to London was the last time I wore my uniform with its Polish eagle and 'Poland' shoulder patches in public. Upon my returned to school, we were required to remove all military insignia of rank and unit and national emblems. We still wore our uniforms; it was all most of us had, but now we mixed in some civilian apparel.

Towards the end of our school year, a British military mission arrived and attempted to recruit the student body into the British Army. This effort was strongly opposed by our teaching staff; nevertheless, the school was obliged to permit the mission to make its presentations. We listened to the offer of good pay, advancement and, after years of service, a grant of citizenship with the possibility of commission. Only three men enrolled.

The school year ended in June and I was promoted into the second and final grade of lyceum. We were advised that our school would be relocated during the summer to a new camp in Ellough, near Beccles in Suffolk. When classes ended, I took a bus to London to visit mother. After a short stint as a hotel maid, she had relocated and established herself as a manicurist in a room she rented in Ebury Street near London's Waterloo Station.

After a few days I left for a farm camp that had been organised by the Minister of Agriculture. Its slogan, 'Lend a Hand to the Land,' came from the Second World War WLA (Women's Land Army) camps. It was near Nottingham, close to Sherwood Forest. Most of the participants were university students, both English and foreign. There were also some young women, who were taking a two- or three-week holiday there. The work was hard. At the beginning of my stay I worked pulling up flax plants and later on the combines. We carried 224lb sacks of grain on our backs. The pay was meagre, food relatively good, but great fun was had by all. It was essentially a holiday. I saved most of my earnings because food and lodging were provided. At summer's end I visited mother again in London.

At the beginning of September I arrived in Beccles, 100 miles northeast of London, and made my way to Ellough. Our school relocated to another camp, again an old USAAF airbase. It was larger, with better facilities. We lived in Quonset huts, which we preferred to our previous quarters. The gymnasium and dining hall were in conventional buildings. The sanitary blocks had tiled walls and the hot water was much more frequent. The gymnasium and tennis courts allowed us to participate in more sports, we were no longer limited to football and volleyball.

The school was now administered by the committee and was renamed the Nicolaus Copernicus Polish College for Boys. The food had improved greatly. The town of Beccles, only 3 miles away, was larger than Thetford and had more to offer. I had more disposable money, due to my summer work; I could afford additional films and food. We made excursions by train and bicycle to the nearby towns of Ipswich and Norwich.

In November the school moved again, to another USAAF base near the village of Bottisham, east of Cambridge, on the road to New Market. The village had less than 1,000 inhabitants, an old fourteenth-century church and a couple of pubs, not much to offer. Cambridge, only 6 miles away, easily accessible by bicycle, was our frequent destination. The camp facilities were the best, with proper classrooms, dining room and sports facilities. We continued living in Quonset huts, four to a room. The rooms had better furniture and real central heating. The four of us got domesticated. We bought an iron and hired a radio. There were no independent radio stations, only the BBC. The only independent station in Europe was in Andorra. It played popular music, which we preferred to the classical music on the BBC. The food improved again. We were no longer hungry. One day we received a shipment of bananas, which we ate for dessert. I had not seen a banana since 1939.

I spent Christmas with mother. She was living near Victoria Station and had easy access to the Underground, making travel through London very easy. I explored the city and its museums during my ten-day stay. London had a large Polish presence centred in Kensington, Knightsbridge and Earls Court. As the Second World War ended, there were close to 20,000 Poles living in Great Britain. By 1949, the population had swelled to 140,000 and many of them lived in London. London was the centre of Polish political and cultural life in exile. The Polish government-in-exile continued. There were combatant associations, all branches of the Polish Armed Forces. The 'White Eagle' and 'Polish Hearth' clubs, with restaurants, bars and ballrooms, were the centre of Polish activity. I liked the city and especially the ambiance surrounding the Polish community.

When I returned, our soon-to-graduate class was given civilian clothes. Everyone received a tweed jacket, grey flannel slacks, two shirts, a tie and a pair of shoes. Every day we continued to wear our old uniforms but on trips to Cambridge we wore civvies.

Our year had close to sixty students and was divided into A and B sections. An unpleasant incident occurred in the other section. The English language lecturer was a Col. Burns, retired from the British Indian Army. He could have been the model for 'Colonel Blimp'. He openly expressed his belief that only God knew the English language well enough to achieve a grade of 100 per cent, the brightest English student could earn 80 per cent, while a Polish student at best could earn 60 per cent. During one of his lectures he made a grammatical error. One of the students, who was fluent in English and whose stepfather was English, stood up and politely asked for an explanation. The enraged colonel walked over and slapped his face. The whole class stood up and left the classroom, refusing to return until an apology was made. The standoff continued for about a week, until a compromise was reached and a new lecturer took over. The students returned to class.

After the spring break, spent in London, we all started to cram for our matriculation exams. The exams were long – three to five hours written in each subject, followed by an oral exam in front of an examining committee. We had exams in mathematics, including algebra, trigonometry, spherical trigonometry and calculus; physics; chemistry, organic and inorganic; Polish language and literature; and history. My cramming paid off and I attained the highest grades ever. To my surprise, I got all As and Bs, except for one C in language. With only three exceptions, all sixty of us passed and matriculated. The night after the graduation ceremony we held our 'Matriculation Ball'. The graduates from the Polish Women's Lyceum came, reigniting the romances that had begun when they hosted the *studniówka* '100 Days before Ball' at their school. Two days later, after exchanging farewells and good luck wishes, I hopped on a bus headed for London.

31

London, June 1949–
8 December 1950

I stayed with mother for a few days, until I found a summer job working as a waiter at the United University Club, along with three other Polish men. Tipping was against the rules at the club, except at Christmas. As a result, all the waiters were Poles, no professional waiter wanted to take a job without tips. Membership of the club, founded in 1821, was restricted to a limited number of graduates of Cambridge and Oxford. It occupied its own imposing building adjacent to Trafalgar Square. There were two dining rooms, one for members only and the other for entertaining female guests. There were twenty guest rooms and an overnight stay included breakfast service. At that time, food rationing was still in effect. All club service personnel ate their meagre meals in a basement room next to the kitchen, where all meals served at the club were prepared. Breakfast plates were sent up to the dining room by dumbwaiter, to a service pantry. Each plate had three rashers of bacon. When the plates reached the pantry we removed one piece of bacon and the guest was served the remaining two. At 10 o'clock, breakfast service ended and the dining room was closed. The four of us retired to a secluded pantry room, where we sat down at a table laden with food. There were rashers of bacon, boiled eggs, grilled mackerel, toast, marmalade and coffee. We sat down with our *London Times* and relaxed. One day we miscalculated. Somehow the last guest had arrived late for breakfast and could not find a waiter. The English steward, a kind, elderly man, served him and then came looking for us. He opened the pantry, took in the scene and was stopped speechless. He lifted both hands to his head and repeatedly said, 'Oh my God'. Without another word, he turned and left. We never heard anything further and continued our breakfasts.

We alternated shifts, breakfast and lunch and then lunch and dinner, six days a week. My schedule allowed for additional time to continue my studies in the English language.

I had already been accepted to the University of Cork in Ireland, the physics department at the University of Amsterdam and to study ship-building at the University of Glasgow. I also considered applying to the newly established Polish University College in London. Their schools of science, engineering and architecture had already gained a good reputation. As it was, I continued to procrastinate before making any final decision. At the beginning of August I decided to stay in London and applied to Southwest Essex Technical College and School of Art in the north-eastern part of London. When I arrived for my appointment at the offices of the department of architecture and building, I was ushered in front of the department head, Professor Aldred, and I said: 'Sir, I would like to be admitted to the structural engineering course.' He looked at me. 'Polish?' 'Yes, sir.' 'Do you have your matriculation certificate? 'Yes, sir.' I handed it to him; he glanced at my grades. 'Very good.' He scribbled something, gave it to me and sent me on to the admissions office.

I took my admission paper to the offices of the Committee of Education of Poles in Great Britain and was granted a scholarship that paid my tuition and provided £20 a month for living expenses. This was the equivalent of a starting wage. I quickly found room and board through the college housing office.

There were many Poles enrolled at the college. Our civil and structural engineering first-year class had five Poles, all ex-servicemen. We all had scholarships from the committee and were receiving £20 monthly. A British Marine in our class resented that his scholarship only gave him £14. Everyone was jealous of the few American veterans, whose scholarships were 'astronomical'. We paid our landlady £3 a week for breakfast and dinner. We were lucky, our landlady worked in a restaurant and somehow we ate much better than other students.

The curriculum was heavy, starting at 9.30 a.m. and ending at 5 o'clock. On Fridays we had three hours of workshop practice and three hours of drafting in the afternoon. The workshop, masonry, carpentry, welding, piping and plumbing were hands-on experiences. We mixed mortar and laid bricks, worked with woodworking tools and machines, we welded, soldered pipes and made lead joints, all under masters of those crafts. I found this very useful later on. Our surveying lecturer was Professor Michalski. Quite often English students turned to us and asked, 'What did he say?'

With the money I had earned over the summer I purchased drafting tools and a slide rule. I improved my wardrobe. We no longer wore our uniforms, except on Fridays for the workshop.

At the end of September I helped mother move to a town house owned by Mrs Zielińska at 46 Penywern Road near Earls Court. She lived there and had a small hairdressing salon for select Polish ladies. Mother rented a room from her and opened her cosmetics salon alongside her. It was mutually beneficial for them. Mrs Zielińska also rented rooms to students from the Polish School of Architecture.

From then on I spent Saturdays and Sundays there. The Polish community had a very active social life. There were evening dances and theatre productions in the White Eagle and the Hearth. A Polish mass was celebrated at Brompton Oratory on Sunday mornings. The wide pavement in front was a place to meet old classmates and friends. We were always there before and after the mass. During the mass we usually retired to one of the nearby pubs for a pint of 'half and half' (ale and bitter). After the mass, we returned for 'Catholic Review'. At Christmas, several of our classmates were in London from different universities in England and Ireland.

In early January, when the carnival season started, there were balls and dances every weekend. On Saturday nights, the balls were at the 'Polish Eagle'; on Friday nights and Sunday afternoons, they were in other Polish places. The balls were quite formal and went on until midnight, when the older people left. Public transportation stopped running around midnight and resumed again at 5 a.m. The younger generation, who could not afford taxis, continued to dance, to less stately music, for the rest of the night.

* * *

The Polish Armed Forces under Allied command had over 250,000 men. They were the largest Allied force after the US and Great Britain. When the war ended, less than half returned to Poland. Others started to emigrate to Australia, Canada and South America.

The United States Congress passed special legislation that allowed Polish servicemen who served in the Second World War under Allied command and were demobilised in Britain, to immigrate with their families. In 1949 the American consulate started to process applications for entry visas. Mother, who fulfilled that requirement, and I as a family member, applied for visas.

* * *

The academic year ended and I started to look for summer jobs. The committee rules provided that scholarships would be paid during holidays if the recipient was working full time in the field of his study. I was offered work with surveying crews or as an apprentice draftsmen that paid only about £1 10s per week. On the other hand, as a labourer on a construction site I could earn £7 or more. The committee agreed that this counted as work in my field of study. I had no problem finding work nearby. It was hard, but with overtime I was making over £10 a week. After the summer I had a tidy sum saved. I decided to improve my wardrobe and ordered a dinner jacket tailored by Hector Poe of Regent Street. That set me back 30 guineas.

By summer we had some indication that our visas would be granted soon. At the beginning of September I began my second academic year. Expecting the level of US engineering schools to be higher than in Great Britain, I took additional evening courses in structural design at the third-year level. Knowing that we would be living in New Jersey, I did some research into local engineering schools. There were four. The highest ranked was the Stevens Institute of Technology in Hoboken, followed closely by Newark College of Engineering, then Rutgers and Princeton. Knowing that we would most likely be living in Newark, I applied to Newark College.

On 28 September our visas were issued and our travel documents identified us as 'stateless persons' since we had no passports. His Majesty's Government provided us with transportation. We embarked on the *Queen Mary* in Southampton on 8 December and arrived in New York Harbor on the morning of 14 December 1950.

I was not yet 20 years old; I had £3 in my pocket; had lived in nineteen places in three different countries, under two legitimate governments and three occupying powers; had attended four grammar schools, five secondary schools, and started my second year of university.

32

Newark, NJ, 8 December 1950– September 1954

We stood on deck as our ship was docking, in New York Harbor, and I asked mother what uncle Henry looked like. She remembered him from her child-hood as a dashing young cavalry officer. She replied: 'He is slim with wavy brown hair.' Below us on the pier stood a corpulent man of medium height wearing a camel hair coat. He removed his hat, revealing a shiny bald head. Pointing at him I said sarcastically, 'Nah, he probably looks like him.' Mother looked offended.

After the immigration and customs formalities had been completed, the same man came forward: 'Niusiu, is that you?' I smiled.

He drove us to his home in Short Hills, NJ. His wife Charlotte and their triplet sons Henry, Richard and Stanley were waiting for us. We were received very warmly and stayed with them over Christmas. Because of the forthcoming Christmas holidays, uncle Henry's meat processing plant, PASCO, the largest producer of Polish kielbasa in the New York area, had been extremely busy. He woke me up at 5 a.m. the morning after our arrival and we drove to PASCO. As soon as we arrived at the plant he put me to work. I skinned frankfurters for the next few days.

Christmas was very like it was at home. We were made to feel like mem-bers of the family. The overabundance of food and extravagance reminded me of the Christmas before the war.

After the holidays I met with the Dean of Admissions at Newark College of Engineering. Looking over my transcript he said that he could give me credits for courses in the third and even fourth year of study, but that I lacked the required core freshman classes. I had no choice but to start again as a freshman. I was to start in February and complete my freshman courses by summer's end. I applied and was granted a full tuition scholarship.

At the same time, I registered at my local draft board and received a 1A classification, available for military service and subject to the draft, later changed to 2S Student Deferment. This was during the Korean War. Knowing that I would most likely be drafted, I decided I'd rather go as an officer and enlisted in the Air Force ROTC.

We moved into a two-bedroom apartment in Newark and mother started work in a garment factory. After Christmas, I found a temporary job as a draftsman and continued on a part-time basis once my classes started. Shortly after, I found another part-time job closer to school, making plastic lenses. I worked twenty-five hours per week through my freshman and sophomore years. Starting in summer 1952 until my 1954 graduation, I worked the same hours for a consulting engineering firm that had designed parts of the New Jersey Turnpike and New York Thruway.

Having registered for the draft, I soon learned that the Selective Service Act provided that all Allied Servicemen who had completed either six months of active service or had endured sixty days of combat during the Second World War, were entitled to be classified 4A, the same as American veterans. I marched myself to my local draft board, was ushered to the office of an important looking woman sitting behind a large desk and told her that as a veteran of the Allied Army, with sixty days of combat, I was entitled to a 4A classification. She took out a large binder, looked up the paragraph I had referred to and asked:

What Allied army were you in?'

'Polish.'

'Were you with us or against us?'

'We were with you, madam. Don't you remember? The Second World War started when Germany attacked Poland in September 1939.'

'No. The Second World War started in December 1941 when the Japs bombed Pearl Harbour.'

'Well ...'

'No problem. Please bring me a certified copy of the treaty between the United States and Poland to prove that Poland was an ally.'

'Well ... that's rather difficult. Why don't you just send my papers up the chain.'

About six months later I received a letter from my local board stating, 'Your case is being transferred to the State Board'; six months later, 'to the Regional Board'; another six months later 'to the National Board'; finally, yet another six months later, a new card arrived from Washington with a 4A classification.

In the meantime, I was advancing through the ROTC ranks. In my senior year I was a Cadet Lt. Col. Wing's Deputy Chief of Staff and member of the Arnold Air Society. Three months before graduation and commissioning, Col. Tudor, my commanding officer, called me to his office:

'Cadet Lt. Col. Hryniewicz. There is a problem. You are not a citizen, therefore you cannot be commissioned.'

'Yes, sir! I know, sir.'

'Do not worry, I've already spoken with both New Jersey senators and they will seek a special act of Congress to award you a commission.'

'Sir! I greatly appreciate your effort. However, I just received a full scholarship to MIT Graduate School. When I finish my graduate studies I will be eligible for citizenship and then I will join the Air Force.'

A greatly relieved colonel replied: 'Congratulations! That is probably for the best.'

I graduated with a Bachelor of Science degree, with honours, in civil engineering. After finishing my summer job, in September of 1954, I drove my second-hand Buick to Boston and began my graduate studies at MIT.

Epilogue

The author today. (Warsaw Rising Museum)

From Stettin (Szczecin) to Trieste in the Adriatic an 'Iron Curtain' has descended across the Continent.

Winston Churchill, at Westminster College on 5 March 1946

I was fortunate that we managed to escape communist Poland just as the Iron Curtain descended. I am most grateful for the help and education I received in England and the United States. The opportunities I was offered and was able to take advantage of allowed me to have a productive life.

My fellow soldiers were not so fortunate. The so-called 'free and unfettered elections' were held a month after I escaped. Their outcome was predictable: many candidates of the opposition parties were disqualified, and the results were falsified. The feeble protests of the governments of the United Kingdom and United States were ignored. The communists took complete control and intensified their prosecution and oppression of former AK members. Thousands were arrested, imprisoned and some were shot. Others were denied employment and access to education. This persecution eventually diminished following Stalin's death in 1953.

Regardless of their youth, some of my friends from the battalion were not spared this fate. Borys, a runner a year older than me, returned to Poland in November 1947. Before he was able to complete his interrupted education he was drafted into the LWP and placed in a penal battalion. He laboured in coal mines for more than two years. Borys considered himself lucky that he wasn't assigned to the uranium mines as everyone who worked there died.

Sten was arrested by the UB in June 1952 while attending the University of Warsaw. He was sentenced to five years imprisonment for 'attempting to overthrow the government'. While in prison, he too was forced to work in the quarries and coal mines. After twenty-eight months, he was conditionally released and rehabilitated in 1957.

Baśka, CO of medics in our battalion, clandestinely completed two years of medical studies during the occupation. Upon return from the *oflag*, she was denied entrance to medical school until after 1953.

* * *

In September 1954, I commenced my graduate studies in the Department of Civil Engineering at the Massachusetts Institute of Technology. At the same time, I found part-time work as a structural engineer in an architectural engineering design office. A year later, when I completed my studies, I continued to work full-time for the same company. Soon after, in 1955, three engineers, all MIT graduates who also worked there, started their own design office and asked me to join them. Always ready for an opportunity, I accepted and became a partner in Symmes, Maini, Hryniewicz & McKee Architects and Engineers.

Cambridge and Boston, with a large number of colleges and universities, were vibrant places to live and work. There were many Poles and some had experiences similar to mine; most of whom had arrived shortly after the war. I met and developed a lifelong friendship with two brothers, Witold and Jacek von Henneberg, both architects. Together with an older brother who did not survive, they took part in the Warsaw Uprising and then went through a POW camp, the Polish Army in Italy and the Polish School of Architecture in London.

Their German name led to a few 'interesting' conversations. During a cocktail party shortly after his arrival in 1949, Jacek was introduced by a hostess: 'Mr von X, this is Mr von Henneberg.' Soon the following conversation ensued:

'Where were you during the war?' asked Jacek.

'In the Luftwaffe', replied von X.

'How interesting. What were you doing in the Luftwaffe?'

'I was a Stuka pilot.'

'On which front?'

'Mostly on the Russian. However, in the fall of 1944, we had a very interesting mission – exterminating Polish bandits in Warsaw.'

'How fascinating!'

'And where were you during the war?' von X inquired.

'Well, it just so happens that I was in Warsaw at the same time.'

'Really, what were you in? … Wehrmacht or SS?'

'No … I was one of the Polish bandits you were trying to exterminate.'

I met a wonderful young woman in the summer of 1957. Her name was Linda Kelly, and she was a junior at Wellesley College. We married in December 1958. After six years of designing buildings, I was ready for a change and resigned my partnership. In January of 1961 we moved to San Juan, Puerto Rico with our newborn son Andrew, where I started up a construction company. Over the next three years, two daughters, Sarah and Elisabeth (Lisa), were born. In 1962 I arranged for my father to come and stay with us for six months. We were reunited after sixteen years of separation. I found him greatly changed, much warmer and less reserved.

We lived in a Spanish colonial house which we had restored in old San Juan. Our neighbour was a young Swede named Lars Odelfelt. As partners, we developed a condo hotel on the San Juan beachfront. This opened more opportunities and Lars went to Stockholm to explore them. In the autumn of 1965, Linda and I spent two months in Europe deciding whether or not to move there. It was my first return to Poland. By that time I had become a US citizen. In order to apply for a Polish visa, I had to fill out a questionnaire and answer 'When and on the basis of what documents did you leave Poland' and detail my military service. I answered 'Left Poland on 23 December 1946 illegally crossing the border' and listed my service during the Uprising. I also mentioned that in 1957, as a partner in Henneberg, Henneberg & Hryniewicz, Architects and Engineers, I won first prize in an international architectural competition in Warsaw. After a month of waiting, the visa was granted. When we arrived in Warsaw that October 1965, we hosted a small dinner party for my family and friends in a local hotel restaurant. There were two gentlemen sitting at a nearby table who nursed the same cold cups of coffee the entire time we were there.

I asked the waiter to send them two cognacs. When they looked towards me I smiled and saluted them with my glass. They sheepishly smiled back and returned the salute.

After nineteen years I reconnected with old friends. I found Pobóg, Borys, Wiera, Dąb and several others while in Warsaw. I also visited Holski, who was very ill and died shortly after. From then on, I stayed in touch with all of them.

Upon our return home, Linda and I decided to move to Europe. I wound up my construction jobs, arranged management of our concrete block plant and sold our house. In May of 1966, with three small children and José, our Puerto Rican houseboy who asked to be taken along, we sailed on a French liner from San Juan to Le Havre and drove to Stockholm. We lived in downtown Stockholm while Lars and I developed hotel projects. We formed a group that acquired the patent rights to a vacuum sewage system that had been developed by a Swedish inventor. I became the managing director of the group and the rights were sold to Electrolux AB. For the next few years I travelled all over the world promoting the system as a special consultant to Electrolux. During that time, we visited Poland a few more times.

Our youngest son, Gregory, was born in October 1970. In 1971 we decided to return to Puerto Rico. I started a new company that designed, manufactured, leased and sold pre-fabricated forming systems for reinforced concrete residential construction. Over the next ten years, more than 10,000 housing units were constructed in Puerto Rico utilising this system. When construction in Puerto Rico came to a standstill following a recession in 1982, I liquidated my construction business. In the meantime, I was a director of a public corporation that owned and operated a 180-room hotel. I was offered and accepted the presidency of the company. We bought and restored another colonial house in old San Juan.

I continued to travel to Europe as a consultant for the vacuum sewage venture. Whenever I had a chance, I made an effort to spend some time visiting my father and old friends in Poland. It was on a return trip in spring 1973 that I learned that Nałęcz had died. I was saddened by his death and the fact that I had not been able to see him again after I had escaped from Poland. He was an extraordinary man. Born in 1914 in Latvia, he was a graduate of the Cadet School and Reserve Artillery Officers School. He had started to make his mark as a talented graphic artist when he was mobilised in 1939. He went through the 1939 campaign as an artillery officer and avoided being taken prisoner of war. He was involved in the Underground from the very beginning. He was arrested in August 1940 and spent several months in Auschwitz concentration camp. After his release was arranged, he returned to work for the Underground. He was a brave man, a natural leader who commanded and led from the front.

In 1974, the communist government first gave and then rescinded permission for the celebration of the thirtieth anniversary of the Uprising. Nevertheless, we met privately, and I recognised quite a few familiar faces. I continued to visit Poland and watched the deterioration of living standards that led to the creation of Solidarity in the summer of 1980.

At the beginning of December 1980, Linda and I were in Switzerland for the annual meeting of the FEI (International Equestrian Federation). While in our hotel room I heard the American Armed Forces in Germany radio network declare: 'The invasion of Poland by Russian forces is imminent.' We had plans to fly to Warsaw the next day. Remembering that the Secretary of the Federation was a high-ranking reserve officer of the Swiss Army, I called him to ask if he knew anything about it. He returned my call a few hours later to say that according to the latest NATO intelligence there would be no movement of Russian forces for the next three days. We flew to Warsaw the next day. It felt like a completely new country. The spirit of anticipation, of change brought on by the emergence of the Solidarity movement was visible everywhere, but food shortages had become even worse than the last time we visited. We left three days later. Martial law was declared a year later, in December 1981, and was in force for almost two years.

In March 1989, while on my way to an FEI meeting in Budapest, I made a stopover in Poland to visit my father in Kraków. On 20 March I returned to Warsaw to attend the funeral of Gryf, the oldest of the Mirowski brothers. Walking through the military cemetery, I stopped by the Katyń Monument, which had been erected by the communist government in April 1987 and included the fallacious inscription: 'Polish soldiers, victims of Hitlerite fascism resting in the earth of Katyń – 1941'. There were two masons there with chisels hammering away the inscription. It was replaced with: 'Polish officers murdered in Katyń'. I knew that the end of communism in Poland had arrived.

The first partially free election was held in June 1989. That precipitated the fall of communism in Poland and six months later the total abolition of communism in all of Central Europe.

I returned in 1989 with my daughter Lisa for the forty-fifth anniversary and the unveiling of a long-demanded monument to the Warsaw Uprising. It was my last trip requiring a visa from the Polish People's Republic. I was back again in June 1991 to bury my father in Andrzej's grave. I would return for another funeral in November 1998; I attended Pobóg's funeral in Warsaw. The last surviving officer of the *Nałęcz* Battalion, he was buried next to its commander.

In June 1992, on the 500th anniversary of the discovery of America, the *Gran Regata Colon* brought together the largest gathering of tall ships ever assembled to San Juan harbour. Close to 250 sailing vessels arrived from Europe and South America. There were thirty three-masted ships, encompassing all of the training ships of the world's naval and merchant marine academies, including two ships from Poland. I was a member of the organising committee in charge of Polish ships. My son Gregory, midshipman of the United States Naval Academy, was assigned to the *Iskra*, a three-mast brigantine of the Polish Navy. Since there was no diplomatic representation of the newly independent Republic of Poland in Puerto Rico, I was appointed spokesman for the Polish Consul in New York. Upon arrival in the United States, the captains of the Polish ships had signed a petition to have me appointed Honorary Consul in San Juan. After vetting by the Polish Ministry of Foreign Affairs and the United States Department of State, I was appointed in 1994. I was one of the first two Honorary Consuls of the Polish Republic appointed in the United States, serving in this position for fourteen years.

In 1994 the fiftieth anniversary of the Uprising was celebrated in a free, independent and democratic Republic of Poland. I was there with my two daughters and my younger son, a newly commissioned ensign in the United States Navy. I stood proudly with them among other veterans and their families and thousands of people. I realised then that what we fought for had finally arrived, that the sacrifices of fifty years before had been worth it.

Since then I have been back to Warsaw many times. In 2004, the sixtieth anniversary, I attended the opening of the long-awaited Museum of the Warsaw Uprising. The names of Andrzej and Wiktor were etched on the Memory Wall with thousands of others. On the evening of 1 August, on the square in front of the old post office building, I attended the commemoration ceremony. I sat in the front row, seated literally 6ft away from Chancellor Schröder, Secretary Powell and other representatives of the Allied Powers (except Russia, which chose not to be represented). After an opening speech by Lech Kaczynski, President of the City, the ceremony commenced with Warsaw's Symphony Orchestra and Choir performing Verdi's 'Requiem Mass', while excerpts of newsreels from the Siege of Warsaw in September 1939, the occupation and the Uprising were shown on a large screen. They became progressively more graphic and disturbing. As the music reached a final crescendo the screen showed two young Polish soldiers, shot by Germans, in their death throes.

The music stopped, the screen went blank and there was complete silence. I looked at Schröder. He was visibly shaken. Then he was asked to speak. He composed himself, mounted the podium and said that it was very difficult for him to speak. It was then that I heard him say, 'Polish pride and German shame' and 'we bow our heads in shame at the crimes of the Nazi troops.'

I was in Poland again in 2014 for the seventieth anniversary with my wife Anne, daughter Lisa, granddaughter Nina, my son Gregory, his wife Megan and my 1-year-old grandson Bryce. Seventy years later, there are about 2,500 Uprising participants left; 400 attended the commemoration. There were four from *Nałęcz* Battalion: 'Nałęcz' Stanisław Tański, 'Janusz' Janusz Maksymowicz, 'Borys' Ryszard Budzianowski and myself. As is our custom, we met at 5 p.m. in the Powąski Military Cemetery as sirens wailed throughout Warsaw and salvos of honour guard echoed between the graves.

The warmth of the general population towards us, particularly among the younger generation, was overwhelming. It reinforced my realisation twenty years ago that, after all, the sacrifices were not in vain. A poll of public opinion taken on the eve of the 2014 anniversary confirmed that 61 per cent of Poles believed that the Uprising was necessary and beneficial to Polish national interest.

Abbreviations

AK	*Armia Krajowa*, Home Army
AL	*Armia Ludowa*, People's Army
Batt.	Battalion
CO	Commanding Officer
Co.	Company
C.Off.	Cadet Officer (*Podchorąży*)
DP	Displaced person
DW	Died of wounds
KB	*Korpus Bezpieczeństwa*, Security Corps
KIA	Killed in action
LWP	*Ludowe Wojsko Polskie*, Polish People's Army
NKVD	*Narodnyy Komissariat Vnutrenikh Del*, People's Commissariat of Internal Affairs – Russian secret police
NN	*Nieznany*, Unknown
NSZ	*Narodowe Siły Zbrojne*, National Armed Forces
PIAT	Projector, Infantry, Anti-Tank
Oflag	*Offizirslager*, POW camp for officers only
PRC	Polish Resettlement Corps
POW	Prisoner of War
PWX	Ex-Prisoner of War
RONA	*Russaya Osvobodityelnaya Narodnaya Armya*, Russian National Liberation Army
ROTC	Reserve Officers' Training Corps
Stalag	*Stammlager*, POW camp for other ranks
UB	*Urząd Bezpieczeństwa*, Security Office
UNRRA	United Nations Relief and Rehabilitation Administration
USAAF	United States Army Air Force
WU	Wounded in action
ZUWZoNiD	*Związek Uczestników Walki Zbrojnej o Wolność i Niepodległość*, Association of Participants of Armed Struggle for Freedom and Independence

Code Names

Battalion KB 'Nałęcz'[1]

Battalion Command				
Nałęcz	Lt./Cpt.	Stefan Kaniewski	CO Batt.	WU 23 August 1944
Poboóg	Lt./Cpt.	Stanislaw Kiersznowski	CO 1st Co.	WU 23 August 1944
Edward	Lt./Cpt.	Tadeusz Łukaszewicz	CO P-20 Co.	KIA 12 September 1944
Holski	Lt./Cpt.	Adolf Hoffman	CO 2nd Co.	
Skóra	2nd Lt./Lt	Henryk Głowacki	2nd in C. 2nd Co.	KIA 30 September 1944
Sokół	2nd Lt./Lt.	Kazimierz Skubiszewski		
Other Ranks				
Abczyc	C.Off./2nd Lt.	Waldemar Uzdowski		KIA 23 August 1944
Alicja	Medic	Unknown		WU 24 August 1944
Baśka	Lt.	Dr Barbara Zylewicz	CO Medics	
Baśka II	Pte.	'Burned' Unknown		WU 23 August 1944
Bohdan	Pte./Cpl.	Bohdan Hryniewicz	Runner	
Borys	Pte./L.Cpl.	Ryszard Budzianowski	Runner	WU 20 August 1944
Czajka	C.Off./2nd Lt.	Jozef Wanarski		WU 23 August 1944
Dąb	C.Off.	Henryk Mirowski		
Dąbrowa	Lt.	Unknown		WU 3 August 1944; DW 4 August 1944
Dębina	C.Off.	Alojzy Pluciński		
Delfin	C.Off.	Władysław Hoffla		WU 20 August 1944
Edek	Pte./Cpl.	Edward Szymaniak		
Grisza	Cpl.	Grigory Siemionow (Russian PWX)		WU 10 August 1944; DW 12 August 1944
Gryf	C.Off.	Zbigniew Mirowski		WU 15 August 1944
Halina	Medic	Unknown		WU 24 August 1944

1   Budzianowski, *Batalion KB 'Nałęcz'*, pp. 111–27.

Jaga	Medic	Zofia Martens		KIA 17 August 1944
Janusz	SSgt.	Janusz Maksymowicz		WU 16 August 1944
Jasia	Medic	Jozefa Kulczycka		KIA 24 August 1944
Jerzy	Lt.	Teofil Pietrowski (Pelerynka)	Quartermaster	DW 2 October 1944
Jur	Lt.	Juljusz Kowalski		WU 3 August 1944
Kmita	C.Off./2nd Lt.	Ludwig Owsiany		KIA 20 August 1944
Kruk	C.Off.	Ryszard Pohorski		
Leszek	Lt.	Czesław Kossak		
Łuniewski	C.Off.	Tadeusz Baranowski		
Mama	SSgt.	Julian Biernacki		
Miki	2nd Lt.	Jan Sobór-Kulagowski		WU 18 August 1944
Mocny	Sgt./SSgt.	Mieczysław Wojcicki		
Nałęcz	C.Off./2nd Lt.	Stanisław Tański		
Ninka	Medic	Unknown		KIA 15 August 1944
Orwid	Lt.	Jan Płoński		WU 24 August 1944
Pantera	C.Off.	Tadeusz Janczyk		
Patriota	C.Off./2nd Lt.	Zygmunt Królak		
Pigularz	Pte.	Unknown	Medic	KIA 15 August 1944
Runiek	C.Off.	Jerzy Kruczewski		
Sten	Pte./LcCpl.	Zdzisław Grzybowski		WU 16 August 1944; WU 5 September 1944
Sternik	C.Off./2nd Lt.	Janusz Wiśniewski		
Szczeniak	Pte./Cpl.	Krzysztof Jachimowicz		WU 21 August 1944; WU 24 August 1944
Szczesny	2nd Lt.	Dr Janusz Harich		WU 23 August 1944; DW 26 August 1944
Tadeusz	Lt./Cpt.	Tadeusz Garliński	CO P-20 Co.	
Tarzan	Pte.	Andrzej Hryniewicz	Runner	WU 17 August 1944; DW 21 August 1944
Wiera	Medic	Weronika Orłowska-Hartman		
Wilk	C.Off./2nd Lt.	Jerzy Mirowski		
Witold	C.Off./2nd Lt	Witold Markiewicz		
Zadra	C.Off./2nd Lt.	Czesław Teofilak		KIA 30 August 1944
Zbyszek	C.Off.	Zbigniew Zieliński		
Zew	2nd Lt.	Zygmunt Zatorski		KIA 24 August 1944

AK Command				
Bór	Maj.-Gen.	Tadeusz Komorowski	CO AK	
Monter	Brg.-Gen.	Antoni Chruściel	CO of AK in Warsaw	
Wachnowski	Col.	Karol Ziemski	CO Group 'North'	
Kuba	Lt. Col.	Stanisław Juszczakiewicz	CO Sector 'Kuba'	WU 13 August 1944
Sosna	Maj.	Gustaw Billewicz	CO Sector 'Kuba-Sosna'	
Radosław	Lt. Col.	Jan Mazurkiewicz	CO Combat Group 'Radosław'	
Doliwa	Col.	Leon Korzewnikianc	CO AK KB	
Sokół	Maj.	Władysław Olszowski	CO Batt. 'Sokół'	
Other Units				
Barry	Cpt.	Władysław Kozakiewicz	CO Military Police Gr. 'North'	
Ognisty	Cpt.	Lucjan Fajer	2nd in C. Batt. 'Gozdawa'	
Jacek	Cpt.	Sylwester Twarowski	Batt. 'Gozdawa'	
Kosa	Lt./Cpt.	Ludwik Witkowski	CO Unit 'B' Kedyw	
Kot	C.Off.	Wiktor Rymszewicz	Unit 'B' Kedyw	WU 4 August 1944; KIA 5 August 1944
Unknown	Unknown	Zygmunt Rymszewicz	Unknown	KIA 1 August 1944

Select Bibliography

Borkiewicz, Adam, *Powstanie Warszawskie 1944* [*Warsaw Uprising 1944*] (Warsaw, 1957)

Budzianowski, Ryszard, *Batalion KB 'Nałęcz' w Powstaniu Warszawskim* [*Battalion KB 'Nałęcz' in the Warsaw Uprising*] (Warsaw, 2005)

Deschner, Gunther, *Warsaw Rising* (New York, 1972)

Davies, Norman, *Rising '44* (London, 2003)

Fajer, Lucjan, *Żołnierze Starówki* [*Soldiers of the Old Town*] (Warsaw, 1957)

Kirchmayer, Jerzy, *Powstanie Warszawskie* [*Warsaw Uprising*] (Warsaw, 1949)

Kaczynska, Danuta, *Dziewczęta z 'Parasola'* [*Girls from 'Parasol'*] (Warsaw, 1993)

Kochanski, Halik, *The Eagle Unbowed* (Cambridge, MA, 2012)

Kulesza, Juljusz, *STARÓWKA Warszawskie Termopile 1944* [*Old Town Warsaw's Thermopylae 1944*] (Warsaw, 1999)

Lewandowska, Stanisława, *Życie codzienne Wilna* [*Wilno's everyday Life*] (Warsaw, 2001)

Lissowski, Jan, Jerzy Szanser and Marek Werner, *Batalion 'Sokół' w Powstaniu Warszawskim* [*The 'Sokół' Battalion in the Warsaw Uprising*] (Warsaw, 2003)

Podlewski, Stanisław, *Przemarsz Przez Piekło* [*March through Hell*] (Warsaw, 1957)

Richie, Alexandra, *Warsaw 1944: Hitler, Himmler and the Warsaw Uprising* (New York, 2013)

Sawicki, Tadeusz, *Rozkaz: zdławić powstanie* [*Order: Suppress the Uprising*] (Warsaw, 2001)

Sztejerwald, Mieczysław, *Kompania Armii Krajowej 'P-20' w Powstaniu Warszawskim* [*Home Army Company 'P-20' in the Warsaw Uprising*] (Warsaw, 2004)

Szubánski, Rejmund, '1 Batalion Szturmowy KB 'Nałęcz' W Powstaniu Warszawskim [1st Assault Battalion KB 'Nałęcz' in the Warsaw Uprising]', *Wojskowy Przeglad Historyczny* [*Military Historical Review*], vol. XXXI no. 2 (1986)

Umiński Zdzisław, *Kanoniczki 1944* [*Convent of Canoness Sisters 1944*] (Warsaw, 1988)

Wielka Ilustrowana Encyclopedia Powstania Warszawskiego [*Great Illustrated Encyclopedia of the Warsaw Uprising*] (Warsaw, 2005)

Suggested Reading

Davies, Norman, *Rising '44* (London, 2003)

Kochanski, Halik, *The Eagle Unbowed* (Cambridge, Mass., 2012)

Richie, Alexandra, *Warsaw 1944: Hitler, Himmler and the Warsaw Uprising* (New York, 2013)

Snyder, Timothy, *Bloodlands: Europe between Hitler and Stalin* (New York, 2010)

Index